FRATER 273

AUTHOR:
Dušan Trajković
dushan.trajkovic@gmail.com

PUBLISHER:
Frater 273

COVER DESIGN:
Stoian Hitrov - Stoianin

BOOK DESIGN AND EDITING:
Dušan Trajković

TRANSLATION:
Vojislav Stojanović

GRAPHIC DESIGN:
Ana Jeličić

PROOFING SUPPORT:
Stewart Cook

ISBN 978-8691520939

∴

Dedicated to Mina

and my Brazilians,
who are always in my heart,
although across the ocean

A∴A∴
Official publication in class C

Issued by Order:

L.	7°= 4▫	Præmonstrator
S.U.	6°= 5▫	Imperator
A.	5°= 6▫	Cancellarius

ANATOMY
OF THE
ABYSS

THE NEOPHYTE'S COMPENDIUM

DUŠAN TRAJKOVIĆ

CONTENTS

Chapter ONE	NEOPHYTE	9
Chapter TWO	AUGEAS	31
Chapter THREE	STUDENT	49
Chapter FOUR	ON PENTACLE AND LAMEN	63
Chapter FIVE	BODY	77
Chapter SIX	THE GREAT MOTHER	109
Chapter SEVEN	WORD	131
Chapter EIGHT	NEUROSIS	143
Chapter NINE	QABALISTIC LECTURE	161
Chapter TEN	POSTCARDS TO A NEOPHYTE	191
Chapter ELEVEN	LUCID DREAMING	227
Chapter TWELVE	LIBER VII	349
Appendix	NEOPHYTE'S PAPERS	385

"If you're going through hell, keep going."
Sir Winston Churchill

CHAPTER ONE

NEOPHYTE

The first step is the hardest one. For everyone, but the Neophyte, for all is opposite for him. His trajectory, and therefore his momentum, is "downward." The Neophyte requires no strength but courage, and he is typically full of expectations and enthusiasm. His mind is strikingly affected by the ritual of the Pyramid, the new Oath he took, the new Motto he acquired. He is full of zest and ready to make progress, emboldened by the ease of his beginning because there is neither hurdle nor height to surmount. Rather, he effortlessly descends. His progress is not necessarily represented by climbing to the stars, but by descending deep inside his being. Deep and down, deep and inside; this thought is so precious, as he will learn, that it needs to be cultivated from the very beginning.

The thought of spiritual growth treacherously provokes his urge to strive towards heights, creating a wholly fallacious and hypocritical pantheon of gods based on something alien, remote and unattainable to the Aspirant. This causes him to spend most of his time correcting himself and adjusting techniques and methods poorly laid out. This misguided effort can even last a lifetime.

Nevertheless, he does not need to aim for the stars, as he shall learn. His upward trajectory will fail sooner or later. He must look before him, refocus upon the here and now. Moreover, he must look into himself, continually searching for all causes and all mechanisms within his being, setting all the benchmarks and all the rules as parts of an inspired monologue. Yet, in all his wanderings, the Neophyte must get lost, and through this way he must find his path. The only way "out" is "in".

The path of the Neophyte in the A∴A∴ is perhaps the most fascinating one within the initiatory paradigm of the Golden Dawn. One can say that the Aspirant's efforts are intertwined with completely new aspects of awareness that he has never experienced before, starting from the very formal entry onto the path that so strongly pressed the Probationer, to such a different and unparalleled experience such as that of the astral projection and the awareness of lucid consciousness.

The Neophyte is a newcomer, but not because he gets new experiences. Rather, it is because he gets right experiences – those which will imprint their seal so heavily on his soul, all the way to the extreme limits of Dominus Liminis. Even the illusion, for the Neophyte, is not an unfamiliar field that is dependent on fate; he embraces it not as part of reality but as part of himself.

A Neophyte who knows his imperfection has an advantage over all other Aspirants who just think they are perfect. The Neophyte prepares his being to become Asar Un Nefer, just by embracing his imperfection; he, therefore, embarks on the path of his individuality rather than that of perfection. Yet, there is something we certainly need to discuss here: We genuinely believe that perfecting all possible weapons is our legitimate path within the A∴A∴, but in a Great Experiment, we ordain an individual to use only those he himself discovers to be necessary. This way of thinking is mainly related to the Adept, who, just moments before taking his Oath, was dedicated to all possible numbers and possibilities. Yet, he was aware that he was just one number and not any other what-soever. The path of individuation is by no means the path to freedom; he does not aspire to be free because he knows that aspiration tends to enslave more than anything else. He is the way he is and embarks on his own particular training within our great Order. He knows that a free man does not aspire to what he already is – only a prisoner yearns for freedom.

The Neophyte is a newcomer, but he does not pass through uncharted lands. Stepping into the unknown does not mean that he will face anything alien; on the contrary, in that darkness, he will discover familiar shadows and the well-known inhabitants of his very own fantasies. Understanding one's own nature is almost impossible while at the Neophyte Grade, yet the perfection of the A∴A∴ path is such that while trying to understand the nature of his grade, the Neophyte is already leaving that grade itself, moving ever closer to Tiphareth. This is the first grade in the real sense of that word, for there is actually no distinction between the Probationer and the Neophyte. Conceptually they are comparable. The Neophyte is a capable Probationer and nothing more. Each and every Probationer is already a future Neophyte, and now it is only a matter of the Aspirant's own Will to realize his "spark" in the present and thus take on something he merely calls "the Oath." In fact, every Oath is the Knowledge and Conversation, broken into what are the characteristics of Ruach – time and space, as well as tangible forms of something that is still to come. By the very act of taking the Oath, as the Aspirant will learn, the Knowledge and Conversation have already been "realized." What he is experiencing now through the grades is merely an optical illusion of his mind. It is a logical game of his nature that experiences the light first and then hears the sound, just as an unenlightened mind perceives thunder and lightning as separate phenomena. Like a brief twinge of pain that has already passed, it is always an afterthought because that impulse is nothing but an electric spark which, when it finally arises in the mind, only shows that what we inevitably feel at that moment is, in fact, long overdue. The Neophyte is profoundly aware of this, and his exploration of the grade indicates a breakdown of reason; he begins to feel higher and more unfathomable realms. He begins to be aware of another self within himself that exists as much as himself, and moving forward, he becomes aware that he is the one who ceases to exist, giving way to another – an apparently different self. But this other self, is really an earlier self rather than a newly discovered one; it is an older self that has not been lived through or perhaps even forgotten. The Neophyte realizes that the new reality he is experiencing is by no means a novelty. All the supposed greatness of his achievement begins to melt and is revealed to be merely a deposit of his unconscious and dormant giant. As previously mentioned, his path is an inward one, not an outward. His method is "again" and not "now," that is to say, "new." Of course, this is expressed once the Neophyte Oath has been taken, but from the point of view of the A∴A∴ Superior, true work is expected from the Neophyte, not the Probationer. The Probationer is just on probation with what is real to the Neophyte. If the Probationer's path was likened to a comet's trajectory, the Neophyte's trajectory is likened to that of a planet; he does not need to burn out but make a full circle. What is important to the Neophyte is completeness, unlike the Probationer who is cloaked in the quantity and perseverance of the vector – now, for the first time, the Aspirant is getting the quality required. His essence is in the need for the completeness of its nature and its aspiration, and the need for the technique to round out rather than to close off, the importance of the need to give judgment and a personal stamp to the completion of the cycle, rather than to the cycle itself. But let the Neophyte always remember that a full circle implies revolution inasmuch as rotation. That particular fullness always implies both a micro and a macrocosm – the completeness of the journey around the sun as much as around oneself. It is essential for the Neophyte to learn to dissect aspects of an idea and, for the first time, learn to distinguish realms and elements, not to define them. To feel the Angel, not to have the Knowledge and Conversation with Him. This sensation is also one of the most fantastic things that he, as an A∴A∴ Aspirant will ever feel upon his being. That sensation is, in fact, the chief architect of all the experiences that are yet to be lived through, and it all becomes one sophisticated mind game that his soul will fall into. All that the Aspirant is going to experience, including the interpretation of these words, will reshape and use that sensation, which will manifest the Angel at the same time, somewhere in the distant corridor of time and space. As the Probationer is simply the one who has not yet awakened, so is the Neophyte an Adept who has not slept enough. The same mechanism is actuated in both cases, like an automobile's transmission placed in drive for the former and in reverse where it pertains to the latter. The Probationer moves forward into waking, while the Neophyte purposefully dreams while yet being awake. It is the same consciousness, but a completely different perspective into which that consciousness is focused. Continuous attention, however, is what we have here, and it is a feature of our great Order.

The Neophyte slowly becomes aware that his attainment is an Awakening rather than a Revelation, that the Will is to be awakened, not found. These are not two realities, but one, now presented in two opposite elements and two different circumstances. He discovers that the Knowledge and Conversation is not found in new or transcendent knowledge awaiting discovery, but rather something that he has forgotten and actually already has. The Aspirant may desire to be "now," but learns that "now" is not a "when." Will is quite a subjective truth, not an objective lie. If the Aspirant meditates carefully on desire, which at first he may not distinguish from the Will, he will realize that the desire is an echo of the present. In other words, when you wish for something, that something is what you have already wanted a moment ago, for something that you have yet to get. The Will is "now," whereas desire is memetic. Desire is the compensation of the Will, which is mantled in both Binah and Malkuth in the same way. In fact, it is fair to say that the moment the Will "blows through" Binah, it was at the same "moment" that is to be found in Malkuth. The Aspirant must remind himself that the 32nd path of the "Universe" has a double attribution: it is an earth element, but also an aspect of Saturn and, therefore, that of Binah. The phenomenon of matter cannot be separated from the phenomenon of time, as it is one and the same phenomenon.

The only true process that happens in your universe is remembrance because you experience one and the same thing in an infinite number of times. But since time does not actually exist everywhere as you perceive it here and now, what, from the point of view of the true or ultimate reality, is then truly remembered? If yesterday did not actually happen, and if there is no yesterday, how can you recall anything? If you are timeless in endless recalling, then who is the one who recalls at all?

Everything you do, you have done countless times before. Each instance is fundamentally the same – you cannot avoid this apparent repetition of one and the same experience. Each time is the same time. Regardless of what you are doing, be it meditating, observing the horizon, or anything else, the trick is to realize that you are not watching it for the first time; it has not been your choice to watch what you are looking at. And finally, to realize it is not actually you doing what you are doing anyway. What is being done is done through you. When you look, you are not the one watching. What you are mistakenly thinking of as corporeal "you" is merely part of what you are looking at. When you look, you are not the one watching – you are what you are looking at. When you eat, you are not the one who is eating, but what you eat. However, the true Self is not the food but the act of eating. You are not life but the act of living. When you attain the Angel, and when you acquire the Knowledge and Conversation you are not the one who Knows and has Conversation. You are already the Knowledge having Conversation with one who is only able to recall that knowledge to a certain extent.

The Neophyte learns whereas the Adept recalls; this specific relationship is only one of the basic aggregate states of the Knowledge and Conversation that the Adept knows so well, out of all those he experiences from the moment of his Adeptship unto the solitary towers of the Abyss. Every great achievement in our Order is paradoxical in itself, as is essentially every Initiation, every transfer of knowledge, and every mental process of learning. Paradox and transcendence is the name and surname of all the work of every true Aspirant. They are the name and surname of the eternal Self – that authenticity which is the only thing we truly seek. Every invocation of an Angel is evocation of a memory. Each experience of the Knowledge is actually a memory and the Conversation is really a remembering. Complete understanding of this process is essential for every Aspirant of the Golden Dawn.

Yet how many memories are there? Memory is only one; there is only one event that happens, only one Knowledge, and one Conversation. There is just one event which you were born for, just one that is worth remembering and could be memorized – one Angel and one Universe. There is only one success, everything else is a failure. There is only one present from which one remembers and to which one returns. Each recollection is the same mechanism of the Great Work. If the Aspirant could understand this game of mind, he would immediately experience the Knowledge and Conversation. If the Adept lives in the eternal present, never will the Neophyte face tomorrow. Tomorrow "is" the present, viewed from a different angle, and every angle is anchored in its corner. All the inherent difficulties typical of the Neophyte's predicament are found in the corner. His problem are corners indeed, since there are as many corners as there are living particles in the Universe.

His truth is inhabited by a single frozen frame of the present – the one he cannot penetrate. That petrified reflection of his own self is where his Adeptship lies, which he is not yet able to attain. But, the reflection of that light is not prevented from reaching him. It is not uncommon for Neophytes to be given a hint of the Knowledge or Conversation. Nevertheless, these are always generalizations that are tainted and, frankly, all wrong – including this one.

Brother Alan Bennett had a lot to say about all of this. He was such a noble soul, and we can safely say, the person with whom Aleister Crowley had a uniquely special relationship – perhaps one of the few true friends and teachers who had an admirable relationship with the Great Beast, as much as was likely possible with Aleister. The Dawn of the New Æon was far from Bennett, who disseminated his achievements throughout the East and imprinted his stamp in Crowley's soul with his insights in such a way that the movement spawned and shaped by the latter as if it were the product of some perfect mechanism, is equally beholden to Bennett for its beginnings. Without Bennett that mechanism would not have certainly functioned at all. Like Crowley, Bennett suffered from severe asthma and would use a wide variety of drugs to combat it, but it would haunt him throughout his entire life. In his late twenties, Bennett would travel to Southeast Asia, primarily in the hope that it would improve his health but also to study Buddhism. He moved to Ceylon (modern Sri Lanka) to study Yoga under Yogi Shri Parananda. Crowley visited him several times during this period, and Bennett would introduce Crowley to a number of practices. One of them was the Samasati exercise, which is used to teach the mind to think backward, which, in fact, allows one to break through the barrier posed by the very idea of death. In its essence, the exercise shatters the phenomenon of self-forgetting as the most severe consequence upon any manifested consciousness. From the standpoint of our Order, this practice is one of the most exalted methods of the Liberated (Exempt) Adept, who performs it in a way that even the Adept Major cannot fully comprehend with any of his wisdom and knowledge. It is the Adept Exempt who realizes that, in its essence, every practice, if done properly, is Samasati in itself, and this insight is initiated by the Neophyte in his understanding of the phenomena of time and the phenomena of consciousness, which define the whole measurable universe.

The progress of the Neophyte to the grade of the Zelator takes place in the complete settlement of life "outside" the Earth. He builds his Pentacle, perceives his body as a consequence and not a condition, and gains the experience of the astral plane. He receives the sensation of the higher spheres and allows subtle energies to flow through his body, which complements the experiences that pushed him further in the direction of Yesod. The Moon is now closer than Earth, and more force is needed to return than to stop. The movement's economy tells him that only one path possible is forward and further – ahead to the Tiphareth Sun. Through his inward journey, the Neophyte gains the power to go forward, which Zelator will use as his momentum. Both terms are used by a future Adept when plotting baits from Paroketh's distance, this inside is no different from forward, but the nature of the Neophyte and the Zelator uses language they understand, so the Angel graciously pulls the strings that match the weight of the Aspirant – strings which would become chains if they were any thicker, but would snap if they were too thin. The Angel pulls these strings in proportion to how deep the Neophyte dives and how determined the Zelator is to push. Meditating on these principles could bring more insight into the Order than all the exercises combined. After all, the grades are only specific forms of consciousness and different levels of their energies, exercises, and methods, which confirm and offer self-affirmation and confidence in the process. Each grade can be attained without a single method, as the knowledge of Pranayama is not necessary for breathing. All of these things require only one thing – that you are simply a living and manifested organism. With confidence we emphatically refuse to believe that there is less holiness in breathing than in Pranayama, as we see the Angel in our daily conversation as much as the Aspirant does during the Great Work.

The Neophyte is necessarily influenced by two forces that equally possess the highest aspects an idea can have – these are the forces of the Moon and the Earth. The Moon actively, albeit with a childlike naiveté, seduces the Neophyte in the form of Yesod, yet simultaneously exhibits the austerity of the High Priestess. Concomitantly, the Earth exhibits the intimate passion of Binah.

Both of these ideas readily point to the Abyss, but in a way for an Aspirant unable to grasp – as if listening to an exotic song performed in an incomprehensible language. Not only will he not be able to fully assimilate the peculiar loveliness of the performance, but it is quite certain that he will be completely unaware of the cultural underpinnings from which evolved the distinct beauty of the singing. Almost involuntarily, he will mix the power of Ares with all the mischief of Mercury. Both of these aspects will render the Neophyte as dismissive and insular, forcing him to fall back on the false superiority of his own predilections. Unbeknownst to him, his attitude takes him further from the Abyss. At some point, his Moon will inevitably eclipse the Sun just when he thinks that an awakening has taken place, and a shadow will be forcefully cast over the simple truth that is being taught to him at all times leaving him oblivious. Both Earth and Moon are equally capable and guilty of producing said eclipse – the Aspirant's Tiphareth, however, is the only constant. This remarkable mechanism is entirely responsible for creating both what we call the Abyss and what we refer to as the A∴A∴ path. Yet it would be quite wrong to say that the value of A∴A∴ is limited, since it relies entirely on that very path. Our goal is religion, and our method is science, but this instruction does not guarantee or describe any of that religion, and more importantly, it takes us away from science. Indeed, the Aspirant is in a completely hopeless situation, being afflicted by all the forces that refract their influence so carefully through the being of a Neophyte, and subjected to the near certainty that he will come to nothing. Counterintuitive as it may sound, this is exactly what he needs – failure.

It is quite certain that in almost all things related to his training, the Neophyte will face failure upon failure, and this is a situation that will fortify itself for a long time. He remains within so many borders and incapable of understanding higher realms and his astral consciousness, for example. Any attempts to rationalize these will distance him from such experiences. The Neophyte knows all this, yet it is impossible for him not to think about it, not to enviously admire others' experiences of astral projection, not to daydream about transferring his consciousness to astral physicality and traveling to the higher realms. As the Probationer, he at least had a quantitative excuse for repeating the practice, which is the essence of that grade. But, at this level, in addition to "doing" things, things now have to "be done." If we accept that this work is something different from anything the Neophyte has done in his life so far, it will be easy to assume the importance of the principle in the A∴A∴ that prohibits work with another initiate, except, of course, the one who introduced him and the other who was introduced through him. Nevertheless, any restriction is indeed most favorable. Let us think about what is being prohibited. More importantly, let us ask ourselves what, if anything, can really be forbidden in something as great as a flock of star wanderers like the A∴A∴ Order.

It is perhaps most important for the Neophyte to languish, to stand still, to advance so slowly and painfully that progress seems almost impossible. Throughout this process, he will hardly understand what is required of him. His progress will seem so abstract that he will often feel like he is not only standing still but also falling behind. Ironically, it is necessary for him to get this impression in order to deal later with the actual value of the work. If the Probationer's task is to persevere within his grade, it is the Neophyte's task to overcome his. These words are much more than a simple instruction; they are more like a finger pointing toward destiny. Indeed, it is equally important for the Neophyte to master his grade completely, but not in any way to stay too much around, precisely because of the surprise of his Binah and its readiness to retaliate upon him in the cruelest way possible.

The Earth is manifested through the Neophyte, but also the Water in its highest form; its sirens are but reflections of the Great Sea of Binah. Every Neophyte is "already" in the City of the Pyramids. Yet, it is not the water experienced in the way of the Golden Dawn Aspirant. It is the Great Ocean, which has nothing to do with elemental water. Neither is it a part of a Tetragrammaton far below the Abyss. It is the terrible Abyss, that dark blue Abyss of the Aspirant's soul which is nothing but the Star. This unfathomable depth is neither wet nor cold; its nature is emphatically and exquisitely empty. Despite all immersion in the Self, no Self is found in that Abyss. Nothing is found – nothing "he" can comprehend. Stars float but do not shine. Only the Aspirant's mind flashes, and he still sees the glare of his Angel in them, for the Abyss merely reflects that splendor, making the Aspirant think that LVX is everywhere except in him – just as the stars are spread across Nu's body. *"There is no part of him that does not come from the Gods"* is a formula of dissolution rather than aspiration.

Indeed, the phenomenon of time is all that occupies a Neophyte – that fracture of the corridors that Ruach calls time, which is actually an infinitely simpler phenomenon – and is present in each and every aspect of his grade. From lucid dreaming, where he has so little time to stay in the astral plane and has to make the most of it, all over to this utterly fictitious notion of the flow of time in a lucid dream, to Asanas and Pranayamas where time so slowly and painfully passes. Even the Pentacle, which is a representation of his

Universe, cannot be static – change and time must be equally present. Only in this way will that representation of the Pentacle be sufficient to persist. The effect of time is an indisputably integral aspect of the Universe represented by such a fragile and tiny object as the Pentacle.

The Probationer and the Neophyte, each in their own way, exhibit a completely different treatment of time; being a Probationer emphasizes the passing of the present; practice that is relentlessly repeating seems to amplify this principle to such an extreme that the Probationer is aware of everything but the present moment. The Neophyte, however, lives in the present. Although he does not experience it, he gets a sense of the Angel, albeit without really knowing him. He may get the Vision or hear the Voice, but it is far from the Knowledge and Conversation. One lives in the passing present, while the other abides in the living present – these are the essential differences between the Pyramidos and the Cadaveris. Yet, both extremes are quite devastating to something as sublime and simple as the Knowledge and Conversation.

We are often completely stunned by a misconception about being a Probationer in the A∴A∴. Surely, being a Probationer is for year. Probation, however, lasts a lifetime. It is very similar to the fate of the Neophyte. The Neophyte is nothing but an able Probationer. Realistically, the unfit Probationer washes out very quickly; therefore, the Neophyte is every Probationer who has resisted the test of time, which is one of the greatest obstacles that will constantly tempt the Aspirant to concede until the attainment of Magister Templi. If one were to early on attain an accurate realization of the truth of his Probation, he would surely transcend the whole idea of the Holy Guardian Angel and, at that very moment, achieve the crossing of the Abyss. Likewise, every Probationer who has passed through Probationer's temptation has indeed already acquired the achievement of the Neophyte in the innermost sense of that word.

First and foremost, the Neophyte, unlike the Probationer, delves deeper into the meaning of practice and comes to perceive the essence that is only visible through said practice. More than anything, he meditates and dives into the parts of his being, learning new laws and new landscapes deep within as well as beyond himself. Along the way, he accomplishes something with this practice and gains completely new knowledge of which he was previously unaware.

The Neophyte's natural method is meditation; each of his rites, even the most traditional one is merely reflection and contemplation. Regardless of how powerful and effective his ritual dance and his conjurations might be, his true lesson will be found in the silence of the aftermath. By this point, the Neophyte clearly knows how to practice the rites and whether he is successful or not, he at least understands what he has to do and what has been omitted from the instructions – that which is clearly indicated in the practices, but also that which is only slightly, or should we say, intuitively visible between the words.

To the Neophyte, in fact, his entire life is one great meditation. He gently begins to understand what Philosophus will fully and finally reveal: the fact that there are actually no fixed practices, just practicing, and the difference is significant. The Probationer has practice, while the Neophyte practices. Each grade fully understands the basic activities of a being, which are implanted in that being by the very fact of being born in this Universe. Every reading of a ritual is as purposeful as its formal performance. And the moment you know you are performing a ritual by reading it, that is exactly what will come to light, even as you are reading these words which are being imprinted into your mind right now. It is all a trick of the mind; every ritual is nothing but a spark thrown by your attention to illuminate the mind with the light of self-realization. Every ritual is a dance of Pan, and it is the sole motive, specific aim, and principle means of the work. The mind is the engine of energy, and every vibration that is controlled and directed by the mind has results. A directed thought, accompanied by the pleasure of the game and intrigued by the inner fascination, which in addition is reinforced by the vibration and mumbling that fills that space with holiness, is the only imperative of the ritual, or indeed any enlightened work. A mild and moderate thought is the beginning of a storm, whereas a strong thought, in its turn, is actually a desecration and the beginning of failure. Every effort of his work through which the Neophyte toils already constitutes the Abyss. Every significant success makes that Abyss deeper and more passionate. It is exactly that kind of nonsense that will engrave two extreme opposites into the Neophyte – the Vision of his Angel and the depth of his Abyss. Time itself provides the rendition of these two heightened experiences to the Neophyte. In fact, he is already aware of it, but that "he" is not "here and now" to understand it. Both of these experiences are, therefore, independent of any method or act – their truth alone is sufficient that if apprehended, the Neophyte would immediately awaken to the Knowledge and Conversation as well as Crossing the Abyss. But it is precisely the effect and influence of Binah that makes him return to the Earth, no matter how enlightening and intense those experiences might be. Every ritual is a dance of Pan, indeed.

In spite of all the practices and experiences he assimilates with his being, there is one idea that is different from everything else that puts so much pressure on his soul; there is one phenomenon of which he has the unbearable impression of knowing it too well, despite being infinitely far-fetched and abstract – the Angel. The Neophyte meets the Angel for the first time, though the Angel meets him always. It is not important what the Neophyte knows or does not know. The point is that he is not able to remember. That is all that matters in the Neophyte grade; one can say that the entire essence of the Golden Dawn is covered by this dark veil based on specific oblivion. The Aspirant must not attach to this oblivion the epithet of knowledge, for indeed, to be able to forget, one does not actually need to know anything other than the characterization of energy. This oblivion is simply the effect of the absence of energy within the Universe as the Will flows through it. Like a computer, which, when it loses battery power, turns off its processes to such an extent that it eventually shuts down. However, within its system, there is one small part that is always running, and that works in a very primitive way. To be able to persevere, the Aspirant must forget. It was that oblivion that helped his Angel to convey his name through what we awkwardly call incarnations, and to keep that name intact. Only forgotten will it remain intact.

While in the grade of the Neophyte, one very often sees the flash of Tiphareth. That is to say, the experience of Knowledge or the experience of Conversation – which can be one particular vision, memory, eureka effect, strange dream, the sense of presence, or the precognition phenomenon of transgression (*deja vu*). To make it all very specific, that feeling, experience, or event must be unique and authentic. It is very difficult for the rational mind to equate these two diametrical settings, that perceive both antiquity and utter nostalgia in this new experience, such as the revoking not of past life but of the true life. As abstract as this experience may be, the practical implication is extremely simple. When the time is right, the Aspirant will know perfectly well what is being said here. This phenomenon of short-term enlightenment and catharsis is also known in the East in the special forms of Dhyana, or Kensho, but what is particularly important in these cases is the more surprising that light-apparition is, the more surprising is the return to the claws of mundane reality and slavery afterward. And as much as the light seemed to be washing away the being of the Aspirant, so terrifying is the descent back into the world of illusion. As the glow of that light fades, the darkness of that shadow of Binah's child Malkuth, into which the Aspirant has fallen, becomes even darker – so dark that he might wish he had never seen any of that light in the first place.

It is not certain if this event is actually a trick which itself creates the Angel afterward, or if it is all part of the same mechanism, giving rise to the consideration that this event could be responsible for creating such a special phenomenon as the Angel. Our program comes across a rather open possibility that the "Angel" is nothing more than a trans-biological-psychological phenomenon of consciousness or time and given this title in a rather naïve way in the three-dimensional world and, therefore, the network of the human mind.

Know yourself. Better yet, meet yourself. There is such a big difference between these similar propositions. "Meeting" yourself is such a drastically different instruction that the question arises as to whether or not "knowing" is even truly possible. Because if it were, an indefinite number of us would have already achieved it. It is the Neophyte's true job to know and accept and open but not to enter the hall of true achievement. The Aspirant knows himself, that is why he is so far from real success.

The Adept, however, meets himself, and in that ordinary act, he becomes aware of how fantastic his failures were in all previous grades – how he erroneously sought light in exceptionalism instead of spontaneity, in the sublime throne of reserved and privileged nirvana instead the unbearable lightness of existence. Success is neither exclusively within nor without. These conceptions are both hopelessly locked into the space-bounded directions of a simple three-dimensional area. Trying to understand them would be like a two-dimensional being attempting to comprehend the noise coming from the pianist from the upper floor. Indeed, there is nothing simpler than human nature, yet nothing more complicated than luring a being to that same nature.

The Aspirant understands that there is an emphasized idea of the being within himself; he sees that all grades are nothing more than different aggregate states of that one being. If we could gather all the possibilities of the Universe in one place, we could only distinguish a very few. In actuality, we would come to a full comprehension of what we call the grades. Therefore, the Aspirant acts in the following roles as:

a) the Probationer – *to obtain scientific knowledge of the nature and powers of his own being,*

b) the Neophyte – *to obtain control of the nature and powers of his own being,*

c) the Zelator – *to obtain control of the foundations of his own being,*

d) the Practicus – *to obtain control of the vacillations of his own being,*

e) the Philosophus – *to obtain control of the attractions and repulsions of his own being,*

f) the Dominus Liminis – *to obtain control of the aspirations of his own being.*

This is exactly where the Neophyte can find the clue that leads him to a deeper understanding of his own Oath. By going through the Pyramidos, making his Pentacle, working with the Earth Element, the Neophyte gains control over the nature and power of his own being. In particular, with the whisper of the Knowledge and Conversation that the Angel often leaves with the Neophyte, this control acquires a very special power. However, certain questions inevitably arise: Does Neophyte really control anything? What really is the nature of the sense of control that portrays his power? Does he control nature, power, or merely his own being? Is it that his own essential being controls "him" through the illusion of nature and power?

We learn that each grade contains these conundrums and that each of the grades change, in small detail, each of the aspects and the types of control. As the Neophyte learns to control the nature and powers of his own being, so does the Zelator learn to control the foundations of his own being too. Beyond this, the Philosophus likewise has to obtain control of the attractions and repulsions of his own being. One does well to recognize what each of these tasks has in common. This precisely illustrates the concept of "his own being." It is as if, in some immediate way, the Aspirant is instructed that contact with his own being is an end in itself and that control is a reward and the natural course of things, once contact has been accomplished. In one fantastic method, the task of control becomes so accursed, that is to say, "restrictive," that the being falls into its own trap and is startled to discover something lying completely unexpected within: instead of obtaining a newfound control, there is only "the being" – tiny and quiet.

What defines this miniature Selfhood, this Genius, is his authenticity and his exceptionality which exceeds all standards of taste and mediocrity, to the extent that the worst vulgarity in his possession easily becomes an object of the highest divine providence. Every movement of Genius is therefore accompanied by authenticity, from the way of his speech, walking, and even in his seemingly corrupt characteristics such as tics; it appears that the authenticity of Genius is magnificent in things that cause an ordinary man to suffer in the eyes of critics.

We can readily conceive of how the testimony of this Genius is always twofold in much the same way as through knowledge of a person's full name; we can simultaneously conclude to whom exactly is being referred and from which family he comes. In terms of the dual numerical designations that delineate one grade from another within our system, the first number shows the current level of the path relative to the Aspirant's starting point, and the other to his current destination. It is a span of a soul between earth and heaven, and you can see that it is always indicative of harmony and balance, no matter what level of achievement to which is being referred. The balance of force is established by the proper setting of the lever (=). The Neophyte realizes that equation of 4=7 is exactly the same as 5=6, except that in 5=6 the being is presented with and balanced upon a lever that means equality between 5 and 6 and nothing else. However, thinking that this equality is just as precise in 4=7 is nothing but a rough approximation of the apparent space occupied by the living Spirit. Its essence is indeed within the mark of equality, but nowhere else. 4 and 7, as well as 5 and 6, are only the states of the moment chosen by the Spirit for its most favorable manifestation. This authentic being is within the equation, surrounded by a differing range of grades and markings, produced by merely by the process of focusing the lens through which he observes and explores his nature, distancing and approaching this lens so he can finally find focus at one moment. This is the substantial reality of the grades in our Order. Unlike the Probationer who has the mark but no grade, the Neophyte has the grade and receives the equation that is part of the puzzle he must put together until the achievement of the Knowledge and Conversation. He knows that his 1=10 contains the instruction of the highest order, far higher than his own grade, and he has only to press on further to learn how that same equation will be expressed through him whenever he realizes himself as the Zelator 2=9 or the Philosophus 4=7 alike. But let the Neophyte consider these apocryphal and blasphemous ideas before him move on.

We could openly say that the connections between the grades are nothing more than the stages of the same dream. Just as the Probationer is the one who falls asleep, the Adeptus Minor will be the one who awakens, and we will talk everlastingly about the process in between. The Aspirant must understand that the grades are artificial creations; they serve only as our milestones in the endless stellar space of Nuit. The awakening of the Neophyte is one of the most crucial responsibilities of our great Order in the amphitheater of stars; yet it is only one role of many which await those who attain – individually unique as they may be but always bearing the same message:

"We are Mystics,
> *ever eagerly seeking a solution of unpleasant facts.*
We are Men of Science,
> *ever eagerly acquiring pertinent facts.*
We are Sceptics,
> *ever eagerly examining those facts.*
We are Philosophers,
> *ever eagerly classifying and coordinating those well-criti-*
> *cized facts.*
We are Epicureans,
> *ever eagerly enjoying the unification of those facts.*
We are Philanthropists,
> *ever eagerly transmitting our knowledge of those facts to*
> *others.*
Further, we are Syncretists,
> *taking truth from all systems, ancient and modern;*
and Eclectics,
> *ruthlessly discarding the inessential factors in any one*
> *system, however perfect."* [1]

Ultimately, we are all in the light, and we are all the light.

---

[1] Aleister Crowley, "Editorial" from the Equinox 1, No. 2.

CHAPTER TWO

AUGEAS

One of the twelve tasks of Heracles was to clean Augeas' stables. Augeas' was the king of Elis and the son of the Sun-god Helios and Hyrmine, the daughter of King Neleus. He was known more for his filthy stables than he was for his wealth, which he cared most about. Heracles served the Mycenaean king Eurystheus who ordered him to clean the Augean stables.

That was the commandment of the supreme god Zeus and was one of the tasks Heracles had to complete in order to redeem his freedom. Augeas also agreed to give him ten percent of the livestock if Heracles cleaned his stables. Heracles got down to work. First, he took all the cattle to a meadow, some 3000 animals. He then dug channels to the rivers of Alpheus and Peneus, and finally let water flow through the stables, thus washing away all the filth. In the evening, he brought the cattle back to the clean stables. However, Augeas being greedy began bargaining and learned from the conversation that Heracles had been obligated to clean the stables regardless of the offer. He then refused to hand over the portion of livestock and drove him away with insults. Those insults cost him dearly because after completing his tasks, Heracles returned with a large army to Elis and killed King Augeas.

Yet, this work is not about Heracles, the greatest hero to have ever walked the earth, who, though being the son of Zeus, succeeded to eternity first and foremost through his deeds. The Neophyte will never be Heracles. His role is neither to be heroic nor to be as bright and enlightening as the Sun. The Neophyte is an antihero; his role is that of crawling in mud and dust; he does not embark on changing the world as a Bodhisattva does. The Neophyte sets out from his yard finding there a creepy pond of stench, backward ideas, covert desires, failed and sluggish physicality, twisted and oppressed sexuality. He never gets out of that yard. He is stuck there in that place because the more dust he removes, the more falls behind him. To his dismay, the Neophyte learns that he is not like Heracles but actually Augeas, and he finds the qualities of Augeas within himself.

The Neophyte is an antihero, wallowing in his own filth, gaining only one positive aspect from being ensconced in such intense darkness – it is now easy to spot the light. Unfortunately, to his limited understanding, that light is a moral freak and a poor analog of the highest path. That light, as bright as it might be, requires that we make it mobile and self-sustaining. Regardless of its reality, brilliance and radiance are what the Neophyte needs to follow and upon which he will then focus his attention. The fact that this mighty darkness around makes it easy to spot the light in the first place is a cunningly planted machination of the Aspirant's Angel. It is of the utmost importance for the Neophyte and the Probationer alike to keep records of everything. Since his Angel is routinely mocking everything, the Aspirant, by writing about it, can begin to see the ridiculing mechanism of his Angel. And in this way, a specific way indeed, he can find out where lies the path that leads to his Angel. For the first time, the Neophyte will add something more personal and concrete to the notion of an "Angel" besides the empty medieval term. For the first time, his Angel will receive an authentic shade and scent. It will become uniquely "his" rather than just any Angel.

The Neophyte will make a list sof his tics, fears, phobias, per-versions, all bodily defects, compulsive behaviors, and in all that range of morbidity, find the one thing that brings them together – the Angel. For every angry person is aggressive only due to the result of the lack of love, and this lack of love is only compensated by the surplus of love. In this surplus of love for everything and everyone, the Aspirant will find a method for spotting the Angel. The Neophyte cleans his stables with the freshness of water, first and foremost, with emotions made self-aware but not suppressed because suppression and oblivion have already brought him to where he is. He consciously experiences, or at least, wants to em-brace all experiences, even the most unpleasant ones, because they are the very feathers of the wings of his Angel, as he is himself. His work with Pranayama will be somewhat helpful in this; indeed, there is no more delicate kind of energy than the Aspirant being empowered with deep Pranic breaths. All this is expected by the Neophyte, and later by the Zelator in particular. But there are so much unnecessary things in that workout: oinking, counting, dif-ferent colors, names, surnames, various heroes, gods, goddesses, lower gods, lower goddesses, chief helpers, less important helpers, and a choir of angels; imagining that all these peculiarities go into his lungs, as well as deep inside his mind. Instead, the Aspirant should devote himself to ultimately simpler things. He can do Pra-nayama for an hour, instead of focusing on, say, an exercise that is extremely simple: his breath must be so slow that it does not last less than a minute, at first. After such slow breathing, his body will already start working and feeling differently, even resulting in a particular sensation on the skin, which is one of the preconditions in the exercise of the first meditation described in Liber HHH. Also, Pranayama without Kumbhaka, intentional and powerful, brings marvelous shifts in consciousness after just twenty minutes, lowers the acidity of the body, and brings back memories from the earliest moments of life soon. Let the Aspirant investigate. He must inves-tigate.

As we have established, the Neophyte is Augeas, not Heracles. Heracles represents his Angel, who has to complete the twelve tasks. In other words, he has to reckon and illuminate every zodiacal house and become aware of the full circle to awaken the meaning of all aspects that refract through his soul, thereby becoming aware of his true nature and his divine order. These twelve tasks just serve to point to the nature of the Sun, the path that the Sun crosses always serves just this one purpose. The tasks are there to point to the only real purpose that a soul has – the Great Work. The Neophyte becomes keenly aware of his neglected life and the inevitability of his death. While the Probationer's path is full of ascending steps, the stage of the Neophyte is a distinctly inferior place – noxious are his dwellings down there. It is far removed from a body into which the eucharist flows. It is an odorous body of stale flesh, like a decomposing corpse. Here he stands still, yet there is just enough movement in him to release the rush of cleansing waters, just as the rivers Alpheus and Peneus cleared Augeas' stables.

At the stage metaphorically implied by this story, the Aspirant is the antagonist; he does not stand for the light or have a path to redemption. Yet, he still possesses the thread that Ariadne cunningly left to Theseus – a mechanism that helps to undo his knot.

What can all this mean for the Aspirant? For his first act, the Neophyte cleanses himself from the futility of the practice which he so zealously performed during the yearlong term of his Probation, wherein he received a "program" and certain instructions. Now, after passing the Probation, he finds himself selected as "eligible" for the Order. The stables of the newcomer are now cleansed by two rivers. That is to say, his Malkuth now twists and climbs upon the Tree of Life, turning from the Middle Path alternately through the Pillars of Mercy and of Severity, respectively. He keeps his physical aspect fresh with various exercises. He makes his Pentacle. That is, he aligns his body with his vision of the Universe, which is the same bodily mechanism. In doing so, he begins to love his body. He slowly rids himself of his physical condition, which the Zelator will experience to the fullest as an attainment in dealing with Asana and Pranayama, through the advent of automatic breathing and stonelike stiffness. The Neophyte introduces "freshness" in his work. He abandons the system he used as the Probationer – doing one practice for a year – and now he brings new vigor and enthusiasm to his grade.

The Probationer is now figuratively defeated by Heracles. Having completed all twelve tasks, Heracles returned and killed Augeas. Likewise, the aspiring being, after experiencing and assimilating all twelve zodiacal phases, inexorably decides to "incarnate" in the aspect of his Pure Will – Heracles "kills" Augeas. The Probationer, having gone throughout his year as the Sun has gone through the twelve houses of the zodiac, now returns exalted as the Neophyte. The Angel appears in the world of Malkuth by birth. The Death of Augeas at the hands of Heracles similarly points to the relationship that Jacob had with the Angel with whom he wrestled. Augeas' death brings about the birth of the Man of the Earth. Heracles is the Lover born to the Man of the Earth – Augeas. All this is obviously a full account of the Ritual of Passing through the Duat – Liber Cadaveris.

Augeas is both an aspect of the Neophyte and the Man of the Earth who is tempted by Binah. His fascination with riches and his filthy stables are the epithets of Malkuth and Binah, made especially clear by the metaphor of the stables being washed by abundant waters. Thus, it is the Neophyte, to his fault, who does not perceive the body as an instrument of Adonai, who does not put the earthly element in the function of the Spirit, and who has tainted his Pentacle with dirt to such an extent that the outlines of the Great Work are obscured. In fact, the Neophyte does not perceive the Universe in a way that predicts the proper use of the Pentacle. The Universe is no longer reflected in him. The Neophyte does not look after his body because he does not see there any means to fulfill his Pure Will. Thus, it decays because it has no proper use, in the same way non-absorbed food goes off. Every Neophyte who refuses to change and reconcile his life with the course of everything in nature, and who in the end refuses to subordinate to the course of his Pure Will, turns into Augeas. His parallel in the Order of the Rose Cross is the Black Brother or Augeas in the Golden Dawn. Heracles must indeed kill Augeas. Even the mere thought of the Angel serves as a support to all work. Without him – without the Angel – all of the Neophyte's work is doomed to futility and failure.

Yet, it may be said that such work of the Neophyte is inevitable. The piling up of dirt and filth justifies cleaning as both sensible and reasonable. Purity, as a term, is very much appreciated in our cause, but unfortunately, one's own opinion is much less so. The Aspirant's impulse to constantly "cleanse" his space from outside influences is so prevalent that we should summarily explore this unique phenomenon. There is, in fact, a misconception about this cleansing. Removing the outside influences merely replaces them with the influences of our own mental apparatus, effectively soiling the space all over again. It is actually impossible to clean the space of work. The only cleansing that has taken place seems to be in our mind. It is there that we store the information that a particular space is pure, by pronouncing certain holy names and drawing appropriate pentagrams along specific cardinal directions. But how clean were we ourselves before we started? The Aspirant knows that every dedication to the highest is indeed the highest act of cleansing in itself. Every action aimed at the Great Work has already been purified by the fire of pure desire, but is there anything more pristine than the desire for the Angel? Does not a particle of dust and ignorance deserve to exist? Is not every unbalanced entity as much of an entity as any other? Do we have the right to ask angels to come to a circle or a demon to fill the smoke inside the triangle with its presence, unless we are ready to both love it and accept it as part of ourselves? Is it possible to just wash off the dirt that we ourselves have been gathering aided by our own stupidity for years? Can you be brave and pure enough to summon demons outside the triangle? Can you be so pure and so dedicated to the Great Work to forget all the danger and embrace the leper demon into your arms with nothing but your love? Let the Neophyte ponder the essence of what is being presented here. Let his apparatus of thought transcend all written rules. Let him identify those who are his. Finally, let him walk steadily and proudly.

Once and for all, let the Neophyte not fear Augeas' death, for it is the crown of everything, even as the bodily death of all that is incarnate. The lethal vengeance of Heracles is inevitable. It is the nature of Augeas to die, and only in this way will he fulfill his divine destiny. The Aspirant must not refuse to face physical death under the pretext of spiritual death, which is ubiquitous in our art. After all, death is the highest form of purification, and it is not uncommon for the Neophyte to go through near-to-death experiences. It is, unfortunately, the only occurrence in the life of the Neophyte that blends the idea of time and the idea of the body. It can be understood that these events are actually lagging reflexes from the Liber Pyramidos, thus keeping some aspects of the body and the soul unchanged in the tomb. This is the rebellion of Ruach under the siege of Tiphareth and is the perfect place to put into action our psychotherapy and Qabalah. The Aspirant does not need to spend time in a thorough analysis of his personality and fundamental refusal to die. What then is the part of us that receives such a passionate reprimand from the Angel? Is it our physical health to which that quiet nature draws our attention, to have the balance restored before we push our body to the extremes in the fire of an alchemical furnace? Or is it a complex lurking from behind and offering the body to save itself and draw attention to something completely irrelevant? It may not even be a bodily mechanism; it may be precisely a psychic one – the one lurking and treacherously sacrificing healthy elements to relieve his diseased syphilis leg. Regardless of the mechanism, we should always be mindful that it is the unconsciousness at stake. We must live through that element as much as through reason. It is always a lever for fear and uncertainty. Still, it can also be the echo of such a tragic phenomenon as anger. The Neophyte must always know that such a drastic choice is the diversion of attention to oneself as a child, which, in fact, is what the Neophyte is in our holy Order. Instead of relying upon himself in the present, the Neophyte can get closer to the idea of death and of self-destruction – where awaits Adonai, not oblivion – though Adonai is death indeed for many parts of the being, including the Aspirant's limited thinking apparatus. In various ways, our nature reminds us that the body needs the spirit and that we should take our bodily aspect seriously. The whole is impossible to comprehend without all the parts. Tetragrammaton is a dead word if a living spirit does not constantly pass through it, as the bodily livingness as well. At times, we, like playful children, find ourselves in need to be brought back to the path by nature and its surprises and persuasive juices. But every Neophyte must know that the nature of Probation is to move on, not to flounder and fail. Failure is just an illusion of an eclipse of the star, where no force of the Universe can stop the motion of the Moon and the star. It is just a matter of time before light will shine upon the soul again. The nature of the progress of the Neophyte is always and only the Zelator. Thus, only the Ritual of Passing through the Duat is the true path onward. Formal performance of a ritual should not be of interest to us at all, as long as our being is turned to the ultimate essence that is only triggered by that ritual. The Ritual of Passing through the Duat is not as much a ritual as it is an actual passage – where further progress lies in the awareness of the meaning of that rite. Therefore, passing further on can be accomplished perfectly without a single spoken word in the ritual. Unless the Aspirant has understood the essence of going through the Duat, performing a ritual by heart even a million times will bring nothing but wasted time, unless he has understood that his passing is changing him, and more importantly, that his passing and his changing also change the Duat itself. Learning the act of Passing through darkness gives you a whole new experience of light. In the end, our understanding of darkness is such a lofty epithet. Darkness is not empty; on the contrary, there is more to it than just light, or LVX itself. Darkness is dark and quiet; it is the potency of all Wills and consciousness in totality. It is the true maternal womb of all stars. But in no way should the Aspirant attach an air of morality to this darkness or even try to understand it from the point of view of his ethics. This darkness is something that is a common epithet of all notions and concepts in our Order – just as light illuminates all things, so darkness serves to perceive differences and uniqueness in that light.

The water that purifies and releases the flow of the Aspirant's Will to the heavens of Tiphareth and the Holy Guardian Angel is purifying just at first glance. Nevertheless, the same water also flows into that great Ocean. Its true estuary is Pan. Above all, cleanliness is a highly relative and fictitious term, both by aspiration and by definition, and purity is too often confused with sterility, which can be devastating to the work of the Neophyte. Almost every act of purification ends in neurosis and projection of sterility, and it is in the line of separation between these two concepts where the Neophyte finds a great lesson that renders the nature of his own grade so brilliantly. In our art, purity precedes dedication, that is, water precedes fire. There is just one aspiration of our being, which is directed by the fire of the Will to the Self. But the whole problem about which we have been talking for so long is that our water can and will put out that fire. Harboring such a great wish for purification causes one to forget that the Will for the Great Work is itself also the most powerful purifier. Is not the will-to-succeed the success itself? Is not the will for the Angel an aspect of the True Will? It can be said that the filth of Probation has disturbed the meticulous Neophyte and that these two grades are actually aspects of one being. An eligible Probationer is already a future Neophyte, the end of Probation and passing through the Pyramidos is also the entry into the grade of Neophyte. Although the Ritual of the Pyramid is undertaken by the Probationer, it is completed by the Neophyte. The very heart of the Pyramid ritual is set by the following verses, which is directly related to the theme of spiritual hygiene:

"Behold! the Perfect One hath said
These are my body's Elements
Tried and found pure, a golden spoil."

The Aspirant should study the meditation referred to as Liber HHH with particular care. There he can find an indication of the nature of the purification through which the Aspirant goes, yet it should be noticed that it is obtained only at the grade of the Zelator.

LIBER HHH

"Two and twenty times shall he figure to himself that he is bitten by a serpent, feeling even in his body the poison thereof. And let each bite be healed by an eagle or hawk, spreading its wings above his head, and dropping thereupon a healing dew."

The Probationer represents suffering, while the Neophyte is pain. But that magnificent Binah, that endless and vast dark Ocean, attaches such great characteristics to that pain that at some moment, that pain will become sadness that erodes the soul, while at others, it will be numbing physical bone pain, then like open wounds burning, and finally, a void that hurts the most. The Neophyte will make friends with all these types of pain.

By studying HHH meditation, the Aspirant will identify corresponding body parts with 22 snake bites. He will go through each part of the body and purify it in his mind, the way he thinks is appropriate.

32.	*The Universe*	ת	Bones
31.	*The Æon*	ש	Teeth (also could be blood)
30.	*The Sun*	ר	Heart
29.	*The Moon*	ק	Bladder
28.	*The Emperor*	צ	Hips
27.	*The Tower*	פ	Muscles
26.	*The Devil*	ע	Genitals
25.	*Art*	ס	Blood (as life, dedicated to the Great Work)
24.	*Death*	נ	Bowels
23.	*The Hanged man*	מ	Saliva and lymph
22.	*Adjustment*	ל	Spine
21.	*Fortune*	כ	Hands
20.	*The Hermit*	י	Legs
19.	*Lust*	ט	Sweat
18.	*The Chariot*	ח	Stomach
17.	*The Lovers*	ז	Nostrils
16.	*The Hierophant*	ו	Arms and shoulders
15.	*The Star*	ה	Head and face
14.	*The Empress*	ד	Sperm
13.	*The High priestess*	ג	Prostate
12.	*The Magus*	ב	Brain and nerves
11.	*The Fool*	א	Respiratory organs

The nature of this purification is like fire, where the lower parts of our being are nothing but the means of sustaining that terrifying flame – terrifying to the very same being undergoing purification without realizing that it remains unchanged while changing in this process. It is precisely in this paradox that the terrifying fear of burning and death lies – an idea that is equally attributable to the phenomenon of cleansing – because he neither burns away a part of himself, nor does he become anything else other than what he has already been. He has just "lit up" what he thought he was or maybe should have been. Indeed, the Angel despises the path of Yoga. He does not seek an "other" to be "One." It is enough for him to be alone with "Himself." For the first time, the Neophyte implants such a passionate thought in himself, realizing the meaninglessness and paradox of the path, and the meaninglessness of purity. He is not yet able to understand, but that is why he accepts his imperfection; he accepts that he alone is the reason for the braking of his Sun boat – him and no one else. And it is in the Ritual of the Pyramid where he underlines this in the finest possible way:

> "Who clutches at my throat?
> Who pins me down?
> Who stabs my heart?
> I am unfit to pass
> within this Pylon of the Hall of Maat."

This is one of the most magnificent moments that any Golden Dawn Aspirant will ever experience. He realizes that it is no one else but himself who plummets down (Malkuth). He is the one who pierces his own heart with his confusing emotions, and who slits his throat by his misunderstanding (Daath), and finally, moping, he accepts that he is unfit to pass further. He finally falls impure and accepts the fall as the ultimate outcome, accepting the truth that he is impure and ineligible.

The magical weapon given to the Neophyte is the Pentacle, and he pays great attention to thinking about this sacred object, which has such a high place in our art. The potent idea of cleaning leads the Neophyte to wonder if the Pentacle can be cleaned? Is the effort itself in designing one's vision of the Universe really the only purifying force that equally creates not only a new view of the Universe but a whole new Universe itself, while destroying the old one, with all of its bad and defective laws such as morality, ethics, sexuality, and ideals? Is not the dust on the Pentacle just part of that same Pentacle? Could it not be about organizing rather than cleaning? We believe that, from the philosophical point of view, this is the only true task that the Neophyte can have. On the other hand, the only real practical task for him is the realization of a lucid dream, that is, an astral projection. All other things are more or less noteworthy, but without this, it can be said that nothing valid has been achieved.

What then is purity anyway? What does it mean to be clean and pure? Is it possible to smear the soul more than it really needs to be? Is not the filth of the soul merely the consequence of a filthy act done long ago? Is not dust just a road sign and a boost on the path to the stars? Is not cleansing just a hoax? Is not just one Liber Resh practice more of a reminder than a cleansing habit? Indeed, all of this sheds an entirely different light on the introductory part of Star Ruby. In fact, most of the search for this grade is not about finding new directions but shedding light upon the old ones. It is about changing and adjusting old techniques to the point of perfection, whereupon we are astonished to see that we had the keys in our hands all this time, but that we merely tried to use them to open the wrong door.

At the very beginning of Star Ruby, the Aspirant is dashing down the hand with a great sweep back and out, crying: *"Apo Pantos Kakodaimonos!"* This bitter movement is often misused in a pathetic pursuit of imbalanced forces. Where would you banish them to, and for how long? Outside of the room, or beyond the city limits? Until tomorrow, or at least until the weekend, maybe? Here we need to look at all this under a different light – we are not turning away any evil. Dashing down our hand with a great sweep back, we are saying to them: *"Get in line! Not away, but behind me – in a row!"* That whole gesture and cry then have quite a different flavor. For us, Thelemites, it is sad to say to our demons *"go away"*; it is far more preferable to exclaim – *"follow the leader, lads!"*

It is not as important exactly how *"Apo pantos..."* translates, but rather what is its underlying meaning. The magick is not in words but in our awareness. We are the ones who give them meaning. One can read Liber Samekh and have nothing happen. At the same time, another can read it and achieve the Great Work – same words, but with totally different outcomes. Barbaric names do not have any meaning at all, yet they induce such a great change in our perception. We can run from stupidity and limitation, but can we really turn away from our light and darkness? As a Thelemite, do we really believe in "demons," or perhaps do we interpret them in some more profound and personal meaning? Putting your finger out and away to compel your demons into a row behind you is not the denial of a child – who closes his eyes when confronted with fear in the dark – but the command of a Thelemite who puts them in order and balance behind him.

The Aspirant will find two basic principles of hygiene in our Order. He should accept both of them as equally correct, although it is natural for each individual to go along with one of the two. They are not opposed to each other, and yet, the difference in their understanding is a philosophical difference in life. But the Aspirant does not need to subordinate his own path to another and regard the other path as more sublime and better. Let him deepen his confidence in his own ideal of purity and apply it in his practical work.

An objection can be made with regard to the Pure versus the True Will. The Book of the Law itself directs us to the Pure Will, but "pure" from what? The True Will is found, while the Pure Will is simply fulfilled. Taking into account such a mishap in today's world about the True Will, and how small a percentage of people have enlightened knowledge of their nature, we can openly ask whether the term itself may have been misconceived. There are no wrong answers, but wrong questions – and when we put all this along the same plane, our question may end up being completely wrong. The very phenomenon of this paradoxical purity in the idea of the Pure Will results in the revelation of a completely different plane wherein we can try to understand this cornerstone of our interest. Only a "Pure" value can be free from both True and False statements.

If we are to accept the concept of a True Will, then the thought of the False Will inevitably arises. Although the central idea in the phenomenon of Will is unity, we must ask – the unity of what? How many things? Is not that a paradox in itself? The True Will has become a beautiful badge to wear on the lapel of a Thelemite's formal suit – the beautiful, glittering, and admirable garment of the public persona. Nevertheless, after a wonderful dinner full of auspicious invocations and chants, we return home and disrobe, all the while wondering, "*What now?*"

But the Pure Will is will because it is pure, and it is pure precisely because it is willing. It defines itself, without comparison to anything else potentially less or not Pure. The Will is, therefore, a value vastly different from the vector, in the manifolds of all dimensions, which acts in each of them in a seemingly different way, yet always remaining the same and retaining a constant in value. Our endless debates poison that "holiness" to such an extent that we inevitably come to a position of discussing someone else's Will rather than exercising our own. All the time talking about purity would be better spent actually talking about light. Yet throughout all this, our allegory gives guidance to the Knowledge and Conversation, along with its paradox, which has always been the one and only true teacher and the method of ultimate experience.

A bit of this sublimity can be found in the story of the Sixth Zen Patriarch:

Hui-neng was a poor young man who supported his mother by selling firewood. On one occasion, while walking through the city, he heard a monk recite the Diamond Sutra. At that moment, his heart opened, and he experienced something he had not experienced before, something he was forced to seek from that moment on along that path, through the Enlightenment. He inquired with the monks and learned that he could join the life of the monks and teach the Fifth Patriarch at Yellow Plum (the Fifth Patriarch, who was called Gunin Daiman (Hung-yen in Japanese) and was based in the North of China).

He traveled for a long time before arriving at the monastery, where he finally met with the Fifth Patriarch Hung-yen. After introducing himself, the patriarch asked him, *"Where do you come from, and what are you looking for here?"*

"I am just a farmer from the south, and I wish nothing more than to realize the Buddha nature."

"You come from the south, and southerners do not possess the characteristics of the Buddha. How then can you hope to experience Enlightenment?" the Fifth Patriarch asked him.

Then Hui-neng said, *"I am from the south, but can one make a distinction between north and south when it comes to the nature of the Buddha?"*

These words immediately appealed to the teacher. He admitted Hui-neng to the monastery, where he did ordinary jobs.

As time went on, the Fifth Patriarch decided to choose a worthy successor and presented his decision to the disciples, saying that whoever hangs the words that most directly reflect the Buddha's nature on the door of his room would assume the mantle of the patriarch.

Shen-hsiu had been the most learned monk by then, and he immediately started meditating to write what he was feeling. The next morning, the door to his room read:

"The body is like the Bodhi Tree
The Heart is a bright mirror on a stand.
Everyday wipe clean the mirror,
So that no dust may alight."

Having read Shen-hsiu's verses, they all felt great delight and somehow felt that he should be the sixth patriarch.

Young Hui-neng was passing by, and being illiterate, he asked one of the monks to read Shen-hsiu's words to him. He then thought for a moment and asked the monk to help him write the lyrics at the door of the Hui-neng's room. What was written on the door was:

"There is no Bodhi Tree,
The Heart has no stand.
When there is nothing whatsoever,
What dust can alight where?"

And so the Sixth Patriarch was born.

The Neophyte will choose well, and he will take an equally right path. He will clean both that mirror and his mind from the urge for purity. He must do the job without passion, cleaning for the sake of cleaning, every moment loaded with dirt causes a detour from the path to the Sun – a detour that the Aspirant will undoubtedly take later, in the attainments of both Practicus and Philosophus. The jewel that makes dreams come true must remain hidden in this great market of the gods. No one should notice the value of this most precious diamond; it must not be stolen because he saves it for just one and equally secret god. It must indeed remain dirty and dusty; it must not reflect the ray that would bounce back to the pupil of a thief who will see it. He will stay low and wait for the right moment to come. Indeed, the Neophyte has nothing to do with his work except to draw paths and develop an awareness of the higher and further planes that lie ahead. The Neophyte does not open the door, by any means. He simply obtains the keys.

CHAPTER THREE

STUDENT

A ll the peculiarity of this place lies in one straightforward fact, though the Aspirant refuses to accept it, which is that he learns a lot more from the Student than from his own Superior. The vast majority have a misconception about teachers. We do not obtain teaching from the Superior – it comes by observation of the Student. The Superior merely provides testimony and validation of our path. Still, the Student is the embodiment of the Superior to himself, and everything he does not like about the Student is indeed what he sees in himself. The Student is Angel's assistant, and the Superior is merely a gardener, even though the holy rose at the center of that garden, from which emerges a cross, does not depend on cultivation. The gardener is only there to lead us with love through the garden of God to our rose, but contributes little to the process. However, the signs and directions he provides are the most wonderful things we will ever see in our holy Order.

In the same way as one's parental feelings simply cannot be explained to one who is childless, the Aspirant cannot be aware of the longing of the Goddess Nuit for her children, or the aspiration of the Will to get assimilated into the great Nothingness of Pan unless he has taken a Student under his wing. It is an entirely natural process manifesting itself in its own way. This process cannot be transmitted to someone else in advance, nor is it possible to be unveiled at a predetermined time.

The role of the Superior is to be a fellow sufferer, a wandering companion, a witness of the sacred act of the Oath which the Student undertakes. The nature of their relationship is commiseration as much as companionship, and not fraternity in the usual sense of that word – to be a witness on the Student's journey and his shadow companion is the true function of the Superior.

The Student is an ever-present shadow reminding him of the constancy of the light behind. One can say that the Neophyte's role has not been fully realized unless he has taken on a Probationer, but that in no way means that the path without a Student is invalid. However, the act of passing the link down to the Probationer completes a full circle. As the Superior moves forward with the Student following, the power seems to be flowing through him neatly and properly. With his signature on two different Oaths – his own and his Student's – the testimony is complete. Yet, this does not mean that his path is destined for such an act. The Superior reflects the Student's Angel, and the whole manner of his relationship is just a pale imitation of the Student's Knowledge and Conversation. Being fully aware of this relationship grants the Aspirant an exquisite epiphany of the Pantheon of our Æon.

A Neophyte must remain aware that there is no good or bad guidance, just as there is no good or bad Student. The Superior's influence is limited to ensuring that the rules of the Order are conveyed zealously and accurately – even though each rule is open to interpretation. It is often said during national elections that who counts the votes matters more than the number of votes counted, but it is inappropriate to suggest that a similar attitude is present in our dealings. Nevertheless, we must always acknowledge one indisputable fact – we are all human beings and everything that entails. We are all prone to anger, fatigue, betrayal, and neurosis.

How on earth are we going to treat the Student then? The Neophyte must consider the relationship with the Student as a dialogue between him and his God – always and on any occasions. As far as details are concerned, everything can be found in our books:

Liber 13 vel Graduum Montis Abiegni
Liber 33 - An Account of A∴A∴
Liber 61 vel Causae
Liber 185 - Liber Collegii Sancti
Liber 207 - A Syllabus of the Official Instructions of the A∴A∴
Liber 489 - One Star in Sight

Memorizing a chapter of the "Book of the Heart Girth with a Serpent" causes quite a unique dizziness in the minds of many Students. They refer to that chapter so often that they forget all else, making it seem as if this holy book was composed of just that one, horrifying chapter. On the contrary, one must consider what happens with those chapters *not* learned by heart. This perhaps is of greater importance than the chapter that was memorized. Therefore, one must make his chosen chapter fuel for the fire arising within his own soul, and a muster field from which he sets off to wage his war. Learning a chapter by heart is not to be a simple act of memorization. The Student must be able to start from any verse, quote the previous verse, and even recount the entire chapter backward if necessary. Inventiveness may be more rewarding than mere learning by heart. I remember that my Superior, once in possession of my diary and practice records supplied after weeks and weeks of preparation and coming to him fully prepared and equally terrified, briefly asked if I had learned a chapter. After I had answered in the affirmative, I took a deep breath and prepared to recite my presentation. Immediately, he only said, "Right." And that was the end of it. In fact, I had recited it many times before – just on my own. But again, every Superior has his ideal way of asking, just as each and every Student has his ideal way of giving. In symbiosis, these two paths indeed find their manifestation in an infinite number of different variants, which, in turn, always point to the same thing.

In a vast number of cases, written parts of the exams represent pressure exerted on the Student, which must be channeled in different and creative ways.

Sometimes it is not a good idea to assign exam questions right after the Oath has been taken, and the grade has just started. It may be beneficial to wait for a month or two before the end of the grade. In some cases, exam questions should be taken every couple of weeks, preferably not before the previous one has been satisfactorily answered.

Of course, the Superior ought to be able to change questions, but without deviating from the plan of progress or its principles. He should recognize which aspects of the Student's being responds to specific questions. For example, one Student can be astoundingly proficient at Gematria and yet so utterly incompetent with dream analysis and interpretation of personal symbols that his presentations will appear childish.

There are Students who are fully aware of their path from the first day of taking their Oath. There are those who simply need time to adjust to new circumstances. There are those of a fighting type who see a plot against their own Great Work in everything, and there are those who are endlessly skeptical. Yet again, they are so utterly frightened with such a concrete sense of fear that their Angel will everlastingly hide somewhere deep in the shadow of terrifying darkness. But they all seem to need only two things: love and confidence.

The Student has a dual function in the life of the Neophyte in that he both servers as his opposite and objectification of himself. The mistakes the Student makes cause the Neophyte to see more clearly, and by teaching the Student, he teaches himself. In this way, the Student is an aspect of the Angel – the aspect that imprints the nature of the Bodhisattva upon the Neophyte's being. The Bodhisattva is the one who refuses to get enlightened until the last being in the Universe is realized in Buddha, therefore choosing to remain in this world and to help other souls. This relationship is a precious psychological machine; a mistake made in our path is something that can be undone with little risk when the Neophyte has a younger and less experienced person with him. The good of the individual Neophyte loses significance in comparison to the good of the Student in charge of him. This commitment to nurturing reveals the high value of this endeavor. It serves as both a brake by continually returning the Neophyte's consciousness to the halfway point and as a constant indication that the Great Work is still ahead. When dealing with others, we are dealing with ourselves. This entire process is a reminder of our morality, as illustrated by this divine instruction for our Order:

> "He is furthermore trained to the one habit essential to Membership of the A∴A∴; he must regard all his attainments as primarily the property of those less advanced aspirants who are confided to his charge."
>
> [Liber CDLXXXIX, Aleister Crowley]

It must be considered essential that every Aspirant works and keeps diaries for the sake of his magical child who will inherit it all. A strong and profoundly intuitive feeling arises when we devote ourselves to thinking about our magical unborn inner child to whom we leave all of this behind. Even if we have children in the physical world, that inner child is someone far more unique, precious, and different from anything else in the physical realm. It is a special urge far beyond being a parent – an urge to leave our heritage to the starry sky. In any case, contemplating this concept can be a great meditation for the Aspirant, if nothing else.

Regarding the Student's oppositional function, the vacuum of his lack of understanding draws upon the inexhaustible strength of the Neophyte's Binah with force and energy akin to the Probationer's original enthusiasm. It is an ideal opportunity for the Great Mother to ground the Student as he ventures into the eternal dream of the unconsciousness and advances from the lack of talent and progress to the first hints of mastery over things he previously had no access to. Nevertheless, the Student's talents are often a major liability to him as he may unconsciously pause along his path to compensate for what he has missed. Yet even as the hindrance of this shadow-fight rages within him, Angel's power will strike and propel him forward, removing dried mud from his wings, so to speak, thus increasing the speed of his ascent. That blow delivered by the Angel is interpreted as pain by the Neophyte, who is yet unaware that such pain is the projection of light. He must recognize that the pain-induced knowledge gained from each event is a specific form of Conversation between him and his God, insofar as there is neither threat nor distress that is not Adonai in essence. Binah will find many ways to mock and counter the perceptions of the Student, which are so unique to each Probationer that it is not worth drawing any premature conclusions.

But how much does it take for liveliness to dwell in the being of the Superior who watches the Student who cuts his own way through jungle and him paving that way with gold? How small is each piece of Superior's own experience in relation to Student's growth? The Superior will find a divine transfer in his own Student, not for the purpose of his downfall or attainment, but for that divine order of things, which like the theatre of the Universe reflects the whole nature of our great Order. It is to receive and to be received, seek and be let in. Their relationship is more exalted than their individual roles in the Tantric ritual; in fact, their relationship *is* the true Tantra. Everything else is just a vague semblance of that sublime game played by the Superior and the Student. Every Superior is an awakened Student, and every Student is a sleeping Superior. The Student, the Superior, and the Angel as well are all integral factors in the game of light and shadows of the great eclipse. Each of them is equally the Moon, the Earth, and the Sun in their own moments.

One thing that should definitely be mentioned is the creation of specific sexual energy, which, when united with the Student's presence in the life of the Neophyte, can have a disastrous outcome. This pressure is equally present in the case of the Zelator, but in a different form, less dangerous, so to say, for he is now directly protected by the Sun and the Angel for the first time, and his path has already moved far beyond so that the power of the Earth cannot have such a terrible influence as is the case of the Neophyte. For the Zelator, the influences of the Moon are already much more significant, while the Neophyte remains firmly under the rule of the great Mother and Binah, who, as the lord of the earthly element, closely watches over his flock in this sphere. This idea presents itself in the form of a Kundry, that is, a Vampire facing the Neophyte and strongly influencing his path. There will undoubtedly be more to say about this particular circumstance.

It is one thing to experience Probation as a Probationer, yet it is quite different to experience it from the perspective of the Neophyte under whose charge the Probationer is. It is a tale so fantastic that it is impossible to convey it with ready-made instructions or words, as is precisely the case with the child – the role of the parent is something that comes as a reward rather than a burden. Therefore, the Student is the prize for the Neophyte; this is really the only correct way to think of it.

It is convenient to ask the Probationer to analyze the particulars of the day he signed his Oath. The Neophyte can then compare the analysis of the day of his own assumption with that of his Student. The aspects of such a comparison will leave a lasting impact.

The Superior should understand the Student's day as a special event within his own birth chart, which he will expand with this information and explore the extent to which it reflects upon his soul. The Superior should also liken this task to calculating comparative natal charts if he so wishes. He should also watch for hidden messages from his own Angel while doing his best to recognize the envoy of light in his Student as if he had caught a spy who was indeed in possession of the information he had to retrieve back under the threat of terrible torture and execution.

It can be observed that certain grades can be of similar nature, in the same way grades themselves have a certain nature that tends to be uniform, so the cooperation between the grades of the Superior and the Student has its own character. Caution should be taken with these observations because they really are nothing more than an analysis of some motivating dream, in which one may or may not find a connection to the Great Event. All that can be said about this theme is contained in the following:

STUDENT

		Probationer	Neofit	Zelator	Practicus	Filosofus
S U P E R I O R	Neofit	FEAR RIGOR FATAL-ATTRACTION PERVERSION				
	Zelator	DISSIPATION SUPERFICIALITY	REVERIE SHAME			
	Practicus	BOREDOM	DISTRACTION	IDEALIZING		
	Filosofus	HATE	FRUSTRATION JEALOUSY	NEGLIGENCE	INDIFFERENCE DOUBT	
	Dominus Liminis	ADORATION	ENVY	IDOLATRY	DEFIANCE	JITTER

Sometimes the crown of a relationship is reflected in the Superior; sometimes, it is in the Student. And just as every relationship needs participants, it cannot be said whether the Student or the Superior is the main trigger here, they both seem to be participating in the phenomenon in the same way. But, of course, every relationship is unique, just as the experience of each grade is itself unique and authentic.

Every transfer of force involves two components: a lever and support. In a broader understanding, these also exist in the interactions of small gears with larger ones. We do not acknowledge attainment until it is transferred to another soul who joins his Superior in his place, or until the transference of one's experience awakens someone else. Two souls, driven by identical motivations, attaining identifiable distinctiveness in their life. The final outcome is always the same thing – the Knowledge and Conversation of the Holy Guardian Angel.

Embracing the Student awakens many aspects within the Superior, of which the pedagogical aspect is but one. The phenomenon of psychological transfer is very important. At first, one is tempted to see this as success, but the nature of every transfer is actually a kind of failure. While it is true that authenticity demands every event to be distinguished from every other event, it is nevertheless correct to present the transference as an integral aspect of the great wholeness that binds all things. The Aspirant needs to confront every idea with its opposite; only in this way can all of this make sense. The Superior is a past Student; the Student is a future Superior. It is the same character reflected in the mirror, who might as well be millions of light-years away, and once that light of reflection returns, he is now marvelously looking and wondering at a beautiful child in the mirror – who is actually himself.

One day, an old professor met a young man who asked him, *"Do you remember me?"* The old man said he did not. Therefore, the man told him that he had once been his disciple. The professor asked him, *"Ah, yes? And what do you do now?"* The young man replied, *"I am a teacher."* *"Oh, how wonderful, just like me,"* replied the old man. *"Yes. I actually became a teacher because it was you who inspired me to be like you."*

The old man was curious and asked him to explain how it was possible, and the young man told him the story:

"One day, a friend of mine came to school with a beautiful new watch, and I stole it from him. Soon my friend noticed the theft and immediately complained to our teacher, and it was you. Then you told all of us in class: "A watch belonging to one of your friends was stolen during today's class. Whoever stole it, please return it." However, I did not want to give it back, so nobody moved. Then you closed the door and told us to get up so you could search through our pockets, one by one. However, before that, you had told us to close our eyes. We did that, and you searched through one pocket at a time, and when you came to me, you found the watch and took it. You kept searching through everyone else's pockets, and when you were done, you said, "Open your eyes. I found the watch." After that, you never said anything to me, and you never revealed the name of the culprit to the rest of the class. That day, you saved my dignity forever. Otherwise, that would have been the most embarrassing day of my life. Thereafter, you never mentioned anything to me about the theft. Although you did not yell at me or give me a moral lesson, I learned the lesson, nonetheless. Thanks to you, I realized that was how a real educator should act. Can you recall that event, professor?"

The professor replied: *"I remember the case of the stolen watch very well and that I searched the pockets of all the students, but I do not remember that it was you, nor could I have known. Because, you see, as I was searching your pockets, I kept my eyes closed too."*

There are two essential transfers in this matter of ours, and both are equally magnificent. Although different, they are both aiming at the same target – the Great Work. The first transfer is the

Motto of the Aspirant himself – representing his first failed attempt at the Great Work. However, the second transfer comes a little later and is presented by the reception of the Student – which is just a shadow of an event to come. But both of these mechanisms, are they anything but reflections of the ultimate Sun? Aren't these "failed" celebration festivities of something that has already been attained?

Yet, as long as there is a need for leverage, as long as there is a need to use any force, we can say that the matter has not come to fruition. If there remains a need for rituals, vibrations, exchange of knowledge, invocations and appeals, incantations, barbaric names, and taking the Oaths, we can reasonably say that we are little more than starving ghosts.

Neophyte's grade is a grade with a significant percentage of loss. Probationers are resigning, while Neophytes are failing, and we often need to think about this relationship. What this all points to is the impact of quantity upon the development of the Proba-tioner, while in the case of Neophyte, it is a qualitative leap that he must make to overcome the task of the grade.

Although it is widespread for Neophytes to desire to take on Students, sometimes those good intentions pave the road to hell. The Student's task is to move on, while the Superior's task is to make that possible, but he can never vouch for such an undertak-ing. Nevertheless, we must always consider that it might not be possible to "fail" at something as sublime as the Great Work. We must make a distinction between the Great Work and the grade. If the inevitable completion of the Great Work is indeed assured, would that mean that passing to the next grade is likewise settled? Failing the grades does not equate to the ultimate fail. At univer-sity, the Student is allowed to take and retake exams under certain circumstances, and it is up to him to determine his own pace of progress and completion of his studies. This matter is entirely left to one's Superior to decide, all according to his Student's personality and affinities. Our standpoint is that you have already achieved everything; you cannot "fail" at something which you already "are." What then do we mean by the term "fail"? Is it a terminal state or just a phase? More importantly, failing in relation to what? Is it even possible that a soul will fail to perform the Great Work, given that he already has the most precious gift and weapon in the Universe – his Will? Do we not keep failing each day and continue to get back up time after time until the final realization? Having achieved this ourselves, can we conceive that this final realization will not happen for someone else? Truth be told, I have never believed one could fail. The Great Work is not someone's condition; it is his claim. There is no failing. There is only the fear of failing.

All of this must not serve as an annulment of one of the highest essential principles of our Order, which reads:

> "Probationers are reminded that the object of Probations and Ordeals is one: namely, to select Adepts. But the method appears twofold: (i) *to fortify the fit*; (ii) *to eliminate the unfit*."

It may be far best to think of this as two limbs of one and the same body. We have to get used to the fact that one principle does not exclude the other. Any generalization and general understanding lead to the total destruction of the progress of an individual. Each case is unique, and all rules must be applied simultaneously to all the cases, which will cause two completely different phenomena to occur in two different individuals. Indeed, an end justifies any means in our work. Since our goal has always been one thing – the Knowledge and the Conversation of the Holy Guardian Angel, so must all means be subordinated to that sacred endeavor. Everything is possible here, and nothing is certain. We have no right but to instruct an individual to proceed further, by all means, and in any way.

Let the Student know that progress is entirely in his own hands, and that both failure and success are his birthrights and his guided choice. And when all the influences and meanness of the Superior, at least in his opinion, crash through him, he is the one who will let it overcome him or let it have a meaningful impact upon his path.

"In a small village, once there lived a wise old man to whom everyone turned for guidance and advice. One day, a young boy decided he would confront the old man with a question that he knew the old man would not be able to answer correctly. His plan was to find a little bird and hold it cupped in his hands, hidden from sight. He would then approach the wise old man and ask him to guess what he had buried in his hands. If the old man answered it correctly, he would then ask him the zinger – whether the bird is alive or dead? If the old man said the bird was alive, the boy would crush the bird with his hands and kill it, thereby proving the old man wrong. But if the old man said it was dead, the boy would open his hands and let the bird fly free, demonstrating at last that the old man was not as wise as everyone thought him to be.

A boy ventured off and found a little sparrow that fit neatly within his hands. Then he approached an old man and said: *"wise old man, can you tell what I have in my hands?"* *"Why, of course, I can,"* the old man responded without hesitation. *"From all the small feathers clinging to your jacket and pants, it is plain to see it is a little bird that you have cradled in your hands."* *"Ah, that is so,"* the young boy exclaimed, *"but is the bird alive or dead?"* The old man paused for a moment then rubbed his chin in contemplation of his response. Looking at the young boy in the eyes, the old man replied in a soft tone: *"whether the bird is alive or dead is inside of your choice. The answer is in your hands."*

We can never really claim that someone is unfit for a grade, or even claim that someone is not fit for the Great Work; quite the opposite – we must claim that everyone could make it. To what extent, it is up to the Superior to provoke and investigate. Nevertheless, he must not put upon himself the weakening need to help everyone in every way equally – one size does not fit all. It is better to help a particular person properly rather than everyone equally, for that one person, having attained, will help everyone else.

But let every Neophyte consider the projection of Binah who, by the time he passed through the Ritual of the Pyramid, has already begun to growl and threaten him. And that growling will grow into the rigor of the Neophyte, and though it is all in the spirit of our Order, he must not project that same rigor onto his Probationer. Yes, indeed – being the Probationer is for one year. Our Probation is, however, for the whole life.

CHAPTER FOUR

ON LAMEN AND PENTACLE

Tell me, what is Lamen exactly? What is it for? Is it a special form of Pentacle? What is the difference between the two?

Lamen is eidolon of your True Nature, your Great Work. It is a specific form of awareness of yourself as a star; it is your personal identity card in the Universe. By making your Lamen, you are not creating anything new or special. You are directly shedding light on the completeness and essence of your being. As with the Pentacle, you will make Lamen using a minimalist approach without excessive details or decorations unless it reflects your True Nature. Dear Brother, Lamen is of the same nature as the one who carries it. It represents the direct transmission of the truth of your being onto a magical tool. If you wanted to duplicate your Great Work, you would make a Lamen.

Pentacle is a representation of your understanding of the Universe; it is a weapon. Lamen is the counterpart of your True Nature. It does not serve anything that is not in harmony with that nature. Therefore, it can be a weapon but need not be. It all depends on the nature of the one who carries it.

In order to make a perfect Pentacle, you must possess the perfect consciousness of your own nature; you must know how your

Lamen looks like. What for? To have true knowledge of the Universe, you must have true knowledge of yourself because you are a part of that Universe. If you do not know yourself, you are devoid of the full knowledge of the Universe. In order to know the whole, you must know all the parts. Enough is not enough. It must be all or nothing. Perfect knowledge of the Universe implies perfect knowledge of yourself, the one who acts within it. Moreover, true knowledge of yourself is to become aware of your Pure Will. To know who you are, you must know who you are not; you must have a defined relationship with the things around you to differentiate yourself from them. To know your own place in the Universe, you must know the place of all the others.

These two are in a close relationship, and the perfection of the one implies the perfection of the other. But no, they are not the same thing.

Meditate on what you are and what you are not.

Meditate on yourself and everything else around "it."

Meditate on Lamen and Pentacle.

Does anybody else could use my Lamen?

Dearly beloved Brother, could anybody else do thy Will instead of thyself? Could anybody else use your own body to move, your own mind to think, your own emotions to feel, or act instead of yourself? Could anybody else discover your own True Nature instead of yourself? Lamen cannot be used; Pure Will has no use.

If anybody would try to use your Lamen, whatever that might mean, it would depend on him solely. How much does his Lamen demand your Lamen? In other words, how much does his nature need to use your own nature? Be free of worries: if your Lamen is perfect, all of this would be in balance. If that be your Will, you could give over to him, which would be perfect, as long as you stick to your Lamen and what is inscribed on it. You will know that perfectly by then. As long as there is doubt within you, nature is not in balance. You must strive towards the balance of your Lamen. Your True Nature uses your body, emotions, intellect, and will. Your Lamen uses your Pentacle, Sword, Cup, and Wand. Dear Brother, if somebody is using your Will, is not it a sign of adoration of you? You can think of that one as your own limb, detached from yourself Æons ago, which is now trying to find a way to join the wholeness of the divine body, once again.

Is to serve something generally good or bad?

Don't you serve the whole Universe, isn't your own nature a condition of the Universe as a whole? You should not think of service as slavery.

Your Lamen should be available to everybody, let it be seen by everybody, let them be aware of your Great Work. In that way, you will make better conditions for its manifestation and fulfillment. There is no threat and should be no fear. Let every Star know about other Star. Let everybody know the Lamen of their Brother and Sister. People call each other by their names, but there is no danger of being possessed. The only danger is not to do what is being depicted by your Lamen. And that is solely your responsibility, and nobody else's.

Is there a danger I become possessed if somebody else gets to own my Lamen?

Egyptians believed that if somebody knows your true name, that he might get control over your soul. It is an ideal example of the recognition of the magical link. But do not forget one thing, dear Brother, that there is one factor involved in that process of the magical linkage which is above all other. That is fear. If somebody steals the name from a frightened person who assumes that bad consequences would follow, that would most likely happen. But it was because the magical link was created, not because of general principles. Do not be afraid, and the link would not manifest.

Dear Brother, the fact you have the Lamen is not a guarantee for your consciousness of the Great Work. Is it enough to build a house, neglecting the foundation? If Lamen is perfect, is there any danger? Yes, but only one: it is to neglect to do what is implied by it. Lamen is not your True Nature. It is only its eidolon. The possibility that you be possessed is in obverse proportion to how free and awaken you are. If you happen to be possessed, it will be a sign of your unconsciousness and weakness. Therefore, as long as you truly contemplate your True Nature, you cannot be possessed. In fact, you do not have to contemplate only that. As long as you think, it means you are aware, and then there is no room for possession. And even if you happen to be possessed, maybe that was exactly in harmony with your true nature or somebody else's nature. Think of how each one of us is being possessed all the time and right now by all those ideas, thoughts, obsessions, obligations, imposed perversions, all the things that are not in harmony with us. There is only one nature; everything else is Everything Else. Do not be afraid of the Black Brotherhood; be more vigilant of your own black thoughts and black doings. There is only one Success. Everything else is a failure.

Is it necessary to obtain the grade of Adeptus Minor before I make a Lamen?

First of all, what do you mean by necessary? That the Lamen is going to be recognized and expected only after you obtain the grade, or that the Lamen will not have strength nor functionality before you achieve the Adeptship?

If I was a painter and accidentally made one painting, among a million others, which is identical with your Lamen, does it mean that I acquired your True Nature? The representation and form of Lamen mean nothing unless there is included awareness of the meaning and nature that is being manifested through Lamen.

However, there is no reason against obtaining certain qualities of consciousness characteristic for Adeptus Minor even before you take the Oath of that grade. There are no rules; things happen according to their will. Anyway, the Lamen knows what your Oath was, and it works once it has been properly constructed.

You could start making your Lamen anywhere and anytime, but will you be able to finish it? Will you succeed or not depends on the work itself, not taking the Oaths of certain grades. Dear Brother, success in one thing is dependent only on one thing, and that is the perfect success of that thing and no other.

Lamen demonstrates your awareness. The essence is in the firmness of its construction, in the fact that it represents the Will that you became aware of.

Aren't you an Adept already, if you construct your Lamen properly? And if you are already an Adept, you will know how to construct your Lamen. One follows the other, having one thing in common, and that is the awareness of your True Nature. Attain that awareness, and you will have both things.

Do the Circle and Pentacle point to the same thing?

Both the Pentacle and the Circle are closely related to the Universe. But the Pentacle is more determined by your understanding of that Universe. There are as many Pentacles as there are different points of view and different understandings of the one mind and its infinitude of change.

A Circle is the symbol of endlessness, and therefore of the Universe. But, while the Pentacle describes how you see the quality of that Universe, Circle impartially describes its quantity or size. Circle describes your aspiration towards the endless, while the Pentacle describes how the object of your aspiration looks like. However, take note that the quantitative characteristic of the Circle is the same as its quality. None of the two could exist without having the other immanent in it.

The Circle around the magician defines the field of his action, his protection, and security. But, isn't the Circle endless? Is there anything "else" around it? There is no "fear" around the Circle because there is no "around." Your own limitations and your own fears put your Circle under pressure, distort it, and make it a symbol of limitation instead of a boundlessness. Calculate the square of the Circle, dear Brother. In the beginning, it is probably convenient to stick to a specific size of the Circle that makes it comfortable to work within it, but isn't the true nature of consciousness its continuous expansion? As you work and progress, so you will expand your Circle.

In fact, there is no symbol for the endlessness. The endless Circle is as endless as it is an endless square, as long as they are the way they are comprehensible endlessness. Infinitely small and infinitely big is of the same size. A pound of iron and a pound of feathers have the same weight. Try not to represent the endless by a symbol, but experience it. Be endless; let your Circle be an enchanting dress of a Goddess. Do not be afraid; our Circle is our limitation; it is our cage. Stop the inclination of your mind to fathom the endless by any previously defined measure. It is much less than anything you might expect; the infinite is only one, while there is an endless multitude of finite things. We made the Circle a symbol of limitation and human misery. The essence of the Circle is not in drawing it and defining it perfectly, but it is in its expansion. While you are drawing the Circle on the floor, are you expanding your being beyond the boundary of the Circle, or you remain inside of it? Beyond the Circle is the True Circle. Therefore, go for it. The Sanctuary of all of our works is "there." And when they ask you which work is ours, among all the others that exist, you will tell them: our work is our cause.

How perfect must be my Lamen? What must be the amount of my awareness of myself in order to make my Lamen right?

Dear Brother, what is the amount of consciousness necessary to be aware of your True Nature? You either know or not. There is no intermediary grade. The consciousness of Self is always and only the consciousness about Self. The accent is on Self, not on consciousness. You are not what you think you truly are, but that what you truly think. Be aware of "who" that one is, and you will become aware of your Great Work. What is enough? Nothing, but the perfect success. What is enough to be aware of Self? Just to be aware, only that and nothing else.

In what way the daily performance of the ritual of the Pentagram strengthens the Circle that I draw around myself?

The most efficient way to strengthen the Circle is to perform that ritual daily but inflamed in passion. Dear Brother, it is of no worth to do the ritual unless you do it entirely, inflamed by prayer. Any ritual you do, you should do as it was your last action on earth. Pretend that after work, there is nothing; there is no next time. There is no next performance. Do not rehearse. Thy Pure Will is not to be rehearsed but to be done. Do not practice anything, but do it. Learn to act in this way. Can you, or should you, strengthen something which is endless by its nature? Let everything in, and let everything out from your Circle. Infinite remains the same, with or without your individual limitations. Infinite disharmony is of the same essence as infinite harmony.

The Circle could protect you from "evil," but what will protect you from your personal stupidity and limitations? Your drawn Circle will always be a symbol of your limitation. Therefore, strive towards infinite, with devilish boldness, and the Circle will grow by itself.

However, are you able to grow big enough to reach the stars?

What is the basis of the strength of Pentacle as a weapon?

Dear Brother, the strength of every weapon lies in the control of it, in its proper use, and in knowledge. So the tiniest blade could be deadly in the hands of the one who knows how to handle it and understands its nature. The strength of all magical weapons is reflected in this principle.

A weapon is as strong as the one who carries it. Now, ponder the meaning of strength itself. It is about harmonized action, a precise and defined way to use the force. In other words, it entails the perfect knowledge of that upon which the force acts and where the leverage is to be placed. Still, it is not enough to have a weapon and leverage only. It is also necessary to know where, when, and how to use them. Only one single method corresponds to a particular action, which will turn it into a visible result. All others are more or less proper methods, but not the perfect ones. The strength of a weapon is in the balance of its nature, the nature of the one who uses it, and that upon which the weapon is used. If perfection is discovered in the interaction of these three, we could say that the weapon demonstrated strength and firmness. But those are just the observations of one balanced whole, which is interpreted by our mind as strong and firm, attributing its qualities to the weapon only, or the one who is using it. Full and comprehensive truth includes all elements, so if something is strong, it means that the manifestation of the interaction between the weapon, subject who uses it, and the object that the weapon is used upon, is strong. When people glorify David, they rarely think of the strength of his weapon or the strength of Goliath himself. David could never defeat Goliath with the same weapon if Goliath was even for an ounce weaker than he was.

What is Pentacle? Is it attributed to Earth and the work with elements only? Does it have any other use?

Pentacle, or Disc, belongs to basic elemental weapons of an Aspirant and corresponds to the Earth element. It is the weapon that is assigned to the last letter of Tetragrammaton and represents the manifestation of the force and magician's Will in a condensed, earthly form. If you look at other weapons, you will see that each one of them got a specific purpose, or, better said, specific nature manifested in an elemental form.

Pentacle corresponds to Earth, it is firm, and its image is carved to be permanent. The Sword cuts the Air, the Cup carries the Water, the Wand spreads the Fire.

Let us go back to Pentacle. As I said, it is an elemental weapon, but it still conceals some other uses that we must be aware of. A symbol or picture of the Universe, as the magician sees it, is carved upon the Pentacle. Pentacle is an aphorism of Reality, its arabesque miniature. At first sight, you can ask me how to represent the endless Universe, with all its parts and realms, upon something so finite, small, and seemingly fragile? Remember now what we have spoken about weapons. A weapon is as strong as the one who uses it. If someone possesses the knowledge, and demonstrates sincere effort to represent the Universe on a piece of clay or wax, isn't that will equal to the will of the Architect of all the Worlds who built and measured all that is? Isn't that already the measure of Success itself?

> Let not the failure and the pain turn aside the worshippers. The foundations of the pyramid were hewn in the living rock ere sunset; did the king weep at dawn that the crown of the pyramid was yet unquarried in the distant land?
>
> There was also an humming-bird that spake unto the horned cerastes, and prayed him for poison. And the great snake of Khem the Holy One, the royal Ureus serpent, answered him and said:

I sailed over the sky of Nu in the car called Millions-of-Years, and I saw not any creature upon Seb that was equal to me. The venom of my fang is the inheritance of my father, and of my father's father; and how shall I give it unto thee? Live thou and thy children as I and my fathers have lived, even unto an hundred millions of generations, and it may be that the mercy of the Mighty Ones may bestow upon thy children a drop of the poison of eld.

Then the humming-bird was afflicted in his spirit, and he flew unto the flowers, and it was as if naught had been spoken between them. Yet in a little while a serpent struck him that he died.

But an Ibis that meditated upon the bank of Nile the beautiful god listened and heard. And he laid aside his Ibis ways, and became as a serpent, saying Peradventure in an hundred millions of millions of generations of my children, they shall attain to a drop of the poison of the fang of the Exalted One.

And behold! ere the moon waxed thrice he became an Ureus serpent, and the poison of the fang was established in him and his seed even for ever and for ever.

LIBER LXV, Chapter V

How to build Pentacle, and what materials should be used in its construction?

Its essence is the only material it is built of. Its construction is the perfection of its design. Did you measure the entire Universe? Did you establish its full proportions? Did you explore all of its hidden parts? And finally, how much are you certain into all of this? Pentacle corresponds to Earth, so isn't your own body, in fact, your own Disc? What is inside corresponds to what is outside. As it is above, so it is below. Explore and measure yourself, and it might be that you will discover the perfect proportion by which the Great Architect constructed all things. How firm is your body, how resistant and valuable, upon which foundations was it built? How much do you care about it? Answers to these questions are part of a perfect design. Pentacle shows the picture of the Universe. How do you see the Universe at all, how well do you know it? How big is it, what are its boundaries? How big are you, and where are your boundaries?

All these are the things you have to take care of, dear Brother, and exploring this, you will discover what the perfect proportions of your Pentacle are. There are as many Pentacles as there are Wills, and as there are bodies. Are there two same bodies? Are there two same Wills? Are there two same beings that perceive and understand the Universe in the same way? Dear Brother, what is your way? Work on that to know what is to be carved upon the Pentacle: if it is perfect, would it matter what is its size or color or how likable it is? Isn't the Universe endless itself? What material will you use to construct it? Something hard and heavy? But it can be fragile too. Something elastic and bending? But it is fleeting and unreliable. Dear Brother, do you know what your own body is made of? Are you aware of all of your organs? Are you aware of all the internal pits that your breath visits daily, each time after you inhale?

And besides all of this, you can find some general remarks in Therion's Liber ABA and Liber A vel Armorum.

How could I use the Pentacle?

Dear Brother, a perfect Pentacle proves your royal ancestry. The first question to a beggar would be what the embroidery of the prince's pillow was. If you were king yourself, you would perfectly know. Dear Brother, if you represent all by the one, then by one single act of yours, you could achieve all. If you become Universe, what would you do as the Universe?

Pentacle is a link toward your Dharana, and toward your certainty in truth, as well as toward the way of your Great Work. If you were so certain and noble in a thing which is totally abstract, and if you were persistent and firm in counting to infinity, how yet certain and firm will you be in finite, small things? How certain will you be while counting until a finite and known number? But, how are you going to number the infinite? Isn't the largest possible number still infinitely away from the infinite? Do you think you can reach the stars by climbing the stairs?

Dear Brother, be persistent, work hard, and enjoy the fruits of your labor. Draw your Pentacle by your labor, count to infinity by the magnitude of your success, by the fire of your devotion. As a being, are you a finite idea? Or are you something more than that? If you want to count and draw the infinite, maybe you have to be the infinite yourself. Then, you simply draw the Pentacle upon your face. The key to this riddle is in your work and success only.

Remember that when you succeed in this, you will have a perfect magical link in your hands. By acting upon your Pentacle, you will be acting upon the Universe itself. Yes, it is strange that by acting upon that small and fragile piece of clay, you would act upon the whole reality. But, if by chance you change the Universe, will your Pentacle change also? Even if you destroy it, it would not be the same Universe you previously drew upon the Pentacle, and therefore it would not be perfect. The Pentacle must be perfect, and one and only. One is the Pentacle, one is the Universe reflected in it, and one is the star that uses the one Pentacle in the one Universe. Create all the possible and impossible coincidences, but more than anything work. Remember this also: the problem is caused by even the slightest misbalance between the factors, and pain and suffering ensue from that. If the one who uses the weapon is out of balance, it could happen that he drops down even the sword of fiery God, due to excessive swinging. If his method is out of balance, it could happen that his sword becomes blunt because of excessive blows. One blow is enough to cut one head. If the weapon is misbalanced, it might be that weak fire would be drowned by the strong rain shower and vanish completely.

Even if I Succeed in this, in what way I could be sure that the Universe I experience now will be the same Universe in a few years? Does the Pentacle change in that process?

The only constant is the constant of change. You mention "few years," you mention time. What is the time in the eye of the Universe? What is the time in comparison with the eternal? Your Pentacle represents the certainty of your insight into the nature of the Universe. If your insight was perfect once, it would be perfect forever. Do not fear change. Isn't it part of the Universe too? Isn't it on your Pentacle also?

I am going now to measure my Universe.
Yes, indeed, measure your Universe.

CHAPTER FIVE

BODY

The very first phenomenon concerning the Neophyte is the body. The Neophyte is indeed the vehicle of his star, as much as the body is the instrument of his Angel. His body is a body precisely because it is His, thus finalizing a circle in the Universe. Only the shallowness of our narrow understanding of that circle creates an illusion of incarnation, or life after death, or life and death in general. It is futile to talk about the beginning or the end of something like a circle. It is even more futile to say such things at the sphere level, and it is utterly devastating to mention them at the planes or dimensions level. The perception of reality changes reality, but it is the understanding of reality that reshapes it completely, just as understanding a magician's trick in the circus devalues the ticket purchased entirely. This elaborate move is so precious to the Neophyte that his entire grade can be filled with bewilderment at this insight.

The Neophyte must be of a healthy and robust physicality, the way his constructed Pentacle is steady and strong. His best sketch and depth of understanding of this cosmos, which he would be able to portray on it, is utterly meaningless unless he is in good health. However, let us address the notion concerning both health and the body. There are so many trivial instructions that have been written for a healthy body that any individual would get seriously ill if they were taken into account seriously. Nevertheless, all of them are equally valuable to one Neophyte, for he must really understand the difference in all these frantic approaches, he must see that spark of nonsense in the search for something as natural and effortless as human health and a vigorous body, and understand the Universe as a concept of space-time, as much as his existence is the wholeness of body-spirit, and that all his physical turmoil rest in the existence of a zero patient of his contagion – human neurosis.

To be able to restore his health completely, the Aspirant must understand his own twisted position and accept it as part of his tangible unreality; not reality, but unreality indeed – which is based on pain and a spasm of slipping into neurosis, when we lose things, gifts and people in our lives, for instance, while we actually lose what we just think is ours. Every illness of the body is a disease of the soul, and each of them brings a sense of contamination. But all of our focus is on how to remove sludge from water – by letting it settle. It is precisely the action and efforts to purify water which stir the sludge lifting it from the surface and muddying that very water. So great is the wisdom to learn to be calm, especially in the days of putting your apparatus to probes, which has a wide and deep dimension within the A∴A∴.

Despite the existence on the inner plane, our neurosis finds its way in our walk and gestures, so each move that the Neophyte makes should be subtle, imagining that he is in a play, as a part of some cosmic cabaret or a divine carousel. Let him rejoice in every move he makes; let everything be gentle and smooth. Even with everyday movements, let him be like a ballet dancer, walking with a scent of royal nobility. Let him breathe the same way, with full lungs and actively inhaling, and then let him end his lung movements indulging in passive exhaling. Let him pay attention to his breathing in moments of disorder, let him stop the striving of his mind to funnel his breathing to the shallow throbbing of his lungs.

Let him enter the deep and wide amplitude of the breath actively and eagerly, sensitizing both physical and psychic moves which have been brought on by his neurosis inflicting spasms upon his physical lungs.

There is such a divine thing of doing nothing but breathing slowly and consciously in all stressful situations because by doing nothing, we do best for ourselves. It is the very action that creates spasms, each action contributing to contractions, stretching, or spasms, and each such action aims at a more derogatory reaction, which has always been directed toward us and within ourselves. Every breath has already been exhaled; every step to the left has already anticipated the right one. Only he who stands is at peace indeed. Let the Neophyte meditate upon these observations during his unrest; his Binah so cleverly urges him to move, but most of all, he drives him to that neurotic spasm leading to the wrong conclusion that it is Karma, which is nothing but what we long for deep down inside ourselves, which is but love and acceptance. Each move of ourselves is a child moving; each step is a step of a child striving for the light. The Neophyte must feel this well and, above all, find that child within himself.

Every Neophyte must take care of his Binah in advance, which can always turn into fear-ridden aggression in an instant. He must shy away from pursuing justice because he is not in a position to fight anyone other than himself, nor to win and fight someone else's battles as much as his own ones. He is obliged to pay back neither his nor anyone else's debts – these are all but well-prepared positions of his neurosis tightening the siege around him. There is no debt, just as there is no merit. There is only one debt in the entire Universe, and that is the debt to Buddhahood, as the Bodhisattva vow, which is but the last name of love.

Pranayama and Asana are just a bunch of circus warm-up exercises unless they engulf the pure and living energy of the soul. Indeed, they are presented ventures for the next grade of Zelator, but this must not be the reason for the Aspirant to start stretching, warming up, and resorting to that kind of flexibility that is so desperately needed for all variants of the lotus pose. But this stretching has to show affection in its nature and be followed by love, as her majesty cat does. Watching this magnificent creature for a few minutes, the Aspirant can profit more than from a decade long lesson of listening to a fakir, only if he is eager to see.

We have to think differently and find the term for what is dormant and lost in our bodies; like with other notions in our lives, everything that goes without saying is pure rubbish. What often slips away from the notion is a decree of immunity; we can understand that the relationship between immunity and the body is like the one between Yesod and Malkuth; the relationship between a subtle force and a form, which we are going to deal with in more details later though. Both things are supporting pillars of our temple, and understanding both concepts is a prerequisite for many spiritual systems. Within Raja Yoga, the body is dealt with before the Aspirant is subjected to Dharana; even a one whole type of Yoga is dedicated to the body – as it is the case in Hatha Yoga. We could debate whether Pranayama is a natural offspring of Asana or whether it is an entirely different class; nevertheless, both things nourish the body in a unique way – be it physical or subtle. Of course, both Asana and Pranayama affect the preservation and culture of the physical vehicle in their own unique way: Asana is mostly found in bone structures, the spine, ligaments, and tendons, while Pranayama correlates to the purity of Nadis, Chakras, and the human energy system, including the immune system. In fact, almost all of our quest for health begins and ends with work on the immune system; this area is so broad, yet our knowledge of the field is very narrow – partly because it involves knowledge of psychotherapeutic mechanisms that would simply have to interfere with other branches of medicine in a living and self-contained way. Unfortunately, it will take a long time before these branches start working together for the benefit of mankind. The very names "health house" or "health center" are entirely wrong. It is the home and center to sickness and unawareness, first and foremost. The health center should be the center to learn about the vitality and co-operation of energy and the body, about life and the Universe, where a doctor's office shall always be – Love.

If we were able to comprehend our own immunity, we would be closer to the Knowledge and Conversation than we could ever imagine. All of our spiritual aspirations are, in fact, an astonishing mixture of biological and physiological elements, those which we so often reject in disdain, thinking that they are not worthy of our aspiration.

The proper approach to immunity is in close encounters with particles and the experience of illness but in small quantities. Health is therefore not safeguarded in isolation but, on the contrary, while being exposed to the broadest possible but carefully balanced doses of impurity. Encountering illnesses is the way to find our health, not in looking for shelter. Sterility is the worst thing we can pursue in developing immunity; avoiding diseases at all costs is a sure strategy to ruin human health. How questionable is our approach to Abramelin operation! True Abramelin does not last for six months, for these months are actually the time of incubation. Real Abramelin operation lasts a lifetime; we have to relate continuously to the ultimate experience of the Angel, in all aspects of life, in spiritual and occult practices the least. In heavy traffic, the first snow in the season, or when paying bills. Always and in the same way, we have to remain healthy with healthy thoughts of the Angel at all times, even in the filthiest statements of insults, masochism, aggression, stress, and suffering.

The purity that is related to human health is of transcendent attribution; it really has nothing to do with purity in the physical or moral sense of the word. The Pure Will is the more straightforward and much purer idea than the True Will is. Understanding the term purity naturally implies the notion of Will and vice versa; realization of that Will fulfills the key to complete Purity. The naming mechanism of the ultimate substances in our Great Work is very interesting, and we often witness that the most natural things have such dull and clumsy names. Yet, those completely straight experiences in our lives have no names at all, which does not prevent us from implementing such nameless experiences into our own lives. Sometimes, a single human life can result from an utterly inexplicable urge experienced in childhood, which can be transmitted later on to the entire life of an individual. But are we not all victims of such actions? Isn't this illogical and unspeakable urge what we strive to declare as the Will? Also, let us remember the definition of Adept Minor's great Oath embodying the attainment of the Great Work – he undertakes "to attain the Knowledge and Conversation of the Holy Guardian Angel," – an utterly complicated mumbling presentation of quite a simple and natural thing.

Much of this has already been said, as is the case in Therion's book Moonchild, chapter IV, 1917, but also Magick in Theory and Practice, cap. XIII, 1929, Magick Without Tears, Letter A, March 19, 1943:

> "In an Abbey of Thelema we say "Will" before a meal. The formula is as follows. "Do what thou wilt shall be the whole of the Law." "What is thy Will?" "It is my will to eat and drink" "To what end?" "That my body may be fortified thereby." "To what end?" "That I may accomplish the Great Work." "Love is the law, love under will." "Fall to!" This may be adapted as a monologue. One may also add the inquiry "What is the Great Work?" and answer appropriately, when it seems useful to specify the nature of the Operation in progress at the time."

This hides quite clearly what we are striving for and the role of a healthy body in the Great Work concept. It is certain that Nigredo is pointing at the body, but that body has nothing of the Osirian afterlife stiffness. It is the bearer of light and bringer of joy; it delivers amusement, nervous pleasures, and experiences, in which the ultimate experience resides. The body itself is an orgasm of the Sphinx, every sensation hides the phenomenon from which the entire cosmos originated. Each and every moment, we receive the same information about the Knowledge and Conversation. However, our perception refuses to process that wisdom.

The Aspirants of our Order do not have a strong and penetrating Will. Their Will is, if anything, Pure and free. Their bodies are strong and penetrating, but also supple and, above all, they are conscious and aware. It is precisely here where our Great Work begins – not in libraries browsing through pages of written truth deep into the night, but the truth that is alive and residing within us. Awareness begins with the awareness of our body as well as our sexuality. The fact that we all know we have bodies does not make us aware of them. Every day we cover and rediscover our genitals in the morning and evening, but are we really pure carrying them around? Would we really be pure while standing naked in front of our boss or our parents? Is purity a biological term being defined as a certain quantity of germs per cubic milligram, or is it a peculiarity of Pan's goat to skip the paths of ordinariness in insane decisions of our will, which should always and at every step be accompanied by our flexible body? To what extent is our final leap into the Abyss a leap into complete chaos when we have transcended the purity itself and fell over into a state of complete nothingness? How paradoxical it is to jump into the unknown completely free, without any hesitation or doubts, without reflection, without any zeal or passion. Is such a leap in itself the Abyss, touching the bottom the very moment when we dare to make such a leap? With all this in mind, the Neophyte should approach his body, like a bird of paradise, slowly enough not to chase it away, but bold and straightforward enough not to let it fly away. For the body is always and in every place influenced by that horrid betrayer Binah, with his time and blight. For his body is becoming old and heavily, by each second of his limited time on this plane. Even so, one Neophyte will not be detoured from the path of light, for he knows that it is exactly this time and understanding of this phenomenon where the most precious jewel that the Great Mother could give her child lies. No matter how conscientious and passionate her threat is, he always knows that the very threat is the path to salvation at the same time, which she will always strive to conceal and hide with symbols, words, oaths and experiments, intellect, temptations, phenomena, and fascinations – everything to keep her child forever with his mother, not to take the long and unknown path, but to stay home with the mother who loves him most and cares for him most and knows what is the best for her child. The body, time, and death – the close and horrible sisters of the Great Mother are her best strategy to keep the child by her side.

Too often, our body is everything but ours; it is governed by an unconscious mechanism which we often wish to be at war with, condemning it while being ashamed of our own shadow, putting it in Osirian curses. However, one Aspirant makes plans for mastering the Universe while being unable to influence his own pulse. Just think for a moment about the fact that one cannot control the beating of one's heart. Although we all know that our reactive mind is at stake, let us really ask ourselves what it is. As long as you are reading these words, your heart is everything but yours. And even now, it is beating in the rhythm that some other "you" has set, upon which you do not have the slightest power. How aware can you be of your own Pure Will when you are unable to control something as simple as your heartbeat? You expect terrifying Ra-Hoor-Khuit to strike upon your enemies, but you are not influential enough to control your own breathing or pulse in the rhythm you want. Halt the heart, slow down the heart, speed up the heart. We are powerless in relation to ourselves – how do we expect to have an influence on some major events in the Universe when we are not capable of having an influence on such personal occurrences? We expect to perform the Great Work, to realize the Knowledge and Conversation of the Holy Guardian Angel, and we are not even capable of asking ourselves what these nonsense terms really mean? Do we perhaps see a trap within them, or maybe a riddle? Indeed, we expect the Great Work, and we cannot influence our own heart, and even now, as you are reading these words, it is beating in its own way regardless of you. Each of our organs is separate from ourselves, yet we declare it ours. What is "ours" at all? And in the end, what is "other"? Our body is just a border between the two, our skin is the last stop of our Universe, or, better said, the only Universe, while everything else is just a mirage and an illusion. Anything outside that membrane no longer belongs to any truth, except the truth of lies and deception, which is based on our senses and the mechanism of how those senses are classified and connected in a network of knowledge about the world around us. An average person does not know the exact location of their organs. Do we really know what the lungs look like? Where exactly is the pancreas, or where is the liver? If I were to give you a single needle, would you know to puncture through the exact center of all organs, or would something like that be done in a completely arbitrary way? When we hear our own voice recorded on the phone, we feel utterly gutted, and it seems so distant to us. Even when we see ourselves in a video, we often notice some movements or the way we walk which we have not been aware of. Our whole body is home to a number of unconscious things; many young and immature children reside in that home. We must bring them up and make them aware. Our body is everything but ours, and it is much more than mere physicality.

Try a simple experiment; try to stop breathing until you die. It is very simple, try not to breathe till the end. We will not be able to because our organism itself triggers mechanisms at the unconscious level that prevent something like this by putting our automatic and reactive mind ahead of what we delightfully call the Will. Yet, is it a sign of weakness of that Will? Alternatively, is this an indication of life's greatness, as if our isolated will is just part of the same, unchanged mechanism of the same vitality and the same unchanged life? Does this indicate that the True Will is a sublimation of all our organism processes however contradictory they might be? It always decides the symbiosis of all factors, proudly calling themselves the Will. A true Neophyte must be the body – a true Neophyte hast to live. Indeed, the Neophyte's body is a cogwheel of his Will. Is not the whole Universe the body of God, with its limbs, star flocks, suns and cells, molecules and consciousnesses, voids known and unknown, each having a particular function in only one body? After all, what kind of mind is in that body? Is it not a single mind, illuminated by the illusion that there are different ones in it, making every created mind of man only one of his neurons, of one great ultimate mind?

Still, can that body grow further, beyond the infinite? Isn't it always the same? The change in physicality is a basic event showing us success in Asana and Pranayama. By working on Asana, the Aspirant will get a different feeling of the body; concentrating on the body, one loses the feeling of the body. It is distorted; you can completely lose your knowledge of the position at some point; even though you know that you are sitting in a Dragon, you will have the impression of sitting in a God Asana. This sweet confusion tends to grow into a trance of incomprehensible proportions, which may but may not be a detour from an expected end. A decently performed Pranayama pours such miraculous sweat that it will leave an equally astonishing effect on the body – of vigor and strength, that, for some time, the Aspirant will have an impression of having a decade's younger body. Working with the body changes the body. But most of all, it changes the awareness of the body – expanding it in the direction of suppleness, strength, and fitness. There is nothing as refining as well-done Pranayama under effectual Asana; nothing brings pleasure to the body like such an occasion.

Yet, it is often the case that after apparent success in Asana and Pranayama, the very next day a completely opposite effect occurs – the body aches, the spine hurts, no strength and zeal is radiating from the Aspirant, and as time passes, instead of being energized, he feels nervousness, boredom, and pain. All of this is undoubtedly a significant step forward, and things are going just well. These two opposite experiences, sometimes alternating at shorter and sometimes at exceptionally longer intervals, indicate the same progress. In general, working with the body always has clearly set amplitudes and shifts between positive and negative transfers, and we will witness this mechanism having its foundation in the furthest corners of the Golden Dawn. Too often, pain in Asana is due to a mental attitude alone, which in no way diminishes the amount of neurological pain caused by stretched ligaments. Thus, there is a shift of such positive and negative days in our work. One day, we can sit feeling well, and the other day sitting is burdened with pain. On the third day, we have already achieved automatic stiffness with sweating. Still, tomorrow immediately, we can no longer sit still for a few minutes due to unbearable itching. In fact, every day is the same, but we cannot perceive that constant, like the difference between thunder and lightning, which are part of the same phenomenon – only thunder occurs later because the sound is simply slower than light. So our suffering is hindsight of success that our being wants to portray as pain to justify the appearance of LVX, the presence of success, merging with the body that is one with the soul. Still, we are neither the soul nor that body; we are an objection to that action rejecting both to understand and perceive it in the right way. Even that pain is always just an electrical impulse in your brain, and the moment you feel it, you will know that the real danger has already passed and that it is just an impulse of your flesh that reaches your brain too late. Every time you feel pain, it has already gone. Grab the moment of the onset of pain, and you will see that there is unity with the body as much as Oneness with the Will itself. To transcend this sense is the condition for the ultimate experience. Therefore, the Aspirant's attention is torn apart by pain, which simply ceases to hurt, losing its purpose when not perceived. What remains is the pure sensation of the pure body – which is always the Oneness and a symbiosis of all the feelings the body endows to the soul. It is an advanced form of orgasm, which has no contractions but presence. The feeling about that body is what contractions and spasms are for an orgasm, which also makes it so pleasing. In this case, there are no contractions in the usual sense of that word. It is just a straight line of ultimate pleasure in the body, in its complete experience of an alive, bright, and constant mechanism.

The Neophyte will certainly undertake trials and experiments on his own body in the way that his Superior proposes. Still, above all, since it is his body, he should show his initiative, intuition, and inventiveness in this work. Lagging about ideas about your own body is a significant brake which always has its clues at deeper, psychological level. Every thought and meditation on this is precious to the Neophyte. One can say that exploration of astral visions and planes is as important as the exploration of one's body, immunity, endurance, suppleness, and strength, and the Aspirant shall notice that the mere observation of these attributes enhances those attributes. Awareness and desire to extend one's own inhale increases that inhale. Every action and success of the body is primarily a success of focusing the Will; the Body-Soul apparatus is connected with all aspects of the grade at subtle levels. It is impossible to remain in the astral vision for long unless it is preceded by fruitful and long Asana; indeed, the Aspirant can guess by now the direction which this friendly remark aims at. During his work, the Neophyte will have perhaps the most striking experiences in his life so far, which, above all, requires a stable psyche and a strong body to stabilize them – above all, thinking about lucid dreaming experiments and experience gathered while working with visions.

There are many different clues to working with the body, and we are going to discuss some of the ideas that the Aspirant himself needs to develop and utilize in further work. The first thing is the idea of starvation, which should be freed of all moral and ethical implications. It is a beneficial discovery that hunger is such a different sensation if one decides to go starving the night before. It is an entirely different type of hunger when you are starving than when you know you will eat. It is the very first observation, and even then, we can notice how the aspiration of the body goes hand in hand with the aspiration of the Will. There is an entirely endless series of positive and extremely negative logical conclusions from nutritive experts, but what we really need to experiment with is exactly what we got on the first day of fasting – the effect changes the way we express our opinion about that effect. If we want the effect to be positive and direct ourselves slightly toward fasting – not with zeal and passion, then we are witnessing it exactly that way. I have often resorted to starvation regardless of any form or advice, completely free to improvise and adapt the idea to a given moment, but always keeping one thought in my mind, which was to make that starvation comfortable. Also, I stayed awake for days, and as long as I was determined to work, as long as my nature was occupied with such relevant research, the need to sleep was defeated entirely, without a single negative connotation. In today's world, we are almost completely deprived of opportunities to get objectively solid and reliable information; it has become fashionable to render a fact meaningless to the very end, with completely fake news being marketed as the ultimate truth. It almost seems that what is true ain't new and what's new ain't true. Therefore, let our only guideline in all of this be our own body and sensations which that body give us – that secure harbor which we have set off on this journey from. The feeling of hunger per se actually comprises much less hunger than neurosis when felt, which cunning always takes on the form of a vessel in which it resides; therefore, neurosis during fasting leads to hunger. If we dissect this neurosis or do something creative, we may notice that hours can pass without the slightest manifestation of hunger. It is when we focus on hunger that we suddenly become hungry. This is such a worthwhile observation for all the starvation experiments, especially during the first 2 or 3 days, after which things unfold much easier. Crises that pop up from time to time are always overcome in the best way by creative action, taking a walk, or, even better, by walking meditation. There should be no slightest aversion to hunger inside our thinking apparatus, but on the contrary, in accepting that feeling of hunger, focusing on it, caressing that feeling, actively breathing through it, we creatively transform it and pass through that feeling consciously; we can make that sense go away with simple satiation.

Drinking water is so magnificent and noble that once the Aspirant has realized how holy this action actually is, he will turn every sip of water into the highest-ranking meditation. Drinking water is Dhyana as much as Bhakti Yoga. As we are drinking, we need to be grateful to water as we create a magical link in that act of strengthening because the pleasant feeling of quenching thirst introduces a new reality, a new feeling of pleasure. Let our being talk to that benevolent water; let us welcome it, as we are largely made up of fluid. May it be welcome in the world where it is already well-known and let it blend in with its element bringing gentleness and, above all, pleasure. Let the Aspirant feel its flow well, let him follow it from when he feels it in his throat, let him smell it,

gently and slowly intake it, let a sip resemble inhaling in Pranayama. Let water reflect our meditation and joy; let it carry
around that joy we feel drinking it so fresh, on and on into our abdominal region. We feel its energy expanding. We feel gratitude
for that circle of consciousness, from the very moment of drinking
to the moment our need for water has been satiated. It is an act of
holiness, with ourselves as priests of that sublime and pure nature.
Enjoy feeling your own life being filled with water, as it is actually
filling with the Self, not with water. Water flows into the body, as
much as the body flows into our Will in the same movement; this
is the actual circulation of water, not that one which involves evap-
oration, rain, and water circling along rivers and seas. Water circulation is an entirely different concept, like circling the corners of
our minds. Both phenomena should have a very special place in
our understanding of things. Focus solely on the feeling of quenching your thirst when thirsty, with thirst fading out with each sip.
When you find yourself suddenly in a state without any thirst, stay
there enjoying something that was thirst a few moments ago, and
now it has been quenched, satiated – the Pure Will. Enjoy this sequence of events that are not aligned by time but by aspects of the
Will.

   We should point to a very simple but truly effective exercise
that helps in cases of painful spots and injuries but can be used at
any place on the body that we want to improve or revive. All we
have to do is push an irritating and tiny, sharp pebble against a
painful spot. The pressure on the body is completely irrelevant
here; what is important is the pressure on the attention that introduces the conscious channel to that part of the body. No matter if
you are going to use magnets, crystals, or rice grains, really. It is
not the material used that matters, but the material of your mind,
which is that of stars. For the most part, I found myself bewildered
while offering people all sorts of nonsense things to put on painful
places – the greater the nonsense, the quicker the relief – we would

not have enough space here to dwell on miracles with spinal problems. Simply stick something you think is interesting and mystical to where it hurts. Be it some magical acorn you have found in a special place; you can put a sharp needle from a pine tree where you have seen a passionate love couple, or maybe stick your own nail that you have cut; the more inventive you are, the more effective you will be. Once you put such an item on a painful spot, just forget about the whole thing. Forgetting is the main fuel, while the passive attention paid to the mechanics of the action which leads to success is the vehicle! You have to want to forget, and that pebble or a needle has to attack that oblivion – focusing the attention back with the help of its discomfort and its touch. That is really where all the magic is.

Starting from the very basic things of our daily life, we genuinely believe that the highest secrets are in the most apparent corners, beyond the shadows of speculation and mystification. What has really been forgotten and lost is ourselves, and as long as we are planning a journey around the world, we are not really going to set our foot anywhere. The moment we take a break and look around, we shall see a handful of the most wonderful spells, from drinking tea to aimless walking around the forest. For the Neophyte, the idea of the body must be of paramount importance – he has to transcend that idea; he must abolish the significance of the subject to the same extent he has previously elevated it – the most incomprehensible heights of his mind. He must explore all possible aspects and paraphrases of this matter; let the body be an obsession of his thinking apparatus for the entire duration of his grade. There are so many diverse and individual phenomena related to him that we will mention only a few that can unveil the Aspirant a chance to meditate.

About Asana

Asana represents a posture, but it requires details. The nature of this posture is reflected in stamina, firmness, and lightness; in fact, understand Asana as attainment, which contains two components – not as a method. The first component is purely physiological, so Asana is a perfect reflection of a stone statue. But, as a living body is necessarily conditioned by movements of lungs, or the heart, or that, no matter how minor – they always exist, so Asana cannot exist entirely in its real sense. Therefore, let us define Asana more flexibly so that every soul can comprehend it. Now, look at the second component that can shed light on the choice of an appropriate definition that is the component of the mental state. It may seem quite inappropriate to discuss this here, in a place reserved for a strictly physical phenomenon. Practice says the following: in a perfectly "calm" body, a perfectly "calm" mind. But vice versa too; these factors complement each other. You can deal with the disorders caused by your body in two ways: by killing the body or by killing the attention that defines and maintains the relationship with the body. The ultimate attainment is the same.

The definition follows from this: Asana is a bodily position that abolishes the consciousness of the existence of the body, but not the existence of consciousness. This is a perfectly appropriate definition that has an exclusively practical analogy. Having removed the attention that brings bodily impulses, consciousness is now directed toward goals that are in line with the nature of work. Think about this: success in Asana is success in changing consciousness, not the body, although the change in understanding the body is quite obvious. As in Pranayama, the essence lies in the control of an automatic process that represents an eternal burden to attention.

The practice has shown that with intense attention and complete dedication to one thing, that one thing vanishes. In short, it is a naive school account of Samadhi, but a comparison certainly fits here. If attention is paid to one bodily position, it will soon cease to exist. The condition for that is the continuity of that position; if it changes, the mind will automatically register it as another position, no matter how much logic dictates that it is one. A millimeter of unconscious leaning leads to the definition of movement, so there are no conditions that lead to cessation of attention. This is about conscious statics. The nature of Asana is actually any position, as long as it is one. Pragmatism leads us to supported positions that do not depend on limiting factors, such as muscles or bones. Asana must be one, both spatially and temporally, and it is but one of the steps toward Samadhi. It makes the mind more attentive in a specific way in order to deal more seriously with the problem of one's own wakefulness.

But there is such a sublime thing in all this, which is far from speculation, based on something so human and pastoral, so fine and convenient. And that is to sit in Asana and deep meditation together with the people you love and see their faces when you come back from those depths, which is such a rare, beautiful, and lovely feeling. In fact, it is inconvenient to so say that we return from drowsiness; quite contrary, we return from true wakefulness, and we become sleepy by returning to ordinary consciousness – such a wonderful feeling indeed.

About Pranayama

Everything I told you about Asana applies to Pranayama, too. It is about controlling an automatic process; what is important is complete awareness of every act, even the one that is performed unconsciously.

Pranayama is the control of Prana, but it is necessary to define what this concept means since, without that, it would be just a speculation. Prana is what may be called force, but not like fuel, rather as nourishment for the spirit. It has many aspects and, what is called, Rupas, so it can be found in food as in blood. But neither food nor the blood is Prana, just as the body is not the spirit. An abstract idea enshrines Prana, and it is necessary to utilize a specific model of thinking in order to understand its true nature. Prana is the prime representative of the magical link. Ingenious Aspirants can see Prana in each thing and pour Prana into any object.

However, Prana is usually associated with a common living factor for all things alive. It is not blood, though it can be, because blood is limited by its color, warmth, and confinement in blood vessels, but the magical link par excellence is the breath. Therefore, Pranayama is breath control, full awareness of the entire apparatus, which is used for breathing. The breath is continuously inhaled, to an extent at which is exhaled. Its field of action is within, as much as without. Life breathes in, death breaths out. Everything inhales, nothing exhales. That one sequence is everything about all, and all about everything, the whole Universe visible and invisible are just modifications of that single sequence – the sequence of inhaling and exhaling.

As in the explanation of Asana, control is also essential for Pranayama, not with burdened attention but with automatic awareness, which you will achieve with statics. With Asana, it is easier, while with Pranayama, it is impossible, as long as there is a biological tendency to breathe. What applies here is static tempo, not the structure. The inhalation pace must be balanced until the attention diminished, and control and a stable rhythm turn into automatic consciousness. Therefore, awareness should be focused on the uniformity of the pace of breathing. Work will give you the best definitions.

There are few experiments with Pranayama that I want you to perform: rapid and deep. Rapid breathing can lead to Royal Pranayama and introduce energy quickly and sharply. Deep breathing is something for which it is hard to believe that there are no enough detailed reports. It is a simple fact: even if you inhale deeply, there will still be enough room for some more air. It is as if we have been taught never to fill that space with air, and as if we had an apparatus of automatism that gives a comfortable feeling of our lungs being full, even though we may fit some more air there.

Furthermore, try one very simple thing: to prolong inhalation for more than one and a half minutes. It will be very unpleasant in the beginning, but very soon, you will get what is described at the beginning of the Liber HHH – a very specific kind of sweat as well as the appearance of tingling on the surface of the skin. Take your breath so slowly that you almost do not move your lungs, as if you make your lungs spread just by thinking about inhaling.

Also, you do not need a lack of oxygen, but more of it. If you do hyperventilate and learn how to overcome its unpleasant feeling, you will feel very interesting phenomena. It is very biological when your body changes its ph as you take more oxygen than you need. This experiment consists of breathing as fast and deep as possible, with active and conscious inhale and passive and relaxed exhale. Try this for about half an hour, and you will get a magnificent experience.

About Hatha Yoga

The branch of Yoga that closely adheres to the notion of Asana as the essential instrument is Hatha Yoga. The emphasis is on the primacy of physical position. It is quite apparent that it is more about the physical aspect, and not about Asana as we take it. As you know, the essence of Asana directs us to the loss and abolition of our attention to the corporeality, to gaining awareness of the limitlessness of the mind-body. As such, it is only one of the steps or branches of Raja Yoga. Hatha Yoga, however, does not primarily require success in such attainment, but rather in the suppleness of bodily characteristics, in order for Asana itself to be adorned with success, and the being of the Aspirant to undergo such shaping up to let each form of energy flow unhindered. Like Asana, it has its aspects – the physical is just one of them. The essence is actually in the purification of "Rupa" where you reside, from the essence your being is made of, which is always a pure light. It can be a method, but also a goal, depending on what you want.

About the use of a Mantra

I want to mention to you right from the start that the Mantra is just one of the steps. What I really want is to understand its parallel in Asana and Pranayama, as well as in all the objects that contribute to Samadhi. As I explained to you in the section on Asana and Pranayama, the same goes for Mantra. The essence lies in binding the mind and increasing the attention. Mantra is a deliberate distraction to all perceptions, except, of course, the perception of Mantra; it is the initiator of the ultimate Yoga which is realized in the Aspirant's mind in the "moment" of Samadhi. The meaning of Mantra alone is irrelevant, though it can sometimes be important – as long as the meaning serves a single purpose – attentive focus.

The use of a Mantra is a risky process. There is twofold danger: the danger of monotony and the danger of intrigue. The proper use of the Mantra will never result in anything interesting, and then again, it will not be anything ordinary. Now you can become aware that Mantra is a deception. It acts on the mind, not with its meaning but with pure mechanics. This may be strange to those who think that Yoga is a goal worthy only of sublime minds who shrewdly interpret dark symbols and understand the speech of unconscious nature. This is not about that at all. The realization of Yoga with the Mantra is a thousand times closer to the most basic physics than to mysticism. Therefore, let us be pragmatic. In its essential form, a Mantra is a signal that disturbs the mind and makes it work differently than usual. Suppose a steady mind is regulated to work at a specific frequency. In that case, a mantra is a tool that will stop oscillations, not by resting but by accelerating the pace until the "wire" that oscillates simply breaks. Silence is not achieved here by turning down the sound but by destroying its sound apparatus. Suppose the mind is a string, then you will tighten the string with a mantra, raising the tone until the string snaps. At that moment, a condition for Yoga has been set. But you should think mainly that the object of enlightenment does not make enlightenment an object.

You can ask me what it looks like in practice. Everything is very peculiar and needs some time to master. Once learned, one understands not only the method of a Mantra but the whole of Yoga. Once you have chosen a Mantra, impartially, you will sit down in your favorite position, the way you have learned and in the way your own experience tells you. When you have abolished the conscious occupation toward your corporeality after a certain time, you can move on, although this can also be skipped if you can focus firmly on what follows. Say a Mantra as slowly as possible. Then repeat in the same way, without any variability in mood or accent; what is required is rough monotony. Now speed up the pace a bit, but just enough to have a clear hunch of acceleration. At the same time, lower the volume of your voice as much as you have accelerated. What happens is a specific feeling about the compression of time that affects the change of consciousness. You will continue like this until you can pronounce a Mantra so quickly that your lips will not be able to follow it with clarity so that you will repeat a Mantra in your mind only. Practice shows that this is much simpler than it may have seemed at first. Also, the volume decreases until it fades into silence. This must be spontaneous, without accent or excessive formality; otherwise, the effect of a Mantra will be diminished or will disappear completely. If this is done correctly, at one point, there seems to be a snap, a mental oversaturation of the whole act. Within that moment, your mind will reach Oneness or the precondition of Oneness, or the precondition of the precondition of Oneness. This is enough because Oneness is only one; a Mantra will remain far behind it. Practical work explains these difficult and incomprehensible instructions.

About the meaning of Ojas

There seems to be a certain kind of subtle energy that contains the identity of the bearer of that force; this kind of force exists within every conscious organism, at least, and its characteristic is in the way it manifests itself. Therefore, it is not Prana, although you can now object to significant similarities. It is wisest not to compare similar things at all, but to be aware of the difference. Ojas can be viewed as a superorganic binder. It is not a force by action but by nature. It brings health and psychophysical balance to the being.

But, like any kind of force, it can be directed and channeled according to the Will. You can get the impression that the entire Kundalini and Kriya section of Yoga is based on this. Ojas wakes up and climbs from the Aspirant's foundation and rushes upwards, waking up all the centers it touches. Much nonsense and many fairy tales have been written on this topic, but practical experiences say that something is definitely happening. If anything can be concluded, it is that the change of consciousness is closely connected with the change and raising of this force. Therefore, both force and consciousness are only carriers, and they can equally be both the consequence and the cause of change.

About cleansing by Hatha Yoga

Hatha Yoga stresses the great importance of body cleansing exercises and lists six types of cleansing accordingly. It is not a bad idea to mention them; you might find it useful.

1. *Dhauti* is the cleansing of the upper abdominal tract, which also includes cleaning the teeth.
2. *Basti* is the cleansing of the colon and rectum by enema.
3. *Neti* is nasal cavity cleaning.
4. *Nauli* is a massage and control of abdominal muscles.

5. *Kapalabhati* or purifying breathing carried out with powerful exhalations.

6. *Trataka* or staring without blinking – used for cleaning and strengthening tear ducts, as well as the whole eye apparatus.

About some hints that Nadis have been purified

There are some very clear indications of this. The whole thing is the question of the subtle vascular nature of Prana. The obstruction of Nadis causes a weak inflow of Prana into a particular part of the subtle body, resulting in loss of vitality. The purity of Nadis is the exact opposite of the above mentioned: Prana flows equally, the body receives as much energy as it needs to, so it is a sure sign of vitality in the furthest capillary cells. Also, on subtle planes, the above-mentioned works to strengthen the Body of Light; thus, its nature is also filled with vitality. Endurance, lightness, complete integrity of the apparatus – from subtle to rough, it is a feature of pure Nadis indeed.

About the Atman

I can tell you little about the Atman; the whole problem lies in the awareness of the term. The concept and essence of the Atman lie in defining reality. Looking directly, everything can be reduced to three things. The first is the subject, the second which is all "around" the subject, and the third, "that" which is in between, which enables them to be understood and defined. The third thing is the distance, without which there would be no relationship or possibility of distinction, but think of distance as a specific expression of Sunyata, or Emptiness. The nature of the Atman is the nature of one of the essential states of the Universe. It is one of the most refined conceptions of the Gunas. Its nature is closely connected with the nature of Brahman. On the one hand, these are pure opposites; therefore, if you understand only one, you will understand the other by the pure negation of the idea. On the other hand, these are exactly the same things.

The Atman is a representation of the Selfness in its essential form, the form of pure existence. However, the insight of Atman indicates its non-Selfness nature. The whole idea of Mahayana Buddhism is reflected in this: Atman is Brahman by realization, Brahman is Atman by expression. Therefore, the notion of Atman can be most closely related to Hadith or the core of manifested existence. Indeed, Atman is Brahman by realization, Brahman is Atman by its expression, as I have already said.

About Chakras

The concept of Chakras stems from the very idea of Prana. Rarely can anyone give a logical, reasonable answer and explanation of what Prana is. Since the nature of Chakras is closely related to the concept of Prana, we encounter difficulties in defining those terms here, but some general observations and conclusions can be drawn. A Chakra is a hub, the crossroads of the Prana flow. The best comparison is a light bulb. Prana is the electricity inside and around. It seems to be looking for a place of manifestation. There is a resistor provoking a conflict of power with its resistance, but under the Will, where the Will for light allows for a possibility to be perceived and seen. But it should be borne in mind that a bulb is not Prana. It only indicates the place where the concentration and charge of force are increased, which is in endless directions everywhere "around." In other words, it is a Chakra – a coagulated concentration of Prana that has the purpose of looking like a rougher skeleton in relation to its shapeless nature, as it is found in nature and outside the body. Prana, on the other hand, is the multiplicity of strings in space. Where several strings intertwine, a lump is formed, which is a Chakra. It is simply a higher order of density and definition of consciousness. The denser the lump, the more concrete its manifestation and function are, with a tendency to increasing and getting more complex on a physiological level. You may think that the densest and largest Chakra is consciousness. This is but a theory; energy phenomena are nothing but ideal tests of Ruach.

About death

Being an aspect of our work, we have to say something about the death of the body. A proper thought of such an experience is as valuable as the thought of Pranayama and Asana; but how wrong the concept of life itself is, because we do not pursue it consciously, but furiously, automatically, as if somebody told us to, like waking up in the morning for an appointment that we hate from the bottom of our soul. This seems to be the last standing general of Binah's defense, but it can also be his traitor, for those who know how to put things right. For a Neophyte, the near-death experience is not such a distant notion, and there are many records and cases of rather brilliant coincidences where Neophytes have had a close encounter with the great adventure of death. That event leads to the awakening of an individual to such an extent that it leaves a mark on all following grades. One might say that it was part of the great architect's plan who triggered by such an act all that the Aspirant experienced later, or it made him quit, though. It is difficult to discern what is the cause and what is the consequence in this great sea of chaos, whether there is such a thing as giving up at all, or is it all just another way of naming the same thing: "love" – in a million different languages and dialects of the Universe. Death, the body, and the immune system are just chapters of one book called life, and living that life is up to us solely, whether living with others or living with ourselves – it has always been one and the same life. The one we have and the one we do not have is always the same life in the same way. The philosophical discussion of life and living is the relationship between the Neophyte and the Zelator, but practical results of all these conclusions must undoubtedly be found in work related to the grade; they will thus form the basis upon which the Zelator will establish himself, and embark on his work on Asana and Pranayama. Thinking about life and death is always thinking about life. Thinking about death is all too often a distraction aiming at not thinking about it, and as long as we have a sadness transfer when our loved ones leave, it is, in fact, always about us. And if we pay attention to the atmosphere of death coming to our neighborhood or our home, we will always have an opportunity to encounter the highest form of consciousness that lies hidden there. But how disguised and cunning is Binah on that magnificent occasion; just as one obtains an object of meditation that can elevate the mind to unprecedented heights – usually death is not talked about in a grieving house, but rather some completely irrelevant things, diverting skillfully from the subject where the same Binah might see his own defeat. For the grave and the shroud of Binah is the cradle of the star soul at the same time. This is all part of nature's play, but we are certainly free to think about all the possibilities and the exploitation of every moment of life – even when it physically ceases. Both sadness and fear are manifestations of Binah, each in its own way and ideally manifested in its own time – just as much as we would have missed an ideal moment of knowing. Both of these things are just a form of his royal majesty – neurosis, but we are free to welcome it with a sign of liberation and joy. Because in that fear and in that sadness, even anger, we see just one way in which the child within, in an utterly non-verbal, awkward, and illogical way, always says the same thing to all the Æons together – "I love you." When a man is born to this world, everyone around him smiles – it is only he who cries. And when a man dies, everyone cries – only he is smiling. A Neophyte must not be brave in this, nor timid, angry, nor even calm. He must dissect all the experiences and observations of this outstanding venture, repeatedly returning as a boomerang thought to himself and about himself. It is all about oneself because all of this hides whispering and teasing the one who projects all these events and happenings, clumsily, continually having a dialogue with our dormant attention that does not respond to him – the Angel.

About Kundalini

You can really understand Kundalini as a form of force; still, I think it will sooner or later cause confusion. It seems that there is a type of action in a person that wakes up in certain and quite specific circumstances and changes the things it encounters. Sometimes abruptly, sometimes mildly, but change is its essence; its energy and nature serve no other purpose but change. Any extension of this view is a matter of speculation, so we will stop here, at least when it comes to mere definitions. You must understand the term, but you must not limit it to anything that is not a certain truth. When it comes to force, it is very easy to stray to the side because your sensors are the least involved here, and that force resides on a very subtle plane.

You need to experience Kundalini as it is in the realm of your own senses and leave its action to a personal experience that can vary and be completely different from mine. Feel free to think about this: Kundalini is a projection of the Middle Path, or better, the Middle Way since you do not yet have a defined relationship toward Paths within your being. It can be said that Kundalini is either a consequence of a change of consciousness that occurs at a certain moment of work or the cause that creates that change. Either way, it is closely tied to the concept of change, and you definitely need to make an effort to understand it and awaken it within yourself. It lies curled up inside your Muladhara and aspires to the heights of your Crown. It seems to be a simple channeling of its action. You should understand this aspiration as directed by Sushumna and all Nadis. That aspiration is not a subjective reaction to the supreme God up there. In fact, the opposite is true; our idea of God above is a consequence, not a cause, of the natural flow of awakening consciousness, and the movement of that experience through some channels, upward. It is entirely irrelevant what of this is before and what is after. The emphasis is on change, and you can think of it as the essence of existence, of that force, and your consciousness. If you behave like that, there is very little chance that you will go astray. Force is not dangerous, but rather, it is a matter of the economy of consumption, by no means in fear of charge; awareness of the proper economy of force creates the freedom to use it properly and without fear. Perhaps we can say that fear is the only thing that prevents control.

About the meaning of two Mudras

Dharmachakra Mudra - Mudra of turning of the Great Wheel – with the thumb and the index finger gently touching themselves at fingertips while the other three fingers be-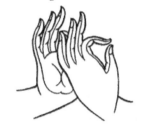ing free and upwards – that is to say, the Aspirant's mind and his being finding refuge in the Buddha, Dharma, and Sangha. But one has to think about this – at first glance, the nature of this Mudra is not static. The hands move as if the Great Wheel is spinning; however, it is about coordinating movement and the right direction of reality; in fact, the hands do not push the Wheel but rather stimulate its own motion, which is unconditioned by inertia or the Aspirant's movement.

If taken from the position of the Wheel axis, the hands are standing perfectly still, and everything "else" is moving, in fact. This is the gesticulated nature of correct Dharana. Therefore, paradoxically, this is the most passive of all Mudras.

Dhyani Mudra. This Mudra imitates holding an oval stone or a shell. It is actually wrapping a being around an oval egg of the  spirit, like a Serpent wrapping itself around the Heart. Thumbs are attributed to the spirit, and their union establishes an endless flow and circulation of consciousness; the only constant is the constant of change.

About Karma

Exactly as much nonsense has been written about Karma as it has been written about the nature of the human being, just because both things are conditioned by the same principles and actually point to the same thing. Karma is a system of connecting gears; if one does not work, the whole thing stops. But that never happens because there is not just one axis, like one Wheel of Samsara. Man is burdened with the isolation of his own actions. Karma is the law of transmission of force, and in the most direct and precise context, Karma is the law of spreading awareness. Not consciousness, but awareness, and there is as much difference as between Karma and Destiny. Awareness of cause and consequence is an consequence, or a cause, of the isolated Ego structure of the human mind. When the Aspirant transforms his awareness into a pure effect and agreement of great cause, when he understands his being as an unchangeable law and the resultant of the action of all forces outside him and within him, when he realizes that every action is cause and effect in itself, he goes beyond change. That relationship is Karma.

About Samsara

Speaking about Samsara is speaking about the Wheel of Samsara. It means acting by the Wheel of Samsara. It means turning around the Wheel of Samsara. But besides everything, you are not on it, nor do you turn or spin, yet again, you act. Understanding

Samsara necessarily implies neither exiting nor not-exiting from the Wheel. The whole wisdom is in aligning your rotation with the rotation of the axis, not in spending the effort on turning the Wheel. You have to understand that the nature of the Wheel is to rotate by itself, so your effort is indeed redundant. Synchronize yourself with the rotation of the axis. By doing so, you will see that the whole reality turns, not the Wheel. The Wheel is proportionally opposite to this conclusion; therefore, its nature is static. This is a paradox itself, as a term and as an experience. Do not turn the Wheel for anything in the world; you should not touch it in any circumstances; therefore, the key of initiation is in the harmony of one movement. The movement of the Wheel and the movement of yourself, which is still One thing. The movement of the Wheel.

"The Great Wheel of Samsara.
The Wheel of the Law [Dhamma].
The Wheel of the Taro.
The Wheel of the Heavens.
The Wheel of Life.
All these Wheels be one; yet of all these the Wheel of the TARO alone avails thee consciously.
Meditate long and broad and deep, O man, upon this Wheel, revolving it in thy mind
Be this thy task, to see how each card springs necessarily from each other card, even in due order from The Fool unto The Ten of Coins.
Then, when thou know'st the Wheel of Destiny complete, mayst thou perceive THAT Will which moved it first. [There is no first or last.]
And lo! thou art past through the Abyss."
[Book of the Lies, Aleister Crowley]

"Therefore, O Sariputra, here in this emptiness there is no body, no feeling, no thought, no will, no consciousness. There are no eyes, no ears, no nose, no tongue, no body, no mind.

There is no seeing, no hearing, no smelling, no tasting, no touching, no imagining. There is nothing seen, nor heard, nor smelled, nor tasted, nor touched, nor imagined. There is no ignorance, and no end to ignorance. There is no old age and death, and no end to old age and death. There is no suffering, no cause of suffering, no end to suffering, no path of ending to suffering. There is no attainment of Nirvana, and no Nirvana to attain."

[Prajnaparamita Hridaya Sutra]

CHAPTER SIX

THE GREAT MOTHER

We are going further with the thought that the Great Sea of Binah has such peculiar manifestations that could be compared with light being dispersed into the spectrum of colors passing through the prism. It has its aspects just as the Angel has its own; every act is equally Angel's relationship with our soul, and every event is actually a form of the same Knowledge and Conversation that the Universe imparts to our soul – the one which responds so lovingly observing that Knowledge and Conversation and thus creating that Universe in which one is able to Know and able to Converse. Just as the Angel needs the elements, so does the Abyss need some of the mechanisms to turn them to its own use in precisely the same way; that remarkable, quiet place where, from the very beginning, paradoxes and nebulas establish their influence along our path.

And just as the Knowledge and Conversation is merely a projection of the experience of Selfhood, in the same way, the Silence is a manifestation of the Abyss. However, both of them are entirely futile attempts by the living being to describe events that are none of those themselves. Moreover, we really do not attribute to those phenomena anything more than their loveliness of existence, they comprise no mystical and magical components in themselves, and if we had to give them a specific epithet, it would first be a notion from the fields of psychology, biology, psychotherapy, and chemistry. There is nothing worse than presenting the simplicity of the Universe to a black magician, which is an entirely illogical and chaotic sequence of circumstances, conditioned by the psychological, neural, and biological connections between cells and tissues, bloodstream, and atoms. He is the one who persists in his ill-begotten wishes to call lucid dreaming an astral projection and make the most natural state of consciousness such as the Knowledge with and Conversation of the Holy Guardian Angel confusing and inconceivable attainment. He will do anything to mystify and introduce vague notions of something as evident as enlightenment to himself; he will falsely try to paint the colorless light of LVX out of his inability to accept that pure light is more magnificent than any colored. He will do everything to do nothing. There are several aspects of this place that deserve to be addressed in our work. This is the idea of Kundry, that is, the Vampire, as well as the idea of the Great Mother, each pointing in their way to a particular action that seems to be coming from the same direction – Binah.

The former rests so conveniently on the Master Therion's observation that: *"I believe then, and believe now, that the Probationer of A∴A∴ is nearly always offered the opportunity to betray the Order, just as the Neophyte is nearly always tempted by a woman."*[2] In that way, it is more than brilliantly presented by the legend of Calypso and Odysseus.

Calypso was a daughter of the Titan god Atlas and Tethys, her mother. She was one of Oceanides sea nymphs, while her name is associated with the Greek word καλύπτω, which means "to conceal" as she controls the forces that divert men from their paths. Calypso lived on the island Ogygia, where she welcomed tired Odysseus, who had been drifting for nine days in the open sea after losing his ship when coming back from Troy. Calypso fell in love

---

[2] "Confessions," Aleister Crowley.

with Odysseus, but Odysseus did not accept her kindness – he was looking tenaciously at Ithaca and his wife, hoping with desire and with a strong heart to meet her again. Calypso loved him so much that she put everything into turning him to her, which she eventually managed to accomplish over time, living with Odysseus in harmony and happiness for seven years. According to some sources, Calypso gave birth to two of their children: Nausithous and Nausinous.

This fantastic romance would have continued if Athens had not interfered, asking Zeus to return Odysseus to his home. Zeus eventually did that; with Hermes' help, he persuaded Calypso to release Odysseus, which she reluctantly did. In the end, she helped Odysseus go home, helping him build a boat and summoned fair winds and sea currents. Finally, Odysseus arrived at his household. Nevertheless, we cannot help but wonder if Odysseus would have stayed with the nymph had the supreme God not intervened? Was Odysseus really enchanted, or was he with Callipso by his Will altogether. Was Calypso at all a detour from his path of destiny, or was she part of that same path?

This whole set is an essential piece of guidelines on our direction; it seems that the Aspirant's trajectory is already seriously threatening to leave under the auspices of the Earth. He is so confident in his journey, ending the ordeal and proclaiming himself "fit" after his one year of Probation. Having passed that period, the dreadful Great Mother had already bestowed significant threats and reprimands for her child, and now, it is time for her to make such a horrendous retaliation upon his soul for the first time, where he least expected it – his sexual energy. With a cunning trick, she will try to make the Aspirant leave the path of light, deploying her vicious debt collector – the Vampire.

What really is this dreadful being, and what is its nature? This, of course, requires such an elaborate presentation before we get into any gullible superstitions. Let us present the model with a very appropriate occurrence: the Aspirant has undergone the Ritual of the Pyramid, he feels empowered and guided by divine providence, he is separated from the Probation by one-year work full of devotion, he started the practice of writing a diary as part of his life, he entered the Neophyte sphere vigorous and fresh, and by taking on a new motto, he was given a new and quite special destiny. In front of him are new practices and trials of Rising on the Planes – every day being a bath in light. However, then, one pleasant day, or even one more enjoyable night, during a walking break after meditating, he accidentally bumps into his high-school love – the one he has never forgotten and has always been dreaming of, beautiful and stunning. This might as well be the last enjoyable record in his diary because immediately after that, there are hellish periods of emotional torture, erotic bacchanalia, crying, and sleepless nights. His diary becomes completely neglected with the self-assurance that as soon as tomorrow, he will make up for an increasing number of diary records he has been writing down on pieces of paper instead of a diary. A complete haze in a magician's consciousness is about to follow; days, weeks, and months of unconscious subsistence go by. Intoxication with all kinds of substances and all kinds of people often goes hand in hand with this phenomenon. Weeks pass like days, while days themselves are filled with endless emotional outbursts, or quite contrary – with complete ambivalence to everything. Once the Aspirant has finally woken up, he could find himself feeling that he has fallen lower than the worst day of his Probation and that it is quite impossible to move on. Yet, both of these claims are equally insane and unrealistic. This is just one of the mechanisms of Binah striking upon the Aspirant; there is an endless number of variants, while the goal is always one – halting the enthusiasm that has flowed so fruitfully through the Aspirant's being, and the main culprit would almost always be the person who has come straight from hell.

It is quite a handy description of the Vampire having entered the life of an Aspirant without asking, striking every healthy leg, striking upon all that is healthy and reasonable, until he has left the Aspirant dry and unwilling to advance further. And so, the Aspirant keeps wondering if Binah may have so wonderfully constructed all this, and in such a perfect way? Is it possible for him to think that this sphere is so powerful in creating such a compelling projection while playing with the fate of humans as with paper figures, yet refusing to realize that the only one who initiates such a projection is neither Binah nor the mysterious Vampire – but he himself. This mechanism is one of the most fantastic creations of our Order, and it is only when the Aspirant has encountered it that he can grasp its horrific depth.

Therefore, what is the nature of this Vampire and the significance of this circumstance, why and to whom it happens, and whether it can be used for further progress; more to the point, is it what it looks it is or is it just a diversion game? In the end, whose monstrous game is this, and who initiates this phenomenon?

It is indeed challenging to judge objectively, given that the phenomenon is hardly objective at all, but what we can agree on is that it is a specific being that feeds on energy. And if we want to be effective, then we will find another specificity there. The ultimate motive is sexual in nature; it is an urge, but completely different from the urge of hunger, for example. It seems that the aspiration of the Probationer has subsequently flown into the vessel of dreadful Neophyte sexual currents and poured out in the form of a demon. It is as if the Angel himself had torn his wings out of his inability to present himself properly, and now, he is tearing up Neophyte's soul. Like a drowning man who, by frenetic movements, begins to drown both himself and the one who is trying to save his life.

This phenomenon does not have its logical appearance, nor is it the resultant force now exerted in its logical direction on the being of the magician. However, one should know that although there might be a case with a Student who has not encountered such an event, it does not mean that the phenomenon is not behind the corner, waiting for an attack in its gravest form, different from everything we still know about this anomaly. All we can pass on are our attempts to frame our experiences, and yet each new one shatters our perception of generalization and sets new laws that can distort our rules to the level beyond recognition. Therefore, the Aspirant should look at all these observations broadly and in principle. In no way must he exclude or automatically accept them just because they are refracted through his life. We follow the path of scientific illuminism, but that does not mean that we gaze in any direction particularly. Despite so many meticulous experiments, we are still not sure that we are even moving anywhere.

This occurrence is not a rare one even in the Student's Probation period, but a complete absence of all this is also quite possible. However, this absence seems to cause a similar problem later, and this phenomenon, like a tsunami, will grow as time goes on and reach Student's secure harbors in their much crueler form. In the first case, it will hit him low but leave him standing on his feet. In the second case, the Aspirant will be left to build much more, and whatever he is allowed to do will be annihilated and devastated in such a cruel way. Loss is inevitable in any case, for it is the nature of every Aspirant to remain genuinely free of anything. The main question is how he will interpret such a phenomenon. Like forfeiture or profit? Is wasting time profit or loss for the one waiting? Is life a gift or a curse for a chained man? Like the grades themselves, each occurrence is nothing but a measuring instrument for something we just expect will happen over time – the same time that has kept striking upon us from the early days of the Neophyte and all the way to the boundaries of the Abyss. Every perceived idea is an illusion because it has been perceived, and we rely on the rules that can be swept away by the morning breeze. Have all, and you shall lose all. Have nothing, and you will not lose a thing. Like a children's song, this is a warning but also a superb instruction.

We cannot but conclude that the Vampire is quite possibly an illusion, and we can dare to say that the Vampire illusion is equal to the illusion of the four great Princes of Evil – both are clues that always lead to the same perpetrator – the Angel. It can even be said that both phenomena are echoes of the same experience, just as the ultimate attainment constructs the Ego now, unconsciously attempting to convey the phenomenon of the Knowledge and Conversation, long before it can even grasp this concept. Therefore, the Vampire is nothing but the cry of a soul desperate to find a worthy rival. This is certainly something like Jacob wrestling with the Angel, while cunningly saying to himself, *"How big I am to wrestle with an Angel,"* at the same time being afraid and refusing to wrestle with any real and concrete opponent. It is a deception of the most insidious kind that deviates from the path, but it serves as the most powerful ballista if well placed.

We really cannot or should not try to understand the nature of the Vampire, nor should we make up any hideous sayings before understanding the true nature of sex. We would instead be wrapped with garlic exploring catacombs of fear than being naked in front of a beloved being. This paradox of shame is an equal manifestation of the Will – if only we could set the correct model of thought, so devilishly cunning – we do not need a victory in a battle but a triumph in war. If we really knew that every situation of shame and every fear is an equally valuable clue that always leads to the Pure Will, all of our teachings would completely lose its purpose. The Universe does not understand, nor is it intended for such a single operation of winning a battle but losing the war. The Aspirant will sooner or later find himself in the City of the Pyramids. As he falls, he will dare to rise. In just one leap, in the wake of the terrible storm of his fate, he shall leap over what seems to be impossible to do. How possible it is for children to jump over their own shadow and how interesting it is for parents to watch, once they have arranged the biggest pile of ice cream if children have mastered that sacred task, so much will the Aspirant be struck by a force that he has not been aware of until now – what this skipped shadow is for the children's mind, that is the Vampire for the Neophyte. Both tasks are equally meaningless, but in no way can this disrupt the level of zest in this illusion. The Vampire's arrival seems to be conditioned by certain minimal spices, most notably the magic mixture of fear, shame, sexuality, spiritual progress, and the desire for the Angel. When mixed up in our odious pot, all of this seems to be the favorite stew to lure the Vampire. And once he has come, he certainly has no plans to stay for just one meal.

The etymology and mythology of the phenomenon itself seem to bring nothing special for us, though the Neophyte may focus on the study of legends and stories – all of this may be a treacherous Vampire call. The Neophyte can never know to what extent and in what way his soul is destined to stand up to the task – therefore, each of his strategies fails. What we need, first of all, is to prepare ourselves to pass through such an event, not to avoid it. Because – this Phantom will definitely come. He is coming.

Some of this can be found in Liber Aleph vel CXI, epistle 100 – On Sirens:

> "Concerning the Love of women, o my Son, it is written in "The Book of the Law" that all is Freedom, if it be done unto our Lady Nuit. Yet also there is this Consideration, that for every Parsifal there is a Kundry. Thou mayst eat a thousand Fruits of the Garden; but there is one Tree whose name for thee is Poison. In every great Initiation is an Ordeal, wherein appeareth a Siren or Vampire appointed to destroy the Candidate. I have myself witnessed the Blasting of not less than ten of my own Flowers, that I tended when I was Nemo, and that although I saw the Cankerworm, and knew it, and gave urgent Warning. How then consider deeply in thyself

if I were rightly governed in this Action, according to the Tao. For we that are Magicians work without Fear or Haste, being omnipotent in Eternity, and each Star must go his Way; and who am I that should save this People? "Wilt thou smite me as thou smotest the Egyptian yesterday?" Yes, although mine were he Might to save these Ten, I reached not forth mine Arm against Iniquity, I spake and I was silent; and that which was appointed came to pass. As it is written, the Pregnant Goddess hath let down Her Burden upon the Earth."

Whenever, wherever, and in whatever form it may turn up – the Neophyte must always remain sure that such a phenomenon of darkness is actually a hint to the path of light; but on the other hand, it is possible that it is a very horrific illusion – because a sick and unprepared soul will even project the entire idea in his life so it can live in the deception of progress. There is just one more perilous thing than the Vampire – the illusion of the Vampire, and, as in the case of one's own stupidity, there is really no defense against it.

Generally speaking, there are only two paths in the development of Neophyte's sexuality – this is by no means sexuality in the usual sense as it is the case in the biological development of a homo sapiens. There is an introverted path, where the Neophyte shuts himself off behind his individual work, the same place where the Vampire manifests, precisely in that part of life where the Neophyte has retreated – the life of the astral plane and lucid dreaming. It is there where the Vampire finds its perfect ground for manipulation, where perfidious sexuality is the ideal projection in something as easy to manage as a dream or lucid dreaming, which is so difficult and utterly important for a Neophyte to master. The second position is of an extrovert kind. Here, the Neophyte is the one who opens up and implements his social life in his magical work. That path is surely admirable; the Neophyte extends the definition of magick and the Will to something completely common, such as driving a car on the street or buying bread at a store. Here he expands his horizons of personal magick by looking for the holiest of beings of all pantheons in every corner of the Universe and consciously goes through all aspects of existence, accepting them as limbs of the body of God. The Neophyte deliberately calls on the Vampire to strike upon the place where he has already entrenched himself thoroughly – which, of course, the Vampire will not do so impatiently. In this case, the Vampire will do precisely the most seducing thing for the Neophyte – which is nothing but wait. The Neophyte will start thinking that he has even passed through the temptation and that he has introduced balance in his life and work so much that the phenomenon simply transcended its own existence and that the idea of the Vampire disappeared before his eyes as if with the first rays of sunrise. But alas, the truth cannot be further away. It is precisely with the opening of the Neophyte that the Vampire opens as well. The Vampire is the being of the shadow – not just any shadow – but the Aspirant's shadow. He will cunningly wait for the Neophyte to strengthen and widen his horizons; he does it so openly for the Vampire. Growing with his subtle body, his head will indeed be in the heavens and his feet far on the Earth, but how large will the shadow be of such a huge structure? The Vampire has grown so much that it has led to a major eclipse. Growing toward the light, he covered the sun. He will become over-satisfied with his own growth; he will praise himself more than his own Self, and yes – he will undoubtedly be on the messianic path. He will start taking on this stinking role and entice all weak Aspirants into it by manipulation, aggression, and intellectualization. By reading and mechanically quoting written works, translating millions of valuable and unworthy authors, learning and fully knowing every inch of Therion's life, he loses his own. So many books and letters made him forget the name and the letter of his own Angel.

The real question is, why is there anything so special in this temptation for the Vampire to act and leave his darkness? We can say with great certainty that these two paths in the development of Neophyte's sexuality are difficult indeed, but far from being more difficult than his one year of Probation, and in both paths, it is the Aspirant who has control. In the first case, the Aspirant has control because the door is always closed; he lets nothing from the outside world into his stagnant hole of life. However, the second case has a trait of his own egomania – even if he had no control, he would be stubborn enough to falsely declare it as his own cunningness or even courage. He will insist on his special and unique holiness so much that even his own filth cannot deter him from such purity. We really cannot say whether the manifestation of the Vampire may belong to the same mechanism of the existence of our Order – in other words, whether it is equally part of the same Order and the phenomenon of the universal A∴A∴ that includes all the cog-wheels of the Universe. Therefore, dissecting this phenomenon is not of particular importance to our progress. It seems that the personal progress of an Aspirant is the cause of this occurrence, which has now come off as a security alarm in our house informing us that there is an intruder. Indeed, for we are the only ones who expand beyond what is our circle of cognition, going further along that circle, and finally across it, out there, into the beautiful unknown. The Vampire does not attack us in our house; with his apparent horror, he just forces us out of that house, out of that circle, out of that nested confinement right there, far into the unknown, leading us into the darkness to spread the light further. The Neophyte does just that – working on himself too hard, staying within himself too much, and exploring his corners, he remains stuck to those corners too much. But beyond that, across the shore of these dark waters, there is a call from the Angel who only uses the Vampire to chase us beyond the zone of our Universe, telling us that there is no "our," nor any "other" Universe. The Universe is just One.

Looking at Odysseus' journey, we might notice another form of distraction, completely different from Calypso's, which is also a form of Vampire manipulation. At one point, it could have been so strong that it almost managed to deter Odysseus. These are sirens; these watery creatures astounding sailors with their singing – the A∴A∴ Aspirants traveling the great sea of Binah, with their howling preventing them from hearing the Word of the Æon – that one Magus will proclaim. This is an equally horrible temptation of Binah, once Aspirants dare to embark on this endless sea unprepared. But Odysseus found a way to resist the sirens, managing to not-listen (a sense of hearing is attributed to the Spirit) to false words of false prophets. He listened to "his own" holy words. The Word of his Angel and the Word of the Æon by which that word vibrates.

It seems that the Vampire is simply a failure of our thinking apparatus which, like an embarrassed mother when being told that they have caught her beloved smoking after school, replies: "*Ah well it's not him, it's someone who looks like him because I know my son perfectly well and he doesn't do such things.*" This is an inability to say the only thing of any value at that moment of new experiences, and more importantly, painful experiences – "thank you."

Finally, it is very important to note the Vampire's very form, which can be completely wrong at first sight. One might assume that a male Vampire confronts a female Neophyte, in the same way as a male Aspirant would encounter a female Vampire. Let us start with the first question that breaks the whole concept: will a female Neophyte be faced by a Vampire embodied in a man? No, not at all.

The Master Therion was extremely accurate in stating that the Neophyte is nearly always tempted by a woman. It is clear that the Neophyte can be of any sex and sexual orientation. However, the Vampire itself is always a woman. Binah simply conditions its archetype toward a woman; a mother is always a mother, as an angel is an angel, and Pan is always just Pan. She is a whore and a lady and a virgin, a saint, an intellectual or a village housewife, a dragon, but always a mother. And her energy is always divine and sublime as much as a woman can be, in no way excluding the idea of aggression, on the contrary – in the Vampire case, this will be pronounced to the maximum. A female Vampire will bite a male Neophyte, and it is the only possible mechanism, with a million of its various details. A high-school sweetheart, or the one from your neighborhood, from work, or even the one of a more rigorous type – your mother's best female friend, all of those are ideal mechanisms for the Vampire to take over. What is so identical in all cases is how a male Neophyte reacts – it is a complete loss of reason, dignity, honor, and even physical health could be ruined by the use of alcohol and all possible substances, as well as his good standing of an honorable member of the biological section, but that certainly should not bother us. What matters to us is what he will get. It is important to see how this will affect the strategy for the Great Work, and certainly, we must continuously think carefully about whether this is not part of that work, indispensable as experience, but not as ultimate stagnation. Simply, the Neophyte must let that energy through himself; he must touch himself with the Vampire; he must allow for her bite. And the moment he lets her do it, not because of his uncontrollable perversion or the sadistic imperative of control, but as a human – in an epic way and worthy of light that must shine upon every corner of the battlefield, pointing to all severed limbs and all spilled blood, only in this way will we know the folly of war and aggression. And only then, indulging in the bite of the Vampire, will we get a kiss of the Angel. And then, all of that will disappear, and all the torments and all rat-race period of life will suddenly end. We will find ourselves stunned by the wonderful energy that has led us so wildly – we will find ourselves a step away from that noble act – the Ritual of Passing through the Duat.

As far as a female Neophyte is concerned, she will by no means face this phenomenon in the form of a male Vampire. On the contrary, she will be the channel through which this terrible force will manifest itself, or more precisely, through the phenomenon of obsession. Suddenly, a female Neophyte will gain such high self-confidence once she has already given up hoping for a prince on a white horse. She will feel the power that overthrows kings and turns princes into daddy's little whiners. A force that will flow so smoothly through her, enabling her to remain constantly awake during the night, and such an unquenchable desire to dominate, conquer, and suck up every form of life. Certainly, in the matter of the female Neophyte, the whole point of this experience is in the phenomenon of obsession, while in men, it is all in fatal attraction. The Vampire manifests itself within a woman, making her the channel of its horrifying archetype. At the same time, in a man, it strikes from the outside, upon an already existing feminine structure – which has only a physical shell. Both cases, though different entities, lead to the same source – Binah.

Both male and female Aspirants must understand that they are equally tempting in the eyes of their Great Mother and that she will do her best to keep her children in her kingdom of illusion. They really need to understand that the power of the Vampire is precisely to be a Phantom – and nothing more, but they should not believe that bringing in the light of their Selves can shatter that shadow. It is much more complex than a mere concept of light and shadow. This Phantom is utterly different from a Buddhist distraction; therefore, a Buddhist saying, "If you meet the Buddha on your path, kill him," can be such a horrible and wrong piece of advice in this case. This is precisely what the Phantom wants – a relationship, even in the form of denial. Yet we are here to think in a completely different direction – that is, we will do everything to refuse him the relationship, at least in the way he expects to have it. Therefore, while sexual energy mutilates Aspirant's enthusiasm, work distorts sexuality in the same way too; therefore, working on grade tasks is disastrous for every detour Binah creates; but it is equally disastrous if, in the exclusiveness of that work, we allow our restrained sexuality to find refuge in that island. But love is always a doing that elevates. It is the only possible thing when all other things have failed, and, in this case, everything will fail indeed. It is such a perfect weapon for defense from love is none. Pure love balanced with the Vampire dirt seems to be the only possible strategy that will further carry the Neophyte.

It seems possible that the Vampire is somewhat conditioned by the appearance of light while striking the Aspirant, that is, in the practical sense of the matter, as long as the Aspirant is in a grade which is under the influence of Binah. It would be wrong to say that this is limited to the Neophyte because the Great Mother controls her child even beyond the attainment of the Knowledge and Conversation. Although the cruelest form is found in the Neophyte times, it is somewhat difficult to assume that he is safe from the impact of this force once he has entered the grade of the Zelator. There is an additional and terrifying element in this mechanism, which tends to be an apocalyptic creation – that is, the Ritual of Passing Through the Duat, which so treacherously awaits him at the end of his Neophyte path. It is hardly possible to say at all that there is an end to any superior experiences in our Order; they only take a different form, even to the level of complete transcendence, but both the Angel and the Abyss have their lacqueys in almost all grades. Just because a full Knowledge and Conversation is realized at the level of Adeptus Minor, that does not mean that the same Conversation has not gone through some other Knowledge much earlier, as the same Angel has been present in every existing sense that the Aspirant has had since his birth. No Oath is limited by something like taking the next one. In fact, our whole life is just one single Oath, one single moment only. Everything that is experienced and everyone who is experiencing is always one and the same phenomenon, but we do postpone culmination in our Order to such an extent that it becomes genuinely unimportant, for the reason that we could be with the beloved Adonai for a moment longer, a day longer, the whole eternity longer. Let the Aspirant be free to think that the Vampire is only an aphrodisiac in the foreplay between him and Cosmos.

In the same way that the Veil of the Paroketh separates the elements from the Spirit, so does the Abyss separate a child from their cosmic mother quite deftly. However, this child does not have typical and classical human characteristics, so how will the term of the cosmic mother be different from everything that our earthly mother means to us? Our ultimate inability to comprehend the Great Mother is exactly what creates the Vampire phenomenon as well as the complete confusion about the Abyss itself.

In this quiet and remote corner of human existence, we have raped this tiny space by a multitude of entities and deities who created Saturday night fever right out of that beautiful darkness. We lit the night of Pan with neon lights of fun, fireworks of achievement, which is an entirely different experience. By bringing in the multitude, we show an impotent willingness to understand "the one." The Aspirant of our Order must, at all times, be aware that every separated consciousness is like the continent in the great eternal Ocean, and no matter how far the continents are, they are all part of the same land at the bottom. At the bottom of that Ocean lies the bond of all things, the ultimatum unity. Paradoxically, it is where things cease to be perceived, in that impersonal and eternal absence of light, down at the bottom.

All women are one woman. Those ideas are our illusions to realize that they are something much more straightforward than what we just want to see in them. The idea of the Scarlett Woman is far more Woman than she is Scarlett, or of any other description.

Our idea of Mother is something dearest and most beautiful, and often much closer to Babalon than Nuit is. How many of us were created in a passionate union, but also by totally unthinkable urges; how many of us were born of rape, coercion, how many of us were unwanted children, hated and cursed ones? How free are we to think about our father and mother's intercourse? In that sacred act, we were conceived; it is the most sacred act besides our birth, yet we so rarely think about it. That very act is the beginning of our most marvelous mystery, our death, as we began to die the moment we were conceived. Let us think for a moment about all sexual acts that ignite the passion within ourselves and how completely absent it is when it comes to the sex of our parents. We do find this to be a deviation of opinion, while it is a perfectly sound and logical question. Are we a result of anything apart from love? What is the extent to which we look for the highest cosmic principles in entirely wrong places? Still, it does not mean that these principles will not echo back – on the contrary.

Every mother can be seen in the Cosmic Mother, and every Cosmic Mother is seen as the Scarlet Woman. Babalon gives birth to the body, while Nuit manifests the consciousness of "I" in that body. Both represent the same ultimate phenomenon diffused and separated through the prism of Ruach.

The Aspirant should always continually think that every relationship is merely a pale imitation of the authentic Tantra, which is the unity with the Angel. Even the relationship with the Superior has some of that imitation, and we must make sure to bring together any other relationship with that ultimate Oneness. As long as the Aspirant has this connection in his mind, any influence of Binah is insignificant. However, the Vampire shall strike the same mind, purging this sacred connection out of it in various ways, or else trying to dim its brilliance with other reflections reintroducing new elements of temptation into an ever-changing flow that moves our sublime soul up to its ultimate estuary.

Binah will certainly try to hold you, as Calypso did. The whole Universe will try to stop you as a good soldier responding to the orders of a great and ferocious mother. Your lower nature does not want anything for you; it does not seek illumination or anything to do with truth. Your lower nature wants you all for itself. Giving all for you while taking all from you. It is often the case that Neophyte loses various aspects of his life while in this grade, starting with material things such as loss of employment, place of residence, financial problems, deterioration of health, troubling emotional relationships, but also miscarriages, as well as physical injuries are just some of the instruments employed by his shadow. Yet, as long as the Aspirant finds discomfort in these words, he will be influenced by that same shadow, for it is nothing but the highest grace when we realize that the Aspirant's soul does not really have anything to lose as it has really nothing to gain. Such a harsh lesson is just an inappropriate and awkward way his soul tells him: "But I love you."

Knowing the difference between the Probationer and the Neophyte is not such an important guideline. It is critical to find a relationship between both things; as much as the Neophyte is free from Probation, so much is Adeptus Exemptus freeing from his Adeptship. It can be said that the mechanism is quite similar and that the cause of both of these manifestations is the same Great Mother of Binah – similarly manifesting her labor pain. The relationship of the Neophyte and the Probationer is reflected in the same phenomenon, in the same way as it is with the calm blue sea of Chesed compared to the vast ocean of Binah; the same idea of water is at stake, but how frightening is the relationship between the sea and the Ocean, the turquoise blue sea and the blackness of the boundless Ocean.

The furthermost fright for Aspirants is the simple fact that Babalon is Nuit and that all the inability to understand this simple equation is the complete defeat of our understanding of the Great

Mother. And if that is the problem, if we cannot know the Mother, how can we understand her child? How can we understand ourselves and our paths when we are not aware of where we came from or if we go anywhere at all. Our art is based on nebulosity and paradox, not mysteries. It is a paradox that we cannot understand. Babalon is only a form of Nuit, and there is nothing out or far from "her." Because she contains every form and every manifestation, born or unborn, every possible or impossible potential – at dawn, she is a girl; at noon, she is the mother; at midnight, she is a whore. She has no name because she is nowhere; just like Pan is everything, she is nothing.

An Aspirant should never try to conceptualize the Abyss. It is not the experience, and it cannot be compared with anything cause the Abyss is not "something" in the usual meaning of that word. Quite contrary, it is not even an experience that could be described as a word. You cannot find the Abyss in the system because the idea of a system is opposite to the Abyss. It is not the question of what the Abyss "is" – the true question is what the Abyss is "not." The true understanding of this would genuinely show such a supreme level of individuality and point out that one does not need any guidance at all.

Babalon wants your attention; Nuit desires your awareness. We always have to follow a holy principle that reads: "The Brothers of A∴A∴ are Women; the Aspirants to A∴A∴ are Men." The attempt of the Vampire against this setting gives an entirely different type of holiness to its task.

We do indeed revise our attitudes according to all experiences, but to design a tale about the Vampire would be such a weak endeavor if we did not reconsider our attitudes about our sexuality beforehand. The Vampire finds stability precisely in our confused understanding of sexuality and our misunderstanding of sexual energy, the energy that gives him so much cruel strength and endurance in such a fantastic way. It is our confusion and, above all, our fear of engaging with sexual energy that gives the Vampire an advantage that an average Aspirant can hardly compensate for. Quite often, we limit ourselves to thinking that we lack that energy when we need it most. But, this divine flow is always here, it has always been present in the same way, but we are the ones whose presence is not always the same. We will perceive our own absence as a fake accusation for the absence of energy. If we sleep the whole day, we might think that during these hours of our absence in our sleep, the whole world sleeps and is absent too. You cannot increase sexual energy. You can raise only the awareness toward that current inside your mind. The level of sexual energy is always the same.

Having sex or not.

Having a partner or not.

If you even have not had a single orgasm in your life, your energy level will be the same. It is up to you to find a way to channel it. People can make love with hundreds of godly tantric partners every day and still have nothing. On the other hand, you can masturbate and make love in your mind with your own God.

Try now to find what that God is.

Is he a male?

A female?

Young? Old? Sweet? Angry? Childish, Wise?

What does he or she look like?

Eyes?

Hair?

Is God an animal, maybe?

Maybe a sound?

He is maybe color and not a being at all?

Which color?

Orange?

Maybe blue?

Go and search each day, adding one new thing which is a part of your God. You will build yourself an ideal lover, an ideal personal God which you will have all the monopoly on, and which will have all the monopoly upon you. Then, when you have constructed him, when you have made this sacred sensual anatomy of your God, start playing with him.

Explore.

Search.

Go fuck with some ugly woman or a guy.

Go fuck with some boy from your childhood.

Go to a completely different town and fuck some very old man or woman.

Go have a threesome, buy a teddy bear and ride him a whole day if you dare.

Play with Lego and your genitalia; try to have an orgasm on the train without hiding.

Call your boss with your number hidden and let him hear you come.

Masturbate, play not with your body but with your mind. Masturbate your mind, let the Universe arouse you in its own way. Your soul is the sexual object of the entire Universe. Let the whole Universe arouse itself with your thinking about the same Universe. Your whole Ego is just an echo of the orgasm of the Universe. But always and constantly try to float on that wind of change which takes you away, away from the shores of ordinary and repetition. Push to the extremes, but always, with everyone and everything, fuck with your God. See where this energy will take you. In this way, your water will not be stagnant like the sea. Let it become a river, wild, fast, and furious – one giant infinite living water of change which will drag your destiny like a little barge on an ocean. Then lose yourself in that open vastness. Yea, in that open vastness.

Know yourself.

Fuck yourself.

CHAPTER SEVEN

WORD

The best spice for any meal is hunger. And a special kind of hunger is the hunger of the soul, which eats every inch of the Aspirant's being, every moment of being awake or sleeping. But of all this, certainly the most expensive spice of the Universe is the word. It gives uniqueness to every existence so well. It shapes reality to be real enough, or less real, or unreal, or unbearably easy for the one who likes it that way. One and the same thing becomes an entirely different thing by applying a different word. Each of our grades is one such spice, one different word that always describes the same condition.

But while words may be timeless, our representations of those words are certainly not. Love is the same word, but with so many different meanings that two different people have very different knowledge about love even in the same era, even though they can both claim to love, and both can be right. Someone can mean completely opposite things by the same word. Therefore, the power of words is based on understanding the one who uses them.

Within our Order, we have a fully respectful approach to words. They are hostages of the most sublime love; we have one knowledge of charms, oaths, formulas, names, vibrations, mantras, or invocations. All of these are words, and yet, there are so many of them that the Aspirant is sometimes left at the mercy of the great goddess to guess what is what. Basically, the main confusion is created between words and formulas, so we will focus on this first.

Indeed, words are different from formulas. We witness a complete substitution between these two things too often, and the end effect is similar to when a sentence is translated literally, losing everything from its punch line or rhyme. Each formula contains a complex mechanism within itself, as much as a word includes a very simple lever of action. For a magic formula, it is thus more important to know the meaning and story behind it, even if it has not been uttered at all; for a word, it is important to know the way how to vibrate it more than to know what it means. For example, the formula IHVH is very different from the name – with many beginners simply forgetting the pronunciation of the last H in IHVH. In this way, they weaken the formula considerably, although the same name can be vibrated in a powerful and enlightening way. VIAOV sounds like everything but the word VIAOV for the one who correctly vibrates this formula. It is actually one sound that changes aliquots. Still, there may be magicians who recite it without any awareness of its meaning. Yet, one should know that knowledge of the meaning of a formula does not automatically make a formula a strong vibration that will act upon the Universe, just as a good vibration is meaningless if there is no understanding of what lies at the root of that vibration.

But the problem is when our head makes them stop being anything but the transmission of our own projections, fears, and expectations. Instead of Tahuti, they invoke a shadow. Instead of opening, the same word now blocks, stops, and prevents the light of the LVX from illuminating the Aspirant. Instead of Tahuti being at the prow while Ra-Hoor abides at the helm, there is now an empty shell on the prow, while the worst excretion of the Moon is at the helm, rather than that of the Sun. And instead of this boat of light sailing the natural path, it now goes chaotically being carried away by the currents and rivers of strayed thoughts and corrupt emotions, distracted from the Great Work.

It can be openly noticed that the phenomenon of the words in the A∴A∴ has a very special place. First, every Motto taken by a magician at every grade is the birth of a word and the Logos, and as much as it is a decree of Tiphareth, it is always through the Father of the Logos, Chokmah. Moreover, as a Neophyte, the Aspirant receives hidden word from his Zelator, then, as an accomplished Adept, he receives the name of his Angel, and finally, as Magus, he obtains the word of Æon. All three grades are pervaded by acceptance of certain words that fulfill the utmost domains of human existence, the words shaking the whole Universe, as the ether through which these vibrations are transmitted, from Yesod to Chokmah.

The secret word of a Neophyte is never pronounced in the outer world, and it is never transmitted in the way as it is done with other words. Above all, one should take into account that M....M is not a word but a formula, which only resembles a subtle inner story, and it is necessary to obtain it through one's Zelator in its proper form. The secret word is the axis of the whole initiation of his, which is fully nourished by the vibration of that word. It never gets transmitted, except to the Neophyte of the A∴A∴, and there are strong reasons why it is so. First and foremost, the very process of finding this word starts much earlier than in Liber Pyramidos, if nothing else, then precisely at this point, reading these words represents an achievement and a valuable process by itself. The very word is a mental arabesque about settling the Aspirant's soul inside the Pyramid, imprinting his mind into its monumental heart. This word is the formula of conversion of two entirely different currencies; those elemental and those spiritual ones. This word is a translator, which turns יהוה into יהשוה; it is a formula that explains life itself. This word, like magical words of the old times used by a necromancer to raise the dead, will imprint the soul into dead things and bring them to life. It is symbolically responsible for our true awakening, our true initiation. And as every Pyramid is a tomb of the body, so it is equally a cradle of the soul.[3]

Vibration is a true expression of the word, and it is represented by a special way of use in this external realm. But there are so many wrong ways young Aspirants approach this venture, and we have to accept our own responsibility with our heads bowed for this. Vibration is a signpost to the stars. It does not carry energy in itself; on the contrary, it carries consciousness and serves only to direct energy, which in that case, unmistakably runs toward the field of action.

It is very important to locate the environment in which the word is transmitted – and that is air. In fact, the entire region of Ruach is suitable to be perceived that way. It is through the air that the Angel and Hermes move equally – the Angel with wings on the back, Hermes with winged sandals or talaria. Even Magus floats carried by a winged helmet, and each of them is carried by the vibration of their own words – the Angel by his name, Magus by the word of Æon, Hermes conveying the words of the supreme Zeus. Therefore, we first guide Aspirants to the correct pronunciation and vibration of words, but we can equally notice carelessly spoken words even with very experienced magicians – words without any possibility of conveying anything of force and power. We can often see that the only purpose there is the purpose of dramatizing – the words are recited, but they do not elicit anything of inner gnosis. The Will itself is an expression of the Logos, asked for by Ruach to resonate with – like sound which cannot be perceived without the air.

Names, as far as we speak about regular practices, are supposed to be used in two main ways. The first is to use them as vibration, but just as an ignitor for an inner engine, which is, of course, your mind. Just as you bring speakers close to your ear and

---

[3] "Anatomy of the Abyss: The Probationer's Compendium," Dušan Trajković.

turn on bass to the maximum, the vibration will start kicking you at the physical level. The second way is quite different. It is meant to awaken your inner nature just as I will wake you up in the middle of the night by calling your name loudly. The first way draws strength from a purely energetic capacity of sound, the second – from the transmutation of consciousness and attention of a magician who is but detoured by the word. To him, it is like being slapped or splashed with cold water – it actually awakens and directs him to a completely different course of a completely new consciousness.

As for the vibration technique itself, the whole idea is to lower the voice much more than we normally speak until we feel the sound coming down from the mouth into the throat. It is an extremely subtle feeling that must be felt primarily with a completely relaxed throat, and the mouth must be open freely. There must be no convulsions of either the mouth or the throat, which have such a destructive effect on the vibration itself. The easiest way to observe this is in the bathroom. Start from the highest pitch at which you can pronounce the sound A or O, and then go down step by step, and at one point, the whole bathroom will ring and resonate. In the same way, you can find the right resonance in any surroundings, using the strategy of lowering your voice tone by tone. In the end, vibrating in the open nature, you will discover your ideal pitch that works best with your body. It is not about any wisdom but simply the resonance created by your lungs, your throat, and your whole body; in this circumstance, your whole body is an instrument that acts united but as a whole too. Just be patient; the most important thing is to relax. Only then will the vibration start to tremble your body. Remember, if you hold a bass membrane with your hand, vibration will not occur.

Once you have discovered this pitch, hold on to it, and remember it. You can try to find out exactly what the pitch is with the help of an instrument so that you can interpret it later in an instant. Play with that pitch for a while, change letters and sounds, but never change the pitch – even a very small difference completely nullifies the impression of shaking that has been created once you discovered your resonance. You will now notice that the vibration and shaking are clearly felt on the physical plane, especially in your ears. Just a slight increase or decrease in pitch and that vibration will magically disappear; you will still sing the tone with the same force, but it will not be nearly as close to that kind of vibrating as it was when you used to do it a moment ago. Start vibrating now A, E, I, O, U, keeping the pitch you have discovered all the time and not letting it out of your hearing at any cost. We can now see that certain parts of the body react and vibrate to certain sounds, either more or less. Thus the letter A shakes the thorax, the letter I shakes the nasal part, E the throat, O the lower part of the throat, while U shakes the upper part of the throat as much as the mouth. Also, play with moving your mouth; open your mouth wide, and then start closing it, discovering ways the vibration changes. You are now an artist with a palette of colors in the form of sound – this is one of the most wonderful discoveries in practical magick. You will be truly amazed by the performances of so many people who find nothing important in this, and where words are repeated only as much as someone would just want to suggest to you that it is now an essential part of the ritual and nothing more. This is so far from the common understanding of music and the art of sound; for us, music is vibrating air; we follow that vibration completely, finding the ultimate path toward our Yoga.

How special is the nature of the word Abrahadabra, which, as a formula, has power when vibrating but contains so many meanings and processes that inhabit our minds when we think of the whole story that just leans on that word. The power is not exclusively in vibrating – but in our consciousness now riding this vibration by its understanding – it can be equally read to ourselves or even in silence, and that sublime instinct occurs just as strongly.

But the word of the Law of the Æon is Thelema, which also has importance, but its power is in a completely different matter. The word is a condition, and the formula is a process, that is the current under which all states are perceived in the laws where the being of the magician resides. Both words and formulas can be vibrated and spoken, shouting, or performed in silence, but one Neophyte must certainly know the difference and relationship between those. Every formula can be a word that vibrates, but not every word can be a formula. This is such an important statement. The difference between words and formulas is exactly like the difference between water and ice. We can control the force of our own impact with ice and shape it so that it remains standing for some time after we have carved it. That carved message can be seen by completely different people – it lasts for a while, and then, the time affects it and changes it to a new form – through a new Æon or new consciousness through some new Law. That ice melts and becomes water – turning into a completely different form, but keeping the same essence. But water is the precursor of all ice and its ultimate end; it is the condition of life itself – tasteless, odorless, epithet-free, colorless – and yet full of pure impulse. It takes the form of the vessel where it finds itself – like the Will, which, when directed to sound, now completely changes the one who uses the very sound. Indeed, that is the whole and true purpose of the vibrations of names and magical words. As ice containing that lovely water, so LVX is in the essence of all words.

So let us do something practical and quite simple, with what we have come up with before. Let us start vibrating the sound of "I," as in "Italy." Let us keep doing it for a while, completely calm, with the throat and mouth relaxed. Let us feel the vibration in the chest area, then the throat, and finally, in the nasal area. Under no circumstances should you push the air out of the lungs, let it pass through the throat in a sound form of the letter I, completely passively and without any additional action other than the exhalation itself. Let us do a couple of vibrations like this and enjoy the sound scratching and shaking us, in a similar way as a cat does while purring. We will now do something quite different, moving the vibration with a completely qualitative leap.

Now, continuing to vibrate in the same way, raise your right index before your eyes, and simply focus all your attention on the tip of that finger, imagining that now all vibration you clearly feel is moving toward that spot. In fact, you do not need to do almost anything. Sheer looking at the tip of that finger makes the vibration feel right in the part where you are looking and where your gaze and attention are focused. It will look as if your throat is in that right index finger and that all the sound and trembling is actually coming from that place. Practice the transmission of vibration from one finger to another by looking at them and imagining the vibration and exhalation of air from that very spot. This is such a remarkable trick that once you have mastered it, and it does take a few minutes to understand, your vibration will never be the same again. The difference is like the difference between scratching and genital arousing, leading to orgasm. It is the same mechanical reaction that leads to a completely divergent physiological response. You can vibrate and shift your attention to parts of the body that are injured or sick. We will go even further – now we will learn to speak through a particular part of the body, through the tip of the finger, for example. In the end, let the spot itself pulsate in silence, without any external vibration, let the only movement be the Pure Will looking and directing its attention to that part of the body. This exercise can be practiced so that the whole body becomes one resonator box for the Will. But we really think that even the vibration itself, no matter how intensely experienced during this simple trick, does not deserve any of our attention, unless it is caused by the Will; that is to say, Will and intention is the only true producer of sound, everything else is just changing a resonator box. Sound is created primarily in the mind, never in the throat, lungs, or right index finger.

Vibration is not the only way to use words in our art; on the contrary, there are certain goals when the method of vibrating cannot bring anything good. Barbaric names draw strength from a completely different psychological effect, which uses a similar mechanism like Mantra Yoga.

There is a great way of pronouncing invocations where they are uttered whispering; it is also a trick of the mind that automatically increases attention when words are spoken quietly. Have the Aspirant read an invocation he usually practices in a complete whisper, almost in silence, and he will notice a delicate change in the quality of his consciousness that occurs after such utterance.

One special aspect of the words in our Order is the magical Motto; too many Aspirants think that it is as strong and fierce as the power and fierceness of the deity, as the Motto is clumsily named. The Motto must never be strong nor anything that has the characteristics of a similar kind. It must be yours, and it must be you in exactly the same way; it must be you long before you realize yourself. It is the name which you had had long before you were even born.

There is a very convenient way of vibrating, reminiscent of goat bleating, where the vocals are not repeated in one continuous breath but intermittently and very rapidly. Not one vowel, but a lot of short bursts of a vowel with minor pauses in between that remind of a goat bleating. It is a mental trick that, when mastered, which really takes just a few minutes, gives a whole new level of vibration of any name, and is eerily effective when used together with the sign of Horus. This way of vibrating can be clearly felt even when you are vibrating in complete silence, only by remembering this method in your mind. This can be perfected to such an extent that after a few times of such imaginary intermittent vibration, it can be felt in a particular part of the body, or even in the whole body to such an extent that the entire body really begins to tremble.

Vibrating with your mouths closed should also be mentioned; try to pronounce A, E, I, O, U while clearly feeling and hearing the difference between the letters. Then you need to move on to more complicated letters. The only condition is that the mouth does not open, not even for a moment. This kind of magical mumbling is exceptionally effective and makes this practice something like mild energy purring. The only condition is to make a larger jaw movement than usual, all with your lips closed.

It is certainly inevitable to mention the Enochian language, which has a very special place in our art, especially since all its greatness lies in the fact that it is quite self-regulatory to each Aspirant. In fact, whatever we pronounce, the result will be the same. Sometimes I skip some parts of keys or say something different on purpose, sometimes I improvise, but whenever I had Will before "change," it seems that Enochian force will pour itself towards that mold in the same manner. It appears that the whole point of Enochian is in a simple mind trick used by children – simply start speaking a language that does not exist, and in a couple of minutes, your being will be drunk by the very specific change in awareness. I tried to experiment, and I read a text from the internet in a language that I do not know at all (try to copy some text with google translate and choose some totally weird language), and after that, I invoke the names. Results are fascinating, as I get exactly the same visions with complete success. As long as I am doing for what I do not know that I am doing, that work always brings complete success, all on the condition that the Will for success has been manifested beforehand.

There are only a few more practical tips related to the Mantra; when you repeat it, imagine there is a dark cave in the center of the Chakra. Try to use the Mantra to call the one who is in that cave to go outside. This small detail only is enough to trigger things in a completely different manner and bring a whirlwind of ferocity that changes the consciousness of the Aspirant so indisputably and to such an extent that he will remain boyishly enthusiastic for days for he has discovered such effective magick.

Also, after you choose a certain Mantra, say it quite slowly at first. Repeat it a couple of times at a slower pace. Try to do the next two things; slow recitation of the Mantra, but also a long pause between repetition. After a few times, and you must not count, say the Mantra a little faster while also shortening the pause between utterances. After several such repetitions, you should recite the Mantra even faster, with even shorter breaks, until the Mantra is so fast that you will say it without any interruption mumbling it with your lips. Now speed it up even more. The mumbling becomes just a miniature movement of the lips, as the Mantra turns into a pure sound. Now, speed it up to the extremes. No lips can move anymore; no sound can be heard; let the whole feeling of the Mantra be within your mind imagining how the inner sound accelerates even more and becomes pure light. It radiates more and more as it keeps accelerating. Imagine how warm and radiant that pulsing light is, and now all your thoughts are like flies clinging to that light. Millions of flies keep on sticking, more and more, all flies from the wilderness of your mind, with that light attracting them faster and faster. Finally, the last step is the easiest one – now, turn off that light.

CHAPTER EIGHT

NEUROSIS

Suppose the whole essence of Abramelin is in the mechanism consisting of the pure enjoyment of consciousness to play hide-and-seek with the Angel. In that case, it seems that this mechanism, in all this waiting, finds a constant of madness instead of ultimate pleasure. And it is precisely this time of waiting in the eternal game of hide-and-seek that leads to the basic phenomenon that accompanies human existence – neurosis – which makes the Abramelin mechanism possible at all. It is precisely neurosis that is the main ingredient of the Great Work; without it, this whole story would be an incredibly tasteless dish. And no matter how invigorating it may be, there will always be something missing that would complement the atmosphere, something that will give an apparent meaning or, better said, an evident impetus in such an abstract and meaningless work.

This story will never be told, for the reason that language and mind are equally the closest generals of this prince of evil. As long as we think about it and lead ourselves to a solution, we will equally be declining. That is one of the greatest truths about our neurosis, which is that it keeps coming back. No matter how much we go forward, we will always go back to the beginning, and no matter how much we think we have learned something, we will still fail an utterly banal test despite being positive about the outcome.

A lot of things are wrong in our work, our entire cornerstone is hollow, and it was done not with intention but out of that human need to continually improve and continuously work on oneself. It is difficult to set up the order and organization of methods in something as varied as human experiences. If the Aspirant really understood the nature of his neurosis, he would experience the Knowledge and Conversation of the Holy Guardian Angel at that moment. Neurosis is the only constant that will take him to the City of the Pyramids. It seems much more apparent than the Angel himself, who becomes visible only toward the end, while his appearance does not even seem to exist in the beginning. With neurosis, it is an entirely different thing. It exists as long as we exist, and its mechanism is always the same. Its actions are exactly the same no matter how high or low we thought we were, and no matter how spiritually experienced and advanced is the person that we find; we will always be surprised at how low he can fall concerning completely insignificant things. All the peculiarities of this observation apply equally to the Adepts, as well as all the other Aspirants.

So many things in our Order are swept under the carpet, and so many things are not perceived as important. Our holy books are full of sublime archetypes, while we refuse to recognize the names of diseases, flaws, and tics inside our own being. And as long as that is the case, can we even believe that we will get closer to enlightenment, as long as we feel uncomfortable when we see a movie with a scene of wild sex in front of our parents, or step in a simple piece of crap on the street with our brand new shoes?

Neurosis is the moment in which a soul is stuck. Therefore, it is a temporal phenomenon. Its real feature is unreality above all, but which got stuck in us at that moment and is interpreted as real and completely true reality; it is the child in us who refuses to grow up because time simply does not fly with him.

Unreal does not mean illusory at all; the nature of its permanence is completely the same as the manifested Universe; the truth of its lie is real like the body. Such unreality is like constellations. When looking from a limited point of view from the Earth, constellations assume the form of mythical figures in two dimensions, but if the same stars are to be observed from some other part of the Universe, it will construct a completely different picture. This does not mean that constellations are unreal; those stars are the same, but our perception of how we connect them leads us to a completely wrong picture of what things really look like up in the skies. Especially since what we are looking at is a picture from a few hundred or thousands of light-years ago, and that now, the situation is anything but the way we see it currently.

A lot about this subject has already been said in the book about the Probationer, but now is the time to understand neurosis more intimately, much more intimately than it experiences us. From that intimacy, the Aspirant must find the strength to fly toward the Sun, not toward the Angel, because the Angel is already intimate enough with the Aspirant. Almost everything the Aspirant is doing at this point is wrong. Instead of striving for intimacy and coexistence with his neurosis, he is intimate with an utterly chaotic idea such as the Angel. From the domain of the City of the Pyramids, neurosis and the Angel are the consequence of one and the same thing, and this claim may even offend many Aspirants. Still, it only shows how important the notion of neurosis is for the work of an individual in our Order.

The relationship between the Ego and neurosis is like the relationship between the Knowledge and Conversation. Neurosis is the energy of the same idea that is embodied as the Ego; these are the two states of the same phenomenon. Just what ice or steam is for the archetype of water, so are the Ego and neurosis a pair of wings of the same Angel.

And just like water, we can generally find three aggregate states of neurosis: fear, anger, and sadness; these are the three main positions behind which each of our ordeals and pain hides. The

Neophyte's task is to find the dominant one in his life, although it can hardly be said that anything is stronger than fear. The Aspirant has one moment in his life when a seemingly insignificant event triggers an avalanche of complexes, tics, dreams, and beliefs – all triggered by a snowball of frozen emotions that is basically one of these three terrible and passionate goddesses – rolling downhill through our lives it has grown into a disaster of emotional chaos, misunderstanding, and suffering.

The essence of neurosis is in the strong and dedicated construction of a new reality, as constant as this reality is. Yet, it is so different from the idea of unreality. Neurosis is not unreal; on the contrary, it is as real as everything else in this world. In fact, it is surreal; its permanence and truth are precisely in that, and for that reason, it is so well rooted and ready to remain forever in our lives. In other words, the Aspirant, being a cause of that neurosis, must eradicate himself in order to eradicate that neurosis, which is a paradox. It can be said that there are only two approaches to the problem – one which solves it, the other which denies it. Both are equally catastrophic and unsuccessful.

Neurosis is an integral part of every grade and a part of every moment of our action, to a greater or lesser extent. We may say that becoming free from neurosis is an utterly impossible thing; it is already very well-known during Probationship, and now it takes on its crueler and concrete form. Partly because of Binah's pressure, but also because of the possible appearance of the Vampire; both make Probation feel as light as a breeze concerning this period. The period of being a Neophyte can be permeated with the suffering of the worst kind, the kind because of which many give up without ever realizing the real reason – which was exactly the goal of neurosis. Indeed, that is the ultimate reach of neurosis – not to come to an end and discourage that dreams can come true. Neurosis does not want fulfillment but procrastination. It does not want a happy ending because it does not want an end at all. It wants to last and not end. It wants the stability of unreality, not the realization of reality or opportunity of real fulfillment. Its scope is as wide as the reach of Ruach, if not wider. The deepest levels of lucid dreams and the astral plane contain all those very same characteristics of neurosis, and we can see that it did not even dare to change – on the contrary, it even gained a deeper meaning at a deeper level and much more brutal impact on the Aspirant's psyche. Indeed, many Aspirants of lucid dreaming find a unique phenomenon that is the same for everyone, and that continues to shock and frighten Aspirants who cannot overcome the specific appearance of the shadow in their experiences for years. This shadow experience, which occurs in its manner of frequency, always brings the ultimate horror, terror, and insurmountable fear into a dream experience where the Aspirant has no control over the projection. Many Aspirants cite this as their worst nightmare, and that shadow usually feeds on their strangest and most ingrained childhood fears, which have such destructive power once they have risen in a lucid dream. But if lucid dreaming brings benefits in anything, it is precisely in the assimilation of this shadow. The very success in lucid dreaming is nothing compared to the experience of assimilating the shadow in a dream – which could be one of the most important undertakings of the Aspirant he may have had before Abramelin once he had found tremendous courage before the projection and managed to present it to himself as the goal of the projection, if he approaches the shadow, embraces it and to feels it illuminate. So little technical knowledge is needed for this, but so much devilish love and courage – the same one that will later take him along the whole of Abramelin operation. We will certainly have an opportunity to talk about this topic in more detail in the area closely dedicated to lucid dreaming experiences.

To understand one's own neurosis and the cause of its onset would actually be Adeptship in the highest form. It can be said that only Adeptus Exemptus can fully understand and overcomes this. Although the Adept approaches this topic quite politely, he still cannot understand that the four Princes of Evil still remain because he still accepts time as an agreed notion in the world in which he still lives, so they really "still" exist. In this "still" lies all their sense of existence. They do not exist because they are emergent, but because they are permanent – not because they happen, but because they still last.

The entire IAO formula contains all the zest of neurosis in its true form; indeed, regardless of the New Æon or Old Æon perceptions, it is precisely this time frame that is the main weapon of neurosis that envelops itself in this framework and upgrades in this way, forever fleeing from the Aspirant. Neurosis has its two aspects equally; lower – in the form of Apophis within the IAO formula; and the second and considerably higher – in the form of the four great Princes of Evil, even after the Great Work has been securely founded in the Aspirant. A distorted Tetragrammaton, perceived as the idea of "four great Princes of Evil," that shadow of the memory of what has been transformed into the gold of Tiphareth, is a negative transfer of the highest kind in the same way. That memory, which serves not to return through time but precisely to create the illusion of time, is the same mechanism of rejection to capture the wave of the present is always the same requirement for the creation of neurosis. We should not mix the shadow with the shape, which gives us a shadow in the first place. The four great Princess of Evil are "just" ruin of the old IHVH temple, which the Angel destroyed by light. There are no "elements" – just our perception of reality, which we just call elements. There are no centimeters in the world; space itself is surely not divided by lines on a ruler. These lines exist in our mind only. They are just an invention of our mind to understand the distance easily. The four great

Princes of Evil are actually a true perception of the elements and the Tetragrammaton. These are not elements but illusions, and now the Adept knows them the way they are. These are obstacles in front of the light that create shadows. We believe and understand these shadows as real things, and in fact, they are just illusions that only have a twisted shape of what blocks the light in the first place.

IAO formula – is "ouch," cried by your Angel stepping over some daring thorn on his path through the light, every time you act "out of him," like a mother screaming each time as her child doing some silly things. Every action of ours and everything we do is just "silly" things that do not have a connection with the Pure Will. You silly, crazy, wonderful child. It is this madness and insanity which is neurosis in its pure form.

The disappearance of neurosis could be attributed to Magister Templi at first glance. However, long meditations and endless thought patterns indicate to us that Adeptus Exemptus is the one embarking on this adventure. He does sail the sea of his neurosis, which is quite calm at first and near the shore, but as he boldly sets out to open sea, it becomes horrible and cruel. The Abyss is the only place which neurosis cannot climb up and leave because, in the City of the Pyramids, there are no values that the mind builds around neurosis. Neurosis will never ascend to that place, simply because there are no dimensions "there," upright or descending, that are so much needed by neurosis.

Some of us might really ask what is the relationship of the Angel and neurosis, and can we get a hint about this relationship that would help our hungry souls? Ultimate phenomena serve ultimate achievements, and, surely, a well-trained Aspirant evokes the idea of the relationship of these two entities in his mind – of which he has no experience, no control, no real knowledge; except that he knows they are both pushing his life like an autumn leaf in a storm. We can say that the relationship between neurosis and the Angel is like between thunder and lightning. Although both things result from the same phenomenon, they have completely different ways of being perceived, which makes them separate things. One is by the perception of our sight, and the other is of sound; even their temporal aspects are different – one is before while the other is after. But neither of these two actually explains the phenomenon itself, which is completely different from the perception of that phenomenon. The moment the human soul begins to be neurotic in childhood, that moment it gets its Angel. Just as both the occurrences of lightning and thunder have had completely ridiculous explanations throughout history and evoked a sublime sense of fear, which is the surname of one neurotic phenomenon, so the Angel and neurosis cannot be viewed separately. Moreover, they must not be observed at all because the very perception of these phenomena brings in confusion. Before we deciphered the Great Question, the way we asked the question was completely wrong because of the simple fact we asked it at all. In the end, we did not even pose it; the Ego posed it, setting us up as the usual suspect. There is no difference between the Ego and the Angel; the Ego is the *difference*. It is hard to explain, but the nature of the Angel and the Angel itself is not the same thing. Every mentioning of Him equally creates the Angel and the illusion of the Angel. Furthermore, neurosis is all the false evidence that benefits the Ego; neurosis is that forged signature that confirms the indictment of the Ego, making the Angel a false perpetrator. Therefore, all three concepts – the Ego, neurosis, and the Angel – are completely unsuitable for statement and practical work. All that remains for us is to try to sculpt these models of abstraction with our minds and call it nothing but art, just an artist's expression in the clay or canvas of the Abyss.

We all have the same dick and the same cunt under our clothes. Some have longer panties, some have tights, some thongs, but deep down, a penis is a penis, and a vagina is a vagina. And we all have the same neurosis mechanism, everybody trying to cover their own by underpants, foils, lies, while for others', we pretend they are not around at all. Again, and again, and forever and ever again, always in circles. This is another feature of neurosis; in addition to being surreal unreal, it is recurrent. Always and in every way the same, always in a spiral. In fact, not in a circle, because it would mean that neurosis is a closed system. On the contrary, it is always alive as much as we are alive; it always adapts to all circumstances. Aspirants often realize that they have remained the same throughout all grades; they even triumphantly express such a discovery. Which, of course, is impossible – that is exactly the definition of one's own neurosis – it is always the same. We are never the same, we are never the same "us," we are many "I," who always live now, always everywhere and with the same illusion of that "always," that "live," and that "now." Our neurosis is the same; it always wants us to be the same so that it would live through us in the same way.

Both fears and dreams come true, sometimes one, sometimes the other, but always and in every way the unreal, the unfulfilled, the coveted. And even when it comes to the realization, our neurosis activates a defense mechanism and rejects happiness right in front of us. Because for it, the reality of joy is poison; it wants to crave chocolate more than to eat that same chocolate, only to dream of a divine kiss rather than dare to kiss, to enjoy its unreality, rather than its manifestation. Therefore, it always wants and achieves nothing. It always calls but never summons.

Let us observe ourselves the next time a fly flies through our field of vision while watching a movie, buzzing so persistently above our heads. Does our attention have to be so special now in dissecting this happening? There is discomfort, but it certainly cannot meet our criteria. We really have to look for higher and deeper attributes. If we continue to pay attention to this discomfort, it will soon turn into anger, a kind of irritation, and finally, the fear of that irritation and the inability to do anything to stop it. As our attention is now less and less directed toward the movie, it would be equally wrong to assume that it is focused on the fly. On the contrary, we have been inside ourselves all the time, and both the fly and that movie are part of an unreal child's fear and desire for love. Within every neurosis, there is as much desire for love as there is a position of fear; it can be said that millions of different types of neuroses are shades of these two ultimate colors, making each one of use have their own personal shade, but the exact same mechanism. We are really unable to fully experience this statement to the proper extent – thinking that it is always a different mechanism. It is an entirely fascinating aspiration and struggle of the Aspirant to keep his neurosis, embracing it and sacrificing everything he painfully finds that can be taken away by that same neurosis. Therefore, an aggressive self-hatred neurotic expresses this aggression towards his loved ones, at the same time expressing the phobia that something terrible can happen to his family. These are completely unrealistic mechanisms, but every Aspirant must accept that equally:

1) he has this mechanism within himself,
2) he shall work on this mechanism and experience it, with an active approach and intense vitality, by all methods and by all possible means – his neurosis is alive, so he must be alive too.

The Neophyte must be a skeptic in his own faith, always thinking that ours is the method of science and the goal of religion. But we must be careful not to choose either of these two; we are not here to choose; we are the ones chosen by the gods and forces of nature as the result of all actions around us and within ourselves to be what we are, in a completely natural and spontaneous, by no means occult, esoteric, or spiritual way. In his work John St. John, Aleister Crowley said the following:

"I further take this opportunity of asserting my Atheism. I believe that all these phenomena are as explicable as the formation of hoar-frost or of glacier tables. I believe 'Attainment' to be a simple supreme sane state of the human brain. I do not believe in miracles; I do not think that God could cause a monkey, clergyman, or rationalist to attain. I am taking all this trouble of the Record principally in hope that it will show exactly what mental and physical conditions precede, accompany, and follow 'attainment' so that others may reproduce, through those conditions, that Result."

In this lies a very appropriate instruction to interpret all things as a unique dialogue of God with our own soul. But that dialogue is always more a whisper and a call than the songs of the foreign languages; this instruction has an extremely simple solution, and that is the cognition of all processes within us, as well as without, as part of one and the same nature, completely open, simple and cordial. All secrets are just our inability to grasp the simplicity of our soul by neurosis; the point of the ultimate experience is by no means in barbaric names, nor in the hours spent in Dharana. Both the Knowledge and Conversation, as well as the Crossing the Abyss, do happen at a single moment – but our neurosis makes all this look like a month-long Abramelin or miles-deep Abyss. The first phenomenon is the phenomenon of time; the second is the phenomenon of space – together, they suffocate entirely every sense of occult science and skill, making it possible at any moment of life or a single breath for the human soul to capture both things without any pre-established standards or preparation. This movement is as mystical as a movement of the lungs to take a breath or the movement of the heart muscle that pumps the blood inside us

– both conditioning life with a completely simple mechanical reaction – and yet making that same simple life full of complications, absurdities, and emotional nebulae due to our completely natural tendencies to believe that we do not understand. Both an ugly and a handsome man are equally neurotic about their own appearance – their appearance seems to have nothing to do with the experience of themselves at all; they both think that beauty is wholly unattainable and complex and such a remote thing for them who are so repulsive and miserable. An unenlightened and enlightened man are by no means opposites. Enlightenment in itself has no counter position. Enlightenment itself is a negation, it cannot be not experienced. One may think that we are not enlightened – that is a correct counter-thesis, but that is the whole point of human enlightenment – not that he reaches, but that he remembers that he has already attained enlightenment. That phenomenon of time, which is the condition of all neuroses, as well as the condition of the creation of the Angel and the Abyss, is the only hidden teacher to whom humanity aspires. It is that immeasurable unit, which means to the Selfness as much as that pumped blood for the heart, or that inhaled air for the lungs.

You are not afraid. You just think you are afraid. Because you think. This is the only motto of the ritual before the Neophyte – the Ritual of Passing Through the Duat – raising Zelator in him with the same holiness as it was the case with the Ritual of the Pyramid turning him into the Neophyte. It seems that all the instructions for this ritual can be reduced to the following: recycle your fear and pass further. This performance is a sublime hyperbole of neurosis; all this ritual has only one element – going through the night. The night of the soul, the twilight of the gods is always poetically depicted in the same way, yet so far away from the silent Self that sails through the darkness. The Aspirant may notice those awfully powerful mechanisms flowing through his being in all their forms and variants, of which fear is certainly the most dominant. All these claims should be taken with a grain of salt by the Neophyte because each Aspirant has a specific case, and all generalizations are wrong – including this one.

Liber Cadaveris, or its full name – the Ritual of Passing Through the Duat, has as much darkness as it has the idea of passage; it is, after all, passing, in no way pausing, never halting. The Sun that inevitably floats in the dark is only surrounded by nature, and its passage through that night is a completely natural phenomenon. Therefore, the Neophyte has nothing to perform by this ritual, as much as it is actually just a poetic play that the Aspirant should only gently follow – with attention and love. This ritual, just like Pyramidos, has completely different content and essence from other techniques and ceremonies, and together with Liber Samekh, it contains a specific mixture of absurdity, abstraction, and transcendence. But the change induced by this ritual is not aggressive; it is not imposed, but something completely different and milder – it is instead a consequence of aligned layering of experiences within a magician, making his life become a major consequence of all previous movements in the Cosmos. His change is not his – he has no right to ask for or demand anything, except for that smooth movement of the Sun across the Universe and its passage through the night. All the trouble of this ceremony is in fear of stopping that Sun; all the power of our neurosis lies solely and exclusively in that fear – the fear of change. That is exactly what Qliphoth is – our inability to accept the constancy of life, and I will be even more insolent to say that Qliphoth is nothing but immobility and retardation of change. Therefore, each and every truth that exists for more than a moment is Qliphoth. Each of "you" individually here, including myself, is a Qliphoth. The only constant is the constant of change. That is represented by the symbol of Swastika, as one of the oldest forms of the cross. Actually, the symbol of Swastika is an active, living form of a cross that is moving and changing. Everlastly. Neurosis is the complete opposite of this, in every respect. It is alive, but its vitality is in conflict and not in coexistence. It struggles and fights because it wants to remain in place; it is afraid of duration because it cannot accept time in a way that only Magister Templi can understand. This kind of illumination of darkness is an entirely sublime phenomenon in our Order – and the whole concept of the Superior and the Student which is so particular to our Order is reflected in this, looking at it as a specific vow given by one Bodhisattva. Only by illuminating that darkness is it possible to move on – illuminating it with one's light. But that brilliance is completely impersonal in nature. It is directed at others because there is simply no "Self" in that place.

> When Buddha lay on his deathbed, he noticed his young disciple Ananda was quietly weeping. *"Why are you weeping Ananda?"* he asked. Ananda replied, *"Because the light of the world is about to be extinguished, and we will be in darkness."* The Buddha summoned up all his remaining energy and proclaimed what were to be his last words on earth: *"Ananda, Ananda, be a light unto yourself."*

But let the Neophyte feel deep inside how many times he has summoned this moment. How many times have you lived through all this in the same way? Ask yourself deeply; you already know all this. You have that feeling, that knowledge. And this time, as you are reading this, you know it is not the first time. There has been at least one before. And then, if you call this one first, as well as every next one, it is anything but the first – how many times have you experienced the same present? Now you can think that you are already an accomplished Adept and that you crossed the Abyss a long time ago, but your memory is over here now, not over there to understand it. In the night of Pan, far away, there are no shadows. So there is no memory of something that has happened an infinite number of times. There is a memory for a repeated thing, two or more times, but endless memory is needed with endless repetition. Endless memories of one and the same Knowledge and Conversation – which, in fact, from the point of Abyss, has never happened.

The greatness of the Passing Through the Duat is not in feeling the power of the Sun, but in the fact that you have already passed its path. The majesty of this path is not in its closedness or completeness but in its multiplicity. It is not strength but ferocity. The Sun that appears in the morning is the same one that passed through the darkness of midnight. Its greatness is not that it is ready to fight in the morning, but that it went through that same fight a long time ago and is now sailing steadily and peacefully, regardless of the trials that await it. It is a great difference in understanding this glorious path, and only in this way will the Neophyte pass on. The Sun will pass on because it is all really its nature – to pass and that it has already passed on, over and over again, continually passing on.

The Aspirant may think that all that blocks him, all the fate of his fall is hidden in darkness. Still, the worst is the fear of light which is indeed fear of his incompetence and stupidity. There are no hidden judges or prosecutors in this place who are blocking justice, who have conspired against us and are holding back our nature by acting together. That blockade is reserved only for ourselves; only the fear of light distances the Aspirant from his attainment the fear of who we are and what we are afraid to be.

Equally, both light and darkness cause blindness, but again, an equally different kind of fear. In the darkness, we are afraid of what may be in it, and there is what we project. Moreover, we cannot even see what cannot be seen, but we are still afraid of what we do not even know is there, and we know very well what it should be. But the fear of light is the worst of all fears; in fact, it is one single fear, because finally, fear is always one and the same thing – the inability to look at the light without looking away because it is by turning our gaze that we turn into darkness. In that glorious darkness, we project again what we are afraid of because we initially looked away from that blinding, radiant, blessed, and living light.

What the Liber Pyramidos had as a vector, here it is a circle. In this ritual, it is essential that the circle is completed and to pass steadily through the night, returning to the birth of dawn. As much as Pyramidos is Bhakti Yoga in its particular aspect, so much Cadaveris is Dhyana. It is necessary to note that Samekh would be a coalition of these two principles, enflaming with prayer and invoking often. Indeed, these formulas have nothing to do with esoteric teachings or occultism, by any means. These rituals do not have their power in the archetypes that will roll through the Aspirant's mind long after he has performed the ritual, changing his consciousness slowly, so slowly that he does not even notice it. These rituals – Pyramidos, Cadaveris, and Samekh are just arabesque miniatures. They are a reminder of what has already happened, of what the Aspirant should remember, not realize. These three sublime things are just the variants of the highest meditation that can be found beneath the Abyss – and that is her majesty Samasati – which our good Brother Allan Bennett passed onto Master Therion so lovingly. Every form of attention, every instrument and magical weapon, every attainment is in itself Samasti practice – by which one does not achieve and know, but recalls. Every new knowledge is just old reshaped knowledge. Every character we meet is always and only one character. Pyramidos, Cadaver, and Samekh are forms of the same Selfness – "me, myself and I"; three aggregate states of one and the same reality.

But we want robes, insignias, charters, recognitions, oaths, and misery so we can be happy. Indeed, it is so remarkable, and we yearn for misery to be happy. Indeed, we are so atrocious to say that the Black Brotherhood is greater than the Aspirant can even conceive. Everything that is not in harmony with True Nature, everything that is distracted from the inseparable essence, is black magic. But, all this is a projection and a part of Adonai's love play, as a process of the highest distraction of postponing the climax with this form of attention. We praise every boldness and proclaim every Aspirant a black magician until he awakens awareness of the Pure Will. Every act is an act of the Black Brotherhood if it is not accompanied by pure success. And even then, the fact that success was achieved subsequently does not make an action aiming at success justified. No act further distances the Aspirant from the Self than does his attempt to attain the Self. This is the whole secret of neurosis that is especially nourished by our occult engagement. It has a very special relationship with the body, like a relationship between death and dying. They are certainly not the same things, and while man generally has a misconception about death, in fact, what he rather thinks about is dying. This relationship between death and dying is specifically considered by Zelator and Neophyte – in the same way as Pyramidos and Cadaveris: the Neophyte in his Pyramid, as the Zelator on his journey through the Duat. The Neophyte in the Ritual of the Pyramid is not in the Pyramid at all. His death is nothing but another life; he is to be found in the womb and not in the tomb. The Zelator, on the other hand, is the same Zelator that goes through the night of the Duat. One is the formula of transformation; the other is of transcendence. In the same way, there is a consistent parallel between life and living. As much as the Aspirant is burdened with life, so much is the Adept alive. The mystery of Pyramidos and Cadaveris is that we are really incapable of understanding the concepts of life and death; even more, we are unable to separate the notions of life and death from the process of living and dying.

Our consciousness is certainly not a factor of the symbiosis of thoughts and feelings in our brain. On the contrary, it is only the result of excluding the Universe and everything that we are not.

That result is what we perceive as individuality. This resultant is the Ego, which is the result of the substitution between us and the Universe. Our Self is constructed not by direct knowledge of what we are, but by the perception of what we are not. There are mirrors all around us, crooked, cracked, and wherever we look at we see a million distorted versions of ourselves in every place around us, but no version consistently reflects what we are. In fact, while looking around, we are looking at a distorted Self. It is an illusion of perception – the illusion of consciousness. The very perception that our consciousness has is an illusion; we perceive everything but not what should be perceived by the one who does everything but perceives.

Kundry gives this whole thing a special confusion, and together with Cadaveris, these ideas will strike a catastrophic blow against the Aspirant's being. This is such a sublime and special topic that we will address it in a special place. But do not be afraid, star child. For it is written: even if everyone gathers to harm you, they will harm you only as much as God has prescribed. Therefore, take your freedom. Because it is free.

CHAPTER NINE

QABALISTIC LECTURE

Malkuth and the Foundation of Qabalistic Dogma

Any comprehensive system must be based on certain principles ruled by universal laws, independent from the outer understanding. If based upon thinking of diamond clearness, such a system could be misunderstood by people only due to imperfections of their intelligence and knowledge.

If the object of interest of a particular system is abstract, it would demand a simpler methodological basis. However, it does not mean that simple branches would develop from such a simple base-trunk. Systems got the nature of mathematical progression, where every next step is higher than the previous one. If the basis is already, in its beginning, founded on an abstract model, how difficult will it be to follow its full development? If the object of a system is abstract, if the basis is abstract, then it is natural to assume that the ending of the system will be abstract of abstractness. Therefore, the key to any system that strives to abstractness and adjustability is in the gradual empowerment of nonsense that it tends to integrate. If we aim to extend the time of inhaling to more than a minute, then we definitely must start with as moderate a rhythm of breathing as possible, without force.

As a system that envelops reality in a single universal glyph, and as a map of all possible and impossible possibilities, Qabalah is one of the shining examples of a great foundation and a glorious crown. Its universality lies in the exact condition of any particular progress, and that is the wisdom of defining mutual relationships. Qabalah defines the whole Universe not by descriptions but by relations. It does not create new terms independent of itself but creates one universal way to integrate the terms into a whole.

If, by any chance, you were misfortune to have a stern literature teacher who demanded you to learn obscure literary works by heart, then you might understand what I am talking about. There are two ways to learn a poem by heart. One is by automatic repetition until exhaustion. The other way implies learning, or better to say, searching for relations that might be applied to the whole of the poem, which would be perceived as a simple mechanism – finding or, better to say, inventing patterns upon which the whole of the poem is based.

Such a search might often be imaginary, as the poem itself need not be constructed according to such a mechanism. To make it clearer, let us have a look at the numbers. If we look at the sequence of 1, 3, 5, 7, and 9, we could see a sequence of odd numbers. But if after 9 there appears some unsuitable number, it does not mean that all of the scheme of linear movement has been lost. If the next number, let us assume, is 132, then the whole sequence is divided into two groups. The first group is a sequence of numbers that follow an odd natural scheme, and the last number is simply 132. However, even for that number, there could be a scheme that attaches it to the first group, making that way one scheme, and not two. So, there is no need to learn every single number by heart. Such a way of learning is significantly slower, not to mention the duration of such learned data in mind.

The benefits of Qabalah are in its natural and straightforward way of defining the relations, which is applicable to all groups of items, regardless of the fact that some items might seem non-connectable. In other words, Qabalah has very clear content from which it is possible to deduce any context. In that way, there are no decently abstract phenomena that could not be classified. According to Qabalah, the glyph of the Universe is of an entirely tangible and pragmatic nature. To state once again, the perfection of the system is not in its complexity or its simplicity, but in crystal clear definition of relations.

Now we can move on to some more concrete things, finally looking at the glyph of Qabalah as it is. In fact, it is necessary to ponder that glyph as it functions in the same reality it wants to define, and not as it "is" or it "is not." We do not attempt to define the historical authenticity of a certain model of thought, nor are we trying to discuss its different variants. Let us try to catch on the essence of the glyph, which could be modified endlessly, but would always remain the same essence. It is the only way to make a pragmatic system out of a dogma, a pure truth out of a theorem.

In order to succeed in this, you need time and eyes wide open. Actually, the most you need is to give it a decent try. And to try again. And again. Apply a scheme, this particular glyph, in all possible situations. As long as there is a single case where you cannot apply this scheme easily, it means you have to try harder. And again. Your tries cannot change the glyph but will only change your consciousness, becoming more flexible and sensitive to the glyph itself. Only then will you experience that way of abstract thinking, which is necessary to understand a map that describes reality.

Let us return to the glyph. It is generally known as the Tree of Life. Like any real tree, it has its growth process and specific morphology, which implies roots, trunk, branches, and fruits. In order to understand it, you must start from the roots, moving upwards. Take note that in this case, a perfect system must have perfect roots. We are not going to describe the structure of the Tree of Life here, as it would take us too much time, and there are already dozens of books published that deal with that subject. They mostly focus on the visual description of the glyph and its essential points.

Our presentation is focused on the basis of the Tree of Life, on examining the basis of this Universe. The basis of our tree is called Malkuth, and in order to understand the glyph or reality, you must understand the basis upon which the glyph is constructed. Once again, we are not to describe what Malkuth is or what the Tree of Life is. Anybody can learn that by heart. Here we want not to discuss but to ponder. Any average Aspirant could dedicate a few days of his life to study the basics of Qabalah and draw the Tree of Life on paper. And after a few more days of dry mental acrobatic, a new, learned Qabalist is being born. I am not going to write about what the Tree of Life is, but where it is around us, here and now. This exertion is dedicated to learning how to integrate knowledge and not how to acquire it. By the mere fact you can read these words, it means you are intelligent enough to acquire knowledge by mere persistence and willpower. But what we try to do here is to learn how to learn. Instead of studying the Tree of Life, we will learn how to water it and finally how to eat its sweet fruit.

As of this point, I am going to assume that the glyph of the Tree of Life is both theoretically and morphologically clear to you. If it is, and there is no reason why it would not be, the only thing you need to proceed further will be to have a list of analogies that might be related, from the symbolical world of the glyph to the world which is around you. In other words, it is necessary to create such a bridge between the world of the symbol and your own world that you can walk upon it safely, there and back again.

A universal dictionary of that kind does not exist, as each one of us perceives the terms in different ways. However, there is an excellent attempt in the form of a book called "Liber 777 and Other Qabalistic Writings." It should be vital for you to understand under what conditions seemingly unrelated ideas could be joined together and for one simple reason so that you could do it for yourself. In other words, we will study all the existing analogies in order for you to set up your own. Whether you are going to accept the analogies from that book in their entirety or only in parts is totally irrelevant. It is crucial to develop a specific awareness that classifies ideas properly. In this lecture, we will deal with the basis of the Tree of Life, called Malkuth, which in translation from Hebrew term means "Kingdom." It is quite necessary to perceive Malkuth around you, here and now. Leave this lesson for a moment and have a look at Malkuth. There is a huge possibility you will not do that, as you absolutely and under no circumstances have an idea of what it means. In other words, you miss the examples of practical attributes or the translation of the language of symbols used by Qabalah. Here, I am going to list some analogies traditionally attributed to Malkuth:

1.	Translation	Kingdom	
2.	Hebrew letters and name	MLKVTh	מלכות
3.	God-Name in Assiah	ADONAI MALEK	אדני מלך
4.	Mystic Numbers of Sephira	55	
5.	Element	Earth	
6.	The King Scale of Color	Yellow	
7.	The Queen Scale of Color	Citrine, olive, russet, and black	
8.	The Emperor Scale of Color	As Queen scale, but flecked with gold	
9.	The Empress Scale of Color	Black rayed yellow	
10.	Practical Attribution of Egyptian Gods	Osiris	
11.	Selection of Egyptian Gods	Seb. Lower Isis and Nephthys (unwedded)	
12.	Greek Gods	Persephone, Psyché	
13.	Hindu Deities	Lakshmi, Kundalini	
14.	Christian Concept	Ecclesia Xsti, the Virgin Mary	
15.	Roman Gods	Ceres	
16.	System of Taoism	Khan	
17.	Precious Stones	Rock Crystal	
18.	Plants	Willow, Lily, Ivy	
19.	Imaginary animals	Sphinx	
20.	Magical Powers	The Vision of the Holy Guardian Angel or of Adonai	
21.	Mineral Drugs	Magical Sulphur	
22.	Vegetable Drugs	Corn	

23.	Scents	Dittany of Crete
24.	Magical Weapons	The Magical Circle and Triangle
25.	Traditional morality	Scepticism
26.	Figures related to Pure Number	Altar (Double Cube), Calvary Cross
27.	Parts of the Soul	Nephesh נפש
28.	Alchemical Tree of Life	Mercurius Philosophorum
29.	Ten Plagues of Egypt	Water turned to Blood
30.	Magical Images of Sephira	A young woman crowned and veiled
31.	Name and attribution of Discs	☿ in ♍, Wealth
32.	Name and attribution of Swords	☉ in ♊, Ruin
33.	Name and attribution of Cups	♂ in ♓, Satiety
34.	Name and attribution of Wands	♄ in ♐, Oppression
35.	Magical Formulæ	V.I.T.R.I.O.L.
36.	Illness	Sterility

Malkuth is the basis, the support of the Tree of Life. It is the last emanation from the absolute. The wisdom of magick is the wisdom of defining proper relations; therefore, it is necessary to understand the idea of the basis. This principle is well presented in mathematics. If we come across the following equation with two unknowns, like $30x + 40y = 180$, there is not much we can do to solve it. But if we come across another equation, where the same x and y are represented like $5x + 8y = 34$, it will help us to find the solution, as we can compare relations.

Similarly, you will seemingly replace Malkuth by its given synonyms, and through understanding the synonyms, you will understand the Malkuth.

The basis as support must be stable and firm. If you look at line number 5 in the column above, you will definitely see that there is something important in the idea of firmness. The name MLKVTh means Kingdom, and every Kingdom must be founded on the King's firmness. Compare other items and find an essence which is common. Although I will briefly comment on the analogies given in the table, I do not intend to obstruct your model of thinking.

I partly explained the first line, while the second one is sheer technical data on how to write the name itself in Hebrew, as you will need it later on if you adopt the Qabalistic method. MLKVTh is spelled by Hebrew letters Maim, Lamed, Cheth, Vau, and Tau.

Now we come to the third line. It is the divine name of Malkuth. Some might wonder what it is for. If on the street you start yelling a name, there are chances that somebody having that name will turn around, although you did not have that particular person in mind. It could even happen that several people turn around simultaneously. Try to do that at some glamorous reception, and as much as it is stupid, somehow, I feel great enjoyment every time I do that. Therefore, if you call Malkuth by its divine name, there is a possibility you might be taken seriously and that it will turn towards you for few moments – giving you enough time to mark it in your mind. The divine name of Malkuth is Adonai Malek, which, when translated, means "my Lord the King." Here we have a full association with the Kingdom and everything related to that idea.

The fourth line is represented by number 55. Malkuth, as the last emanation of the absolute, is manifested as the tenth Sephira (the word Sephira implies singular, while Sephiroth relates to plural). The sum of all the numbers from 1 to 10 is number 55. It is an affirmation of that number as the wholeness of the sequence from 1 to 10. It is also good to remind that $5 + 5 = 10$, Malkuth. Both halves of that number are equal and well balanced. The right balance is the condition of firmness.

The fifth line is the elemental attribution, and in the case of Malkuth, it is Earth. In fact, none of the others, "higher" spheres, includes Earth. This fact emphasizes, even more, the idea of firmness and similar implications.

Lines 6 to 9 give scales of color. The reasons for these colors were explained very nicely in the book "777." For now, I think it is enough to notice the analogy between those colors and the colors of Earth. Later on, after we move through all the other spheres, we can return to this. As I mentioned earlier, you are here to learn how to practically deal with Malkuth and discover why exactly those analogies were used. The reasons will reveal themselves to you in due course of time. Not to mention how many reasons and arguments simply do not apply for some people, considering their mental structure and nature. In the beginning, it is necessary to define basic outlines, to work on a draft, and not on the final product.

Lines 10 to 15 show analogies with various divine principles from different pantheons. There is not too much speculation. It is necessary to study mythologies and understand the nature of a particular deity. Thousands of books were written about it, and you can find them in any library. Study those deities until they become really close to you. Book "777" has the following to say on that topic:

On Egyptian gods
Seb as the god of Earth. Lower Isis and Nephthys as imperfect until fertilized. Sphinx, as it is comprised of four elements or cherubim.

On Greek gods
Persephone, virgin Earth. See legends about her. She is Malkuth of Demeter and Binah. Adonis is a suspicious attribution, maybe the connection with Adonai as Lord of Earth. Psyche is the unredeemed soul.

On Roman gods
Ceres, goddess of Earth.

Line 17 gives attributions of precious stones. Stone crystals are of earthly nature, as they embody the quality of firmness. There is more to say on this, but we will live it until we have reviewed other parts of Tree of Life as well.

On line 18, or herbs, the book "777" says the following:

Willow is a traditional tree of an abandoned virgin, unredeemed Malkuth. Lily implies the purity of the virgin, and ivy its adhering and slender nature.

The obvious presence of the Virgin asks for having some time to study astrology. Virgin or Virgo is a pure earthly sign of Zodiac. Of course, nobody forbids you to study this area further.

Line 20 mentions the vision of the Holy Guardian Angel as one of the magical powers. The Holy Guardian Angel is your Adonai or Lord (in translation). If you relate this to the Divine name of Malkuth, you could find interesting analogies: Adonai Malek, or My Lord the King. Malkuth as Kingdom.

Lines further mention sulfur, wheat, etc. It is not hard to find relations to earth. Now, you can easily find that the surname of Malkuth would be Earth. It also has lovely nicknames like Firmness, Basis, and Kingdom.

Line 24 mentions magical weapons. In the case of Malkuth, those are the Circle and the Triangle. Triangle is the place in which the Spirit manifests itself, according to the magician's Will, while the Circle, roughly speaking, represents the magician's protection. Manifestation is the final goal of creation, the densest form, and a representation of an idea in the solid, material form. Therefore, these weapons were attributed to Malkuth with a reason. We could say that protection, as an idea, finds its justification in it. The Circle of protection must be concrete and firm, or otherwise, it will not be good protection.

Line 25 mentions skepticism. What is it about? Roughly speaking, skepticism is based on insistence upon the irrevocable proofs. The nature of such proofs must be concrete, firm, and tangible, from the standpoint of a skeptic. Aren't these the attributions of Earth, that is, Malkuth?

In a similar fashion, try to solve the other "riddles." The last one, sterility, refers to what Malkuth is not. And that is bareness, the impossibility of manifestation.

I hope that after all this, it is clearer to you what Malkuth is. Now, we have tremendous work in front of us, which is to recognize places where we can find Malkuth. Only in that way can Qabalah demonstrate a certain purpose, and you will turn a dogma into a true map that you can safely travel by and experience what it refers to. Let us emphasize this: Qabalah in itself does not explain how, as much as it explains where. It directs the human spirit in specific directions, but it does not tell that much about exact methods of how to reach the goal. If the Aspirant has crystal clear awareness of the destination, the object of his attention will determine the method itself. Therefore, you will hardly reach an island on foot. Under the condition that you know where the island is and that you got the will to travel there, a trip by boat becomes self-evident as a method.

There are two diametrically opposite ways in which you can find Malkuth. The first one is to find a concrete thing that represents it. That way asks for directness and resoluteness. There is an issue of intrusion of other associations, as it is challenging to find something that represents only one thing. The other way is to analyze one thing and recognize in it all those aspects that correspond to Malkuth. Generally speaking, anything could be Malkuth, just because it is a thing, but nevertheless, look deeper into the essence of the idea that stands behind that thing and because of which it is what it is.

Let us take one object as an example. Let it be a teapot. Is it Malkuth? Try to bring it into relation with analogies described in the table and with other analogies that could come to your mind and that you consider being Malkuth. If your answer is affirmative, then you must know with perfect certainty why it is so. Maybe you could discover the analogy of a teapot as an object that contains something. A solid object that contains liquid. It might be a connection with Malkuth. Or, for instance, its purpose of making tea. Tea is being made of dry plants. If that tea is being made of plants specifically attributed to Malkuth, then it could be Malkuth. I wonder what tea made of willow tree leaves would be like?

Let us take some other object – for instance, a brick. The first analogy that comes to our mind is that bricks are used to build houses. It definitely represents Malkuth. By its shape, it could be represented as a double cube, demonstrating firmness and durability.

Now, let us have a look at a tree. The tree as a living being that takes its energy from the Sun and gives us oxygen to breathe? Not so obvious. Tree swinging on the wind? The tree that delivers fruit? The tree that was cut? Peach, apple, cherry? It is not so clear, is it? But if we consider wood as construction material, maybe there should be some connection. For instance, a wooden house, a cottage. That is much better. A boat seems to be a decent connection, but as it is primarily related to the idea of water and not to earth in the first place.

Have a look at the knight's armor. As a method of firm defense, it might represent Malkuth. Especially the armor that protects the lower parts of the body, legs. We could consider legs as the basis of the human body, which corresponds to the concept of Malkuth.

Now, try to find aspects of Malkuth in some things that do not seem to be Malkuth at first sight. Let us try to develop the second method of searching.

What about a pillow, for instance? Could it be Malkuth, and in what aspect, if it cannot be Malkuth in its entirety? Pillow serves for sleeping, and sleep does not represent Malkuth, but if we consider a pillow to support the body, analogies are not too far away. I just remembered those funny small pillows for feet that you get for free when you buy a giant armchair on sale. Yes, such a pillow could be Malkuth. Support to a grown, firm body. Then, there are legs that are placed on that pillow. All those are analogies that could be related to Malkuth.

A stale tuna sandwich? Something it is stale if not used for long. It became inert. Also, sandwiches are made of bread, and bread is mostly made of wheat, so it could be Malkuth. Tuna fish is not a proper analogy, but it does not matter anyway as we definitely would not taste that sandwich.

Now, let us consider a bicycle seat. The seat as support for the buttocks is Malkuth. And now I remembered a story I heard from some sports fans, that banana bicycle seats are very unhealthy as they allegedly might cause sterility. This is ideal to find a connection with Malkuth, taking into consideration line 35 of our table.

Let us proceed further.

Find a domestic animal that represents Malkuth. Would it be a dog, a chicken, a sheep? In India, an elephant is a domestic animal. So robust, big, and firm, it might be attributed to Malkuth.

What cosmetics would be appropriate for Malkuth? Pedicure tools, as well as toilet paper, although it is not related to cosmetics in a strict sense. Let us use the scale of colors. For instance, black nail polish tinged with gold. Or even better, black stockings embroidered with gold. Stockings are being related to legs, and legs to Malkuth. Talking about legs and feet, black dirt under nails is clearly Malkuth too.

It is interesting to mention what construction material is used in villages, being excellent for thermal and other isolation. It is cow shit. It is definitely a good Malkuth.

The subject at school? Geography, but also could be biology, physics, even a sports class. It all depends on what aspects you find and how much those aspects relate to the attributions of Malkuth.

Cars? Maybe Volvo or Saab, definitely. Mercedes got a logo sign that points too much to the symbolic of number three, so we will leave it for some other occasion.

Could a radiator represent Malkuth? Although it is there to produce heat and make life in a household easier, its essence is in heat and not in the home itself, so maybe it is not an appropriate presentation.

What about drinks? Beer would surely come across your mind because of its Malkuth complexion, especially dark beer that got an appropriate corresponding color.

All right, we dealt sufficiently with simple nouns. Now try the same with verbs. Also, analyze the sentences.

For instance, in the sentence: "Edward Famous lost over 30 pounds while he was writing his new book on human rights," find a word or place where you can find Malkuth. At first glance, it might be a book as something which is the base and fruit of Edward's labor. However, that could be pounds, too. Something happened to Edward; he lost his pounds. It is heaviness, mass, firmness, in other words, Malkuth. You need not seek perfection; it is enough to follow the thoughts in this way and find an answer which is satisfying.

Have a look upon an object that you know the best – have a look upon yourself, and find where there is Malkuth. Maybe your legs were not developed enough; maybe Malkuth manifested more at some other part of your body? Find some talent you got that represents Malkuth, as well as some of your defects or drawbacks related to it.

This is a kind of magical puzzle. All you need to do is to go out and make an inventory of Malkuth. When used as a practical tool, Qabalah is excellent for the mind, and it will not be too long before you notice that you started to view things differently and that you started to find deeper meanings in them. It is necessary to approach this with a certain subtle spirit of playing a game, as intuition and imagination express themselves in this wonderfully, and being too serious or stern would ruin your efforts. It is not necessary to create connections; just put the emphasis on defining the already existing ones. And when you do that, you will need child-ish enthusiasm and sense for a game more than anything.

This is true Qabalah. Go outside. That is the most important step; you have to find something to enter Malkuth. So, where is Malkuth on the street? Look around you. The tram is coming – great! Try to find line number 10; get inside. Then get off at the station where divine providence takes you. Your Adonai will construct coincidences. You do not need intention in the least. You need a coincidence. You do not need order; you need pure chaos. Only in that environment can the germ of your Will give birth to a young plant that will grow to heaven, with its roots in the halls of hell.

Yesod and the Path of "Universe"

Dear Brother,

I am glad the last lecture brought you benefits. So far, you were able to get yourself acquainted with the Qabalistic way of thinking and the basics of its model of reality. Maybe you already started to apply in practice the Qabalistic method and analysis of your Universe. Sooner or later, such an undertaking is awaiting you, and maybe you already noticed that you arrived at a point when you cannot go any further. You managed to combine all the information so far into a specific network of associations; you managed to uplift your own thinking to a level of pragmatic combinations that make your life drastically easier.

Now we will expand your model of the Universe. We will shed light on a new level of the Tree of Life. The whole of this lecture is dedicated to Yesod, a ninth emanation of the absolute.

As you noticed, we are moving upwards, but that ascent is conditioned by the full understanding of the previous lecture. You can assume how much I will ask from you later in more complex problems, but you will agree that the most stupid thing is doing the same thing twice and return to the beginning because the attention was weak. Once when you have adopted the Qabalistic way of thinking entirely, there will be nothing impossible for you; there will be no obvious problem that you cannot resolve. For here, you learn to expand and deepen your own awareness and not your knowledge. Now you can remember why I put an accent on practical experience from your everyday life, not on the books you read. Truly, you have to be a Qabalist not only in front of a book but even amongst the densest traffic jam or in the moments of the worst mundane derangement. You have to be a Qabalist not by knowledge but by the peculiarity of your thinking. Qabalah is not a chapter in a book, nor a separate topic in our science, but a specific approach which ensures a certain transfer of information in a so-far unknown way. It is a method, not an achievement, at least for now.

Now we will devote ourselves to the ninth Sephira, Yesod. It is above Malkuth and precedes it. This is a good point to differentiate between two things that I already notice are hovering in your mind. A "preceding Sephira" is an awkward term that I want to clarify. You see, if I sit on your head, do I precede to you? Or, does the fifth floor in a building precedes to fourth? You must carefully determine which direction you are observing reality. If you watch from above, Yesod precedes Malkuth, but if you are looking from below, then Malkuth precedes Yesod. When we observe reality, it is best to agree that all of its components exist independently and in parallel planes.

Let us have a look at the Tree of Life. Look at its branches high above yourself. Can you see them pierce the sky and embrace infinity? But ask yourself, if you look upon yourself from that same sky, can you see it rushing toward the Earth, disappearing far away in the lower realms? We have a path upwards and an equal path downwards. What the path will be like depends primarily on your destination.

You can use the Tree of Life to ascend to the house of God, but you can also use it to show to God his glory here, down on earth, depending on what method is momentarily in accord with your Will. You can climb into the house of God, but you can also make your house divine if you settle the Lord inside. This is one of the roughest divisions of our art – on the path of mysticism and the path of magick. One should take note that the word "absolute" does not imply a direction as a purely vector value. This simply depends on your nature, or the nature of your operation.

If you want to socialize with me today afternoon, you can come to my house, but you can also invite me to yours. Each direction has two ends. Each force got two ways in which you can deal with it. This a supremely important theory for the beginning and is worth every minute of your thinking, so do not hesitate to study it. To be expedient with time, I will present to you the same thing that I showed you last time, and it is a list of correspondences that can be brought into connection with this plane. There is plenty of new things to be discovered, and I will not waste time on things you already know. Use some time to absorb new correspondences, as you did for Malkuth, in order to use them flexibly.

YESOD

1.	Translation	Foundation
2.	Hebrew letters and name	ISVD יסוד
3.	God-Name in Assiah	ShADAI EL ChAI שדי אל חי
4.	Mystic Numbers of Sephira	45
5.	Element	Air
6.	The King Scale of Color	Indigo
7.	The Queen Scale of Color	Violet
8.	The Emperor Scale of Color	Dark purple
9.	The Empress Scale of Color	Lemon yellow, tinged with azure
10.	Practical Attribution of Egyptian Gods	Shu
11.	Selection of Egyptian Gods	Shu
12.	Greek Gods	Zeus (like △)
13.	Hindu Deities	Ganesh, Vishnu
14.	Christian Concept	God Holy Spirit (like Incubus)

15.	Roman Gods	Diana (like 𝓓)
16.	Precious Stones	Quartz
17.	Plants	Mandrake
18.	Imaginary animals	Elephant
19.	Magical Powers	Vision of the cosmic structure
20.	Mineral Drugs	Lead
21.	Vegetable Drugs	Orchid root
22.	Scents	Jasmine, all scent roots
23.	Magical Weapons	Scents and sandals
24.	Traditional morality	Independence
25.	Parts of the Soul	Ruach רוח
26.	Ten plagues of Egypt	Frogs
27.	Magical image of Sephira	Beautiful naked man, very strong
28.	Name and attribution of Discs	♀ in ♍, Gain
29.	Name and attribution of Swords	♂ in ♊, Cruelty
30.	Name and attribution of Cups	♃ in ♓, Happiness
31.	Name and attribution of Wands	𝓓 in ♐, Strength
32.	Magical Formulæ	ALIM אלים
33.	Illness	Impotence

As you can see, the items were classified as in the previous lecture. However, pay attention to the following: each one could provisionally be classified as an element or concept of your inner nature, which is manifested in a certain way. Also, it could be classified as a planet or a concept that has its own outer "reason" and influence that affects that concept. We perceive elements, which are activated on the micro plane, and planets, which act on the macro level. Both actions are processes that draw their essence from the most abstract. Therefore, do not limit your mind by the understanding which finds shelter in the acquired knowledge. Only two things affect your life: your nature from inside and your fate from outside. In time, you will equalize both of these concepts.

Look at an example of a dog: is its nature fiery? Or maybe watery? Is it more similar to air or earth? When you represent its nature by a planet, think of the force that presides over it. Separate the character and nature of a dog and move it into a more abstract concept. Does it bark at the Sun or Moon?

Try not to confuse two things – Earth as an element and the Earth as a planet. The Earth as a planet possesses Earthy element as much as Watery, and still, its center is pure Fire. Moreover, life would be impossible without Air. Therefore, for you, the Earth as a planet must have a quality that is different from the elemental aspect. Dear Brother, maybe it carries more life in itself and on itself than all the elements altogether.

As an element, Yesod is Air. But its planetary aspect is the Moon, the first celestial body in your travel toward the infinite. Going that way, we will pass in turn all the celestial bodies important for us, and that in a specific direction and in a specific order which should not be neglected. You will ponder it yourself when you get to know the Tree of Life better. It is still early for such judgments, so we stick to Yesod – "only" the second sphere on our way.

The Moon represented Yesod, and as such, it complies with all the ideas and concepts implied by that body. Primarily note that it is very close to the Earth. In fact, it does not have freedom in movement, but it is bound to the Earth's orbit. The Moon is a body that mediates in the knowledge of the Universe. It is close enough to reach it with ease, but far enough for the Earth to influence it. Too close, far enough.

The Moon, as Yesod, is a little "above" Malkuth on the Tree of Life. As Malkuth is a plane of physical action and manifestation, so Yesod is of a subtler, slowed nature. Their relationship is similar to the relationship between a metal bar and radio waves. It occupies the region of sleepwalking, and therefore of all daydreaming, suppressed or manifested thoughts and fantasies – a place of trash of our "true" nature, which makes us live beings. There are the remnants of our awareness, the imprints of our mental, emotional activities, and all the activities empowered by consciousness. As the imprint is stronger, so it remains longer. Therefore, an artist's idea that lived in his mind through many years is far stronger and enduring than an idea related to the choice of dinner.

You will compare this to the concept of collective unconsciousness. But there is a problem, and that is the issue of endurance. During practice, you will find for sure that time is just one of the characteristics of your being, which is always here and now, at the plane of Malkuth, and therefore, that characteristic is lost by the ascent of being to higher planes. But why can't our mind get information from such a marvelous place? Why are possibilities to make a breakthrough into that sphere so rare, reserved only for talented people or liars? The answer is very simple, but the solution isn't. The name itself clearly suggests that it is the collective unconsciousness. Indeed, the term "unconscious" is an answer. In order to get such information, you have to break into such strata. Maybe it is not that difficult, but the real problem is maintaining the information in the awakened state. In other words, you have to be conscious of the unconscious, to be aware of unaware.

Between the Earth and the Moon, there is "empty" space. More precisely, that space is being emptied gradually, subtly losing its vitality. The atmosphere is the last place of life on Earth, the last place of everyday awareness. In order to get to the Moon, you must gradually adapt yourself, as scuba divers do, but in the opposite direction. You must be aware of every change in your awareness, and more importantly, you must always keep your goal in mind. Every change of consciousness brings new awareness, and each new awareness has new laws and tendencies. Those are the categories that are variables in our task, but you have to stick to the only unchangeable constant in work, and that is the goal of your path. Derangement is the deadliest foe here, and you have to go upwards, always and only upwards.

Therefore, mastering the change of consciousness and separation from physical existence is one of the most important achievements here. However, there is only one important achievement in the life and work of a magician, only one success. Everything else is a modification of that one. But, we will have the opportunity to talk about it after we have mastered this model of the Universe with more confidence. In any case, I encourage you in advance in your attempts to transfer your awareness into your Body of Light. Remember to always be open to anything, for the experience of success in this is different from everything you may imagine or expect. The final analysis comes later, and you can only make things harder by doing it now. It cannot be worse at your point, you simply have no results, and only conclusive success can help you understand the processes and laws of your own being. And your failed or successful attempt is just an attempt. Success is the only thing you need, so do not try to strive for anything except that. It will arrive when you realize that it is hidden in the awareness that you are succeeding, independently of a method. Success is not the category of time, but awareness.

The key to this lesson is in the word "change." You must discover the nature of the subtle sphere that is upward and above, you must discover on your own all the specifics of this new area of action, and finally, you must learn to act in that sphere and not merely to observe.

You noticed that in this lesson, I am covering many ideas that apparently are not connected to Yesod. My dear Brother, from now on, you will have to understand the nature of spheres on your own. The basic idea is in the change of consciousness, your consciousness. I will point it out to you and help you develop a particular way of thinking that will release your spirit toward higher and subtler planes. It is an art of pragmatic Qabalah – to define the relationships and their change, which are conditioned by the change of your consciousness.

It is very important to realize the difference between Malkuth and Yesod because that difference is the key to the change of consciousness. The sole difference of Yesod in relation to Malkuth, if you are aware of it at least to some degree, makes your intention turn toward Yesod. From the Earth, you will easier get to the Moon if you focus on the atmosphere itself, and from there, you will easily move upward. Marathon runners understand this very well. Keep up to the momentary difference between two distant objects. That difference is a special element, the third element between those two objects, which is a mediator between the two. Now you can already perceive that one of the central concepts that I am expounding is consciousness. It is a key not only to understand the difference between Malkuth and Yesod, but it will be of use later on too. Ponder that difference. Ponder the existence of hundreds of invisible waves that are flowing through your head right now. Think of what is happening in my head while you are reading these words. My thoughts, now, while you are reading, are as true as yours, but you definitely will never have proof of their existence. To gain experience in the higher energy states of spirit, you have to act in a certain way. When somebody from your classroom is whispering to you an answer to a test question, there is only one danger. A danger that you will not hear it.

You need receptors, in fact, to temper them good, as you already have them by the very fact that you are a conscious being.

Let us compare now the essential ideas of Malkuth and Yesod and find differences. Malkuth is Kingdom, while Yesod is Foundation. Both of them clearly point to the idea of solidity, but if you think more about it, you can notice that Kingdom is based on form, while the idea of Foundation is in subtle strength and energy. Foundations are strong, and the Kingdom is firm. There is an immense difference. Therefore, the Kingdom is more of an Earthy element, while the Foundation is Airy. You can ask me why it is not fiery? Foundation is not an essence but active support. It does not carry an idea but matter. Pay attention to how the wind carries the leaves in autumn, and you will understand how subtle energy we speak here.

One of the essential differences between these two ideas is in the illnesses which are traditionally ascribed to them. With

Malkuth, it is sterility, while Yesod, it is impotence. If you dedicate yourself to this issue and find a key difference there, you will understand both the natures of Yesod and Malkuth, as well as their relationship. If you remember the previous lesson, you will know that we devoted our attention greatly to the firmness and physical manifestation as one of the basic ideas of Malkuth. Sterility is a curse that may befall Malkuth, as sterility makes the manifestation of man impossible, and more broadly, it points to a standoff in the Universe. Sterility carries the idea of disabling the manifestation, which is tangible, alive, and firm. That illness is one of the links to the idea of firmness. Impotence points to a similar outcome. It can also influence the decline in the development of the Universe, but not that much as sterility. Impotence is connected to the idea of energy itself, subtle urge, and it is of airy nature. It is a blockage that prevents action; sterility, on the other hand, prevents the form – form against subtle energy, firmness against fluidity. Think of this, and I am almost sure that from this moment, you have a pretty clear picture of what I want to confer to you.

Yesod and Malkuth are very similar, but you must know the difference for sure. You must classify ideas without hesitation. I am asking you to develop two kinds of consciousness – one for Malkuth and one for Yesod. When you classify the idea, simply recognize the kind of awareness that is initiated.

Only now can we move on to the real problem, which is the next step toward your new way of thinking. By learning about Malkuth and Yesod, you gained knowledge about them, but it remains for you to find out one more crow idea used by the Qabalistic method. Although I had been talking to you about it all the time, it is almost certain that you did not pay attention to it.

Make a short observation of the characteristics of the Universe. Everything that happens, and everything that exists inside of it, interferes mutually and participates in the activity. But do not

misunderstand activity as action, but the sole living spirit. Therefore, it is possible to have an activity without anything happening.
An activity includes subject, object, and a process by which they
are defined as such, fulfilling a particular aspect of Nature. Sometimes, during an activity, you may get the impression that there is
no object or subject. You can even be sure there is no process, either.
Analyze such cases; a good Qabalist always faces miracle, and do
not wonder, but praise the manifestation of God's work.

To tell it simply: there is subject, object, and predicate. As a
Qabalist, apply that to your knowledge. It is clear to you that your
starting point is Malkuth. Yesod is somewhere "up" and should be
reached. Yes, dear Brother, we came to verbs themselves, to the
method. You certainly have two points, so now just draw a line
between them. You can notice that the length of that line and its
nature depend on the nature of the points. Therefore, the method
and path that lead to Yesod will have characteristics of both
Malkuth and Yesod. In the beginning, that path will look more like
Malkuth, but as the travel reaches its end, it will lose its properties
and assume the nature of Yesod.

We are returning to the topic from the beginning, and that is
the adjustment. The adaptation of consciousness happens gradually until the goal has been reached to maintain control and continuity of awareness. You can hear a bunch of nonsense about certain
unfortunate souls that suddenly lost their mundane life and now
are hovering around as confused ghosts because, in their suffering,
they do not realize they ceased their worldly existence. These stories concealed a very good way of thinking, but certainly, you have
also to learn to reject sheer rubbish. Therefore, here you can find
the answer on how to master the technique of the Body of Light in
the fastest possible way. The answer is in the change of consciousness. In order to observe with your astral eyes, you have to start
looking with altered consciousness. You have to acquire a conditioned reflex to change the state of consciousness at the moment

when you step into the new body and look upon things from a new perspective. In the beginning, it is a trick, and you can learn it very fast unless you waste precious time looking for perfection in your visualization. The trick is in determination to make a reach and not to endure. You have to make it happen quickly, not to do it indefinitely. When you look at your body from your astral counterpart, at that moment, you have to acquire all the aspects that the new body has. Dear Brother, it is a Qabalistic method. Remember how I insisted last time we spoke that you learn all the correspondences. Now, apply it here. In the moment of transference of awareness, you have not only to see with your new eyes but also to breathe the air from there, to smell and stand at that place. You have to infuse your mind with the truth that you are really there. You have to switch off your personal censor of reality that tells you it is all nothing but a figment of the imagination, by the simple truth that you are there. Therefore, that truth must not have a single aspect of falsehood. Create success through the creation of magical links. You cannot expect to be there if you breathe and think from here. And even if you are failing, try to fail from there. The whole point is not in visualization at all but in a state of clear resolve. On many occasions, I have achieved success without visualization at all. You will see that you will quickly achieve success in this if you act properly by doing properly.

Let us do a concrete job: pay your full attention to the following. I want you to close your eyes and look into the dark, black space in front of you. Try to understand that black space as a mental polygon where we are to test situations and models of Qabalistic thinking. You can understand it as black modeling clay for your spirit to play with if you want. Look at that emptiness, into that black clay. It is pretty alive, as you can notice, and in fact, it is not so black at all. In fact, there is the least black color. There is a reason for it because this clay is alive. Insert, through your imagination, a picture of the house into that clay, as you use your Will to impress upon it a three-dimensional stamp. Now, you have to know that it is Malkuth. Now, look inside the house. Walk around and finally enter it. In front of you is a big room, and to your left is the staircase that takes down. Have a good look at those stairs; I want you to watch them for a while. They are a very important segment of this story, do not spare your time. After some time spent studying it, walk them downwards. We enter into a basement, spacey basement. Feel moisture, inspect the corners filled with cobweb. You will see a lot of things there. Old coats, old furniture, jars with pickled vegetables, barrels with cabbage. Do you see it now? Can you feel the change of atmosphere down there? Can you see that you are not in Malkuth anymore? Here you can notice the foundations of the house; here, you can see things that were dumped away and left to slow forgetfulness. Here is the foundation of the house, but there is no life in that scenery. You can find a lot of information and things, but the one who uses them lives upstairs, in a warm and dry place. Think of the essence that I want to transmit to you. Also, this can be a valuable example to you that subtler things are not always literally to be found "up there." In this case, they are to be found in exactly the opposite direction.

This change, the introduction of a completely new element into our story, brings us one of the most important aspects of the Tree of Life: the concept of the "paths." They are the methods, mediators that equally contain both the starting and ending Sephira. They are there to make our travel comfortable and, more importantly, they offer us the integration of new experiences and new states of consciousness into our everyday life. The function of the path is like the function of Metatron, the transmitter of live God's word to humans because nobody else could hear God and stay alive. Metatron, as well as paths, harmonize the experience and insight with our individual limitations and old perspective, which are too fragile to understand something as terrible as the new and unexpected knowledge, as the truth, as change.

As before, I give you the list of basic ideas and correspondences by which you will recognize the essence of the path that connects Malkuth with Yesod. I give you a description of the new kind
of awareness that will uplift you There and bring you Back.

32ND PATH - "THE UNIVERSE"

1.	Translation	Tau Cross	
2.	Jewish script	TV	תו
3.	God's name in Assiah	ADNI H ARTz	אדני ה ארץ
4.	element/planet	▽/♄	
5.	King scale of color	Indigo	
6.	Queen scale of color	Black	
7.	Emperor scale of color	Blue black	
8.	Empress scale of color	Black, tainted blue	
9.	Selection of Egyptian gods	Sebek, Mako	
10.	Greek gods	Demeter	
11.	Hindu deities	Brahma	
12.	Roman gods	Saturn	
13.	System of Taoism	Kan	
14.	Precious jewels	Onyx, Salt	
15.	Plants	Ash, oak, ivy	
16.	Animal	Crocodile, bull	
17.	Magical powers	Alchemy, geomancy, making pentacle, traveling astral planes	
18.	Mineral drugs	Lead	
19.	Scents	Sulfur, styrax, all heavy odors	
20.	Magical weapons	Pentacle, salt	
21.	Traditional morality	Envy	
22.	Linear figures	Triangle	
23.	Four worlds	Assiah, world of material manifestation	
24.	Five tattvas	Prithivi	
25.	Five skandhas	Rupa	
26.	Parts of soul	Nephesh	נפש
27.	Metals	Lead	
28.	Order of beings	Ghouls, larvae, gnomes	
29.	Human body	Excretion system, firm structures, tissue	
30.	Illnesses	Arteriosclerosis	

Let us take some examples from everyday life. You know that I consider this section most important; therefore, I ask you to pay attention. Of course, I will assume that you thoroughly studied the tables and that you naturally adopted all the specific characteristics, as well as that you intuitively found differences and similarities among them. Now I want you to find the framework and connection between Malkuth and Yesod, through 32nd path, in each example that I give you. We will move from easier to harder examples, but keep in mind that the model of thinking is the same. If you got the basic model, even the highest modification would not be an issue for you, and it will be only a matter of time when you will have resolved any problem.

I assume that you are reading this letter on your computer. Let us put aside the agony and horror catching on me when I think how much time and energy I invested in creating these tables; what we are observing now is the process of reading this letter. You must clearly define Malkuth, which is not an incredibly difficult problem for you, I hope. Let us assume that Malkuth is, simply, "you." Now, look ahead, and define the final destination, define a subtle goal that you are striving to. It may be knowledge that you are obtaining here and right now. That knowledge you are obtaining through a computer, and all that uses electricity and telephone cable. Now you got both remaining elements: Yesod as information, represented by this lesson, and 32nd path of Universe. Ponder how you obtain new information by computer observing the monitor. Between me, who knows, and you, who wants to know, is a single thread that connects us. Observe the cables. Inside them is electric current that carries the information and knowledge. Yesod as information, inside of a cable – which is 32nd path.

Let us examine the other ideas from everyday life in order to determine where Yesod is and in what way the path of the Universe manifests.

Maybe it is good to describe to me what you had for breakfast this morning. Let us not annoy ourselves with lies about a healthy life. I suspect that your breakfast was so silly that you cannot even remember what it was. But I am sure you treated yourself with a cup of good coffee, as yesterday was Friday, and you probably came home pretty late. Coffee keeps you awake, which is related more to Malkuth. But why not? Why wouldn't you observe a reversed process? Assuming that you were sleeping, then it was the plane of Yesod. Now you are awake, and it is Malkuth. Coffee is the mediator between the two; it takes you back to the plane of Malkuth, into your defined reality. It is the path of the "Universe."

What animal would you allocate to Yesod? Could it be a cat? Or a horse? Maybe it is better to think of birds as they correspond with the element of air. You see, you are watching birds from below; they are above us – attributes of Moon, astral plane as subtle, "higher" plane. But what particular bird we could focus on? Moon, astral plane, fantasies, dreams, shells. Raven, or better, vulture. It does not matter how precisely you classified things; you still cannot make definite estimates because you do not have knowledge about the other aspects of the Tree of Life. But, the model upon which you develop your thinking is important.

Now, from the following list, extract the terms that point to Yesod:

sea, attic, rose, bend roof, summer clothing, ice cream, musk ox, shallow pocket, deep pocket, empty pocket, wedding ring, zebra, wine, saber, hunting gun, sorrow, star, purple.

The next assignment is somewhat more difficult: I want you to determine an aspect of Yesod contained in each of the given concepts. You must assume that Yesod is present in each of these ideas, somewhere more obviously presented, and somewhere hidden. You must train your mind to penetrate into the meaning of apparently insignificant terms:

cave, prison, lottery, Italy, Austria, baroque, jam, static electricity, flat bicycle tire, ruler, yellow raincoat, molehill without moles, molehill with moles, New Year, Popeye, Michelangelo's David, god, God."

At the very end, I point to the most challenging problem. Could you find Yesod in the following term:

Malkuth

When you answer this last question with absolute certainty, we can advance further.

CHAPTER TEN

POSTCARDS TO A NEOPHYTE

Cara Soror,

I have read all your previous letters rather carefully, but I have refused to reply to you until now. I will try to compile one comprehensive letter, including all the individual topics. There are so many wonderful points that you have tried to point to and so little time to sort them all out, so little time for anything at all indeed. We can only hope that these are voices of a sleepless night, and you really have to understand them that way, as byways of a dream. Because no matter how you understand them, the end is at your inevitable awakening.

About the Opening

One of the key elements of the work is an introductory or a preliminary opening. It is highly desirable for the Aspirant to determine the truth of these claims himself. The purest dedication is a dedication to the Truth. Any attempt to represent your Universe by someone else's model is doomed to despair and failure. It can be said that such a model is not a part of the Universe in relation to the Aspirant. Each event is a personal relationship of God with your soul only. Can that relationship be represented by another relationship mimicking it? Is there a lie in relation to one Truth? Does God have a reflection?

Therefore, let your introductory work be as pure and true as possible and let it make a dramatic depiction and an allegory of your Pentacle. Instead of the Qabalistic Cross, there can be a representation of what is depicted by the Sign of the Beast, that is, what your being accepts it in its own way. Ask whether this way of preparatory work is necessary when experience constitutes and makes a sketch of the whole reality? Such a constitution contains components that are freed from any predetermined form if understood within the living Spirit.

Is not the only introduction to work, the Will to work itself? Is it not work itself, the Will to work? Is not the very attainment, the Will to work?

If all things are reduced to one thing, what will that one thing be reduced to? For man is not what he truly thinks he is, but what he truly thinks. So how are you going to act?

Announce the Will before, forget it meanwhile, enjoy after. This is the secret of all magick.

After all, there is nothing so effective as the nature of silence; the full effect of the ritual is only after its last word, never during the performance; in that silence, when words remain as an echo in the mind which is drained from active desire, once when the Will have already been invested previously in the awareness of the goal. Success is found in the end, as all ends are crowned by silence. What is the common conclusion of all books, stories, songs, and fables? That is the full dot in the end, and no matter how magnificent the saga is told, that full dot has more to say than all the letters and words together.

About Yoga

Let us turn to the East to the extent crucial for our journey, without insisting on unnecessary details. The issue of Yoga is challenging to put on firm ground. Yoga is not a method. Yoga is attainment. It wrongly indicates the concept of Unity, or rather Oneness. Most of Yoga practitioners define the highest state of consciousness as a unity of the Aspirant with the object of work. In other words, when the subject and object become one. This is mainly a brief definition of Samadhi, not to go further into the discussion of this theory because it is not our intention here. And because I like to think differently, I would be skeptical about this definition. Being one with another is quite inconvenient. Each of us feels Unity with himself at this moment. Even in the absence of that feeling, Oneness with yourself is undoubted. Why do you think that Unity with another is different from Unity with yourself? Man finds external reasons for natural urges which are purely within. He complicates his own life because he is unable to comprehend himself properly. This is the paradox of Yoga. You cannot practice Yoga. You cannot practice achievement; it would mean that you have already achieved it. Yoga is not even Oneness; it only suggests the attainment of Oneness. It cannot be practiced and, therefore, cannot be more or less attained. Yoga is not a method. Yoga is attainment. What moves you away from Yoga is your intention for failure, nothing more. What drives you away from Yoga is your practice of Yoga, like exercise and striving are the essence of every failure.

About Raja Yoga

The particularity of Yoga is reflected in the specificity of its path. Too often, even the most zealous practitioners forget that the emphasis of their Yoga is in the way itself. The goal remains the same as long as it is the idea of Yoga. Therefore, always emphasize Yoga, not the prefix; Mantra Yoga is the same Yoga as Hatha. What is different is the way, but that difference is insignificant once Oneness has been attained. In its specific way, Raja Yoga is a recapitulation of Yoga as a whole, in relation to its existing methodological branches. It directly strives to the goal through concrete work and training, so it can be perfectly applied by Western minds.

In a way, the pragmatism of our maxim *"by the method of science, to reach the goal of religion"* is where it has been mastered most successfully. Perhaps it can be said that its success lies in gradual attainment and progress towards the absolute. But this is a superficial observation; experience shows that its essence lies in a far more straightforward fact.

Some thoughts related to the magical link

Very slowly, we come to the key issue that I want to convey to you, as you will see that our entire art is based on it; if you do not understand it fully, you are nothing but a lousy spiritualist of the worst kind. It is a matter of days when all your virtues will disappear, carried away by the germ of the plague of your own distorted opinion. Magical link – how dangerous this term seems! You can now fantasize of heavy, steel ropes in your mind used by a magician to tie beings around him, forcing them to subdue to his perverted nature to the fullest. My dear, the essence is simple, though it usually takes practice to understand and apply this in your own magick.

The magical link is the minimum condition for the transmission of force, to put it simply. The simplicity of the definition does not diminish its truthfulness. But the greatness of our art also lies in the fact that the definition is left with one broadly variable factor that we can freely modify, and that is the quantity of that minimum condition. In fact, the only boundary set is within your mind. I will be pragmatic. If I want to let the force go through your body, I have to make sure that your body comes into contact with that force. If you are then in contact with another body, the same force will be manifested through that same body. One crucial principle applies here, which is that the idea of the body can be in the domain of the broadest abstraction as long as it exists. The core of the message is in a terrifying discovery that the whole system of magick and our understanding of reality is a prearranged model of information, in

fact, a network of models, where your current position is determined by the rules within the environment in which you operate.
In fact, one network does not exist as such. Rules and principles are
illusions of individual projections. The magical link is a mediator,
and the more it is in harmony with nature, the more successful
your magick will be. The magical link as a mediator is actually a
translator; look at his role for a moment. You can see that it is two-
sided. One line of force connects it to you. The other line connects
it to what you do not understand. It is neither here nor there; that
is, "both here and there" would be a more precise statement. Think
about this concept – good magick, like any masterpiece, requires a
good sketch. In fact, our whole art lies in finding a suitable translator. After some time, which we call experience, the need for a translator becomes less and less for the simple reason that you begin to
understand a foreign language; therefore, you become that ideal
mediator for your Great Work. But the language used by our art is
universal; once you learn its rules, it will always apply to everyone.
I will tell you a few more things here. Let them be guidelines for
your Dhyana Yoga.

You will see that basically every mistake in our art is based on
a wrong assumption about the location of the force, which means
that the force is assumed from the inside instead of the outside, and
vice versa. I often made such mistakes in my youth, mixing planetary and elemental influences. For specific and unique reasons, our
Ruach can replace these roles so effectively that it is noticed too
late. Then, instead of change, failure comes through. In fact, it is
very difficult to say that it is a matter of mixing concepts. I will be
free to say that no action can be manifested unless the forces are
mobilized from within as well as from without, in precise relationships specifically required by Pure Will. The problem arises not
when the forces are forgotten or mixed, but when there is an imbalance in the relationship of their parts. Too much emphasis on
one aspect of force will result in failure, but not because there is no

other aspect, but simply because it is forgotten. In other words, a mediator disappointed his own principle "both here and there" because he was either too here or too there. The magical link did not even exist, so failure was inevitable at the very beginning of the work; you will see that in our work, there is no notion of "lack," but only "imbalance."

Never spare time or effort to choose the right mediator. Once you have gained the knowledge about the use of the magical link, only then will you create opportunities for the manifestation of true magick. In the end, you are the greatest and most valuable of all magical links indeed. Your own consciousness is the finest and most adaptable link of all, but it will take you a long time to get to the true meaning of it.

About the nature of Ruach

You have had the opportunity to encounter one specific phenomenon, and I think it is time to consider it extensively. We came across this idea at our last meeting, and you have asked me about it many times. Namely, everything has certain qualities; and one cannot talk about one aspect without mentioning another. Each thing in itself contains a huge number of forces that are manifested through it. Besides, there is a certain kind of force that radiates from within as a result of external influence. It is very ungrateful to say what precedes what and what is conditioned by what. Suppose you notice that the nature of Water characterizes something. In that case, it does not exclude the possibility that Fire is also present. Also, regardless of the elemental aspect, you will notice specific planetary attributions that affect that subject. The problem sometimes arises when we think that the nature of a planet is opposed to an element. But do not worry about it. The problem exists only within your knowledge of defining relationships. You have to understand that aspects are regulated by planes of existence, so the conflict of forces exists if you look at them closely and from one angle only.

Observe the sphere of Hod; it was assigned the element of Water and the planet of Mercury. You will see that our program in this sphere implies the development of thinking as well as the development of intuition. Mercury is Airy in nature, and the nature of thinking right is the nature of an ingenious mind that is adaptable like Air. In fact, moving is perhaps a more appropriate word. Is the nature of this sphere, therefore, Water or Air? The Deity of Hod is characterized by Mercury, a god with winged sandals, a divine messenger. If we stick to the last characteristic, we can also find an idea of a mediator between the Supreme and all that is under it, similarly to Metatron in the Qabalistic hierarchy of beings. Like Thoth, he is the master of wisdom, defined by the wise word and the meaning of the record. A mage's word is exercised instantly and without delay because what is embodied within it is the truth and nothing but the truth. But such wisdom is fundamentally different from the one established in Chokmah, which you will have an opportunity to study at the right time. The word is transmitted by the Air where the winged Mercury rides, so the Air is a transmitter of wisdom – is it nothing less than a perfect magical link? If you connect Air with the human mind, you will realize that it is the only true possible link. Only the mind is capable and gifted to create a connection between things that are seemingly completely unrelated.

Suppose you pay attention to other divine attributions. In that case, you will notice another aspect that is different from Thoth and Mercury principles – at first glance, at least. You can clearly see that the attributes of the jackal and Anubis are equally assigned under Hod. As you already know, he plays the role of a kind of guide through unknown parts of the Universe, like Tuat; he is the guide of the soul through the afterlife, all the way to the heavenly fields of Amenti. The role of a guide is an important thesis of every work, which implies passing through the unknown astral planes. He is a true mediator between a magician and the unknown. From your records, I see that you have already had experiences of communicating with them, which makes me particularly happy. They seem to be completely separate beings from those inhabiting higher planes. They are, so to speak, "somewhere in between"; too close to us, but not too far away from them. You can view them as projections of our own Ruach, anyway. Still, I think it is important to experience contact before making a judgment about the nature of such "beings."

I will point to an example of the most important and sublime practice, in my opinion, which, in its simple and effective way, illuminates the role and nature of Ruach, the magician's thought, and the mind quite pragmatically. With this method, all these ideas are connected to the nature of a guide, as much as to the nature of wisdom, the one that illuminates the path of the mage and prevents him from deviating from it. Think of the following worship that the Aspirant carries during the day, in certain aspects:

Liber Resh vel Helios
SVB FIGVRA CC

0. These are the adorations to be performed by aspirants to the A∴A∴.

1. Let him greet the Sun at dawn, facing East, giving the sign of his grade. And let him say in a loud voice:

    Hail unto Thee who art Ra in Thy rising, even unto Thee who art Ra in Thy strength, who travellest over the Heavens in Thy bark at the Uprising of the Sun.

    Tahuti standeth in His splendour at the prow, and Ra-Hoor abideth at the helm.

    Hail unto Thee from the Abodes of Night!

2. Also at Noon, let him greet the Sun, facing South, giving the sign of his grade. And let him say in a loud voice:

Hail unto Thee who art Ahathoor in Thy triumphing, even unto Thee who art Ahathoor in Thy beauty, who travellest over the heavens in thy bark at the Mid-course of the Sun.

Tahuti standeth in His splendour at the prow, and Ra-Hoor abideth at the helm.

Hail unto Thee from the Abodes of Morning!

3. Also, at Sunset, let him greet the Sun, facing West, giving the sign of his grade. And let him say in a loud voice:

Hail unto Thee who art Tum in Thy setting, even unto Thee who art Tum in Thy joy, who travellest over the Heavens in Thy bark at the Down-going of the Sun.

Tahuti standeth in His splendour at the prow, and Ra-Hoor abideth at the helm.

Hail unto Thee from the Abodes of Day!

4. Lastly, at Midnight, let him greet the Sun, facing North, giving the sign of his grade, and let him say in a loud voice:

Hail unto thee who art Khephra in Thy hiding, even unto Thee who art Khephra in Thy silence, who travellest over the heavens in Thy bark at the Midnight Hour of the Sun.

Tahuti standeth in His splendour at the prow, and Ra-Hoor abideth at the helm.

Hail unto Thee from the Abodes of Evening.

5. And after each of these invocations thou shalt give the sign of silence, and afterward thou shalt perform the adoration that is taught thee by thy Superior. And then do thou compose Thyself to holy meditation.

6. Also it is better if in these adorations thou assume the God-form of Whom thou adorest, as if thou didst unite with Him in the adoration of That which is beyond Him.

7. Thus shalt thou ever be mindful of the Great Work which thou hast undertaken to perform, and thus shalt thou be strengthened to pursue it unto the attainment of the Stone of the Wise, the Summum Bonum, True Wisdom and Perfect Happiness.

Notice well the part of the text that is repeated with each worship. This is the following statement: *"Tahuti standeth in His splendour at the prow, and Ra-Hoor abideth at the helm..."* Tahuti is at the front, like an observer. He points to what he sees ahead and reports on all the external influences acting upon on the boat of the Sun. Ra-Hoor, as Will, considers all of Tahuti's statements and then decides on an action that steers the boat. It may be that wisdom and free, impartial opinion in harmony with nature are, in fact, the only trustworthy guides on the voyage of your Sun-boat, dear Sister.

How that boat is going to sail in the beginning depends on what Tahuti notices on the bow. Once true nature has awakened, the movement of the boat will depend on the "action" of Ra-Hoor at the helm. Ruach is "there" in front, the will "withdrawn" in the back; thus, acting, the magician safely sails the waters of the Nun.

More on the nature of Ruach

Dear sister,

Now, we can take a long step further; I never really liked small and too careful steps because they are slow, and at the same time, tiring. Do not be brave in your art; you should be rude instead. Yet again, radiate kindness as your nature is the nature of the Fool, not the Knight. Care should not be identified with sluggishness. A safe move can be made at full speed equally, so your attention is more important than the intensity of your Spirit.

We will now consider some aspects of the Tree that group its parts into specific models, but these aspects are different from the three you have learned so far. I am telling you now about what you have once mentioned to me spontaneously. Still, I skipped it without commenting, saving it for the present. Every little model you have adopted so far is based on gradual and, so to speak, imperceptible progress and change. The Ten Sephiroth with 22 paths is a great model for thinking and working on. If working with such a model brings some results, then it is certainly not wrong to assume that working with a smaller one brings some other fruits; you can ask me why all this when you have one clear goal in front of you. All I can tell you is my question of whether you really have a sure goal or just a definition of its coordinates wrapped in symbols. The fact that you see the path does not secure the goal, or at least not the one you aspire to. You can be a Thelemite in only one way – following your Will, not the Thelemic system. The fact that you support Thelema and follow that system is worthless if you do not have awakened the knowledge of your Pure Will. Therefore, it does not matter. Within our art, the adaptability of your tool is of great importance, and you should not spare time to realize that talent.

We will narrow the model of reality with a single goal: decreasing the scale creates clarity. Admittedly, accuracy is lost.; what we gain is speed. What I ask from you is to learn to walk in magic boots. Think of the powers of the mage; he moves and acts according to the Will and without restrictions. His mind is the Universe, and all the laws that are there are nothing but the laws of his mind.

I mentioned to you one sphere of action, which we call Ruach. It is often quite poorly mentioned and explained as intellect. This may lie in the eternal problem of defining the inner reality that our Western minds have. Concerning the parts of the soul, Qabalah sets one model, among many.

1	Kether	
2	Chokmah	NESHAMAH נשמה
3	Binah	
4	Chesed	
5	Geburah	
6	Tiphareth	RUACH רוה
7	Netzach	
8	Hod	
9	Yesod	
10	Malkuth	NEPESH נפש

It is easy to notice the spatial dominance of the Ruach sphere, notice the center that is inhabited in Tiphareth. Now let us get back to what I am going for, and this is the idea of the antithesis, which is attributed to Ruach. You have noticed that it intensifies with your ascent; in Yesod and Hod, it was noticeable, in Netzach quite conspicuous. In Tiphareth, it might be unbearable. Here, I am telling you in the future tense because, for you, this conclusion should be only a logical conclusion based on pure speculation, so do not rely too much on this. In any case, we have narrowed the model of reality to only three notches.

Think of the following: the center of Ruach is Tiphareth, like the Sun, but beneath it lies Yesod as the Moon, and it is one pair of the opposites. The other is hidden below, in the form of the first horizontal path at the ends of which are the Sephiroth Hod and Netzach, like your Cup and your Wand. Finally, the third opposite is expressed in the pair of Geburah and Chesed, in the form of Strictness and Mercy. At first glance, the sphere of Ruach indicates everything but harmony and unity. Think about the way you think. Do you notice the unity of your thoughts? Is the nature of any part or aspect of your mind a unity? As Qabalists, can we state that the unity of the whole Tree is inhabited in only One place?

Opposition as an idea is a method, not the attainment. For centuries we have been trying to define the notion of the unity of opposites. But nowhere is it better described than within the first stanza of Dao Te King: "*The way to go is not the eternal Way...*" The unity of opposites is a clumsy expression that creates only unnecessary confusion in our art. I have always been so frivolous in these matters: if they gave a task to eradicate slavery, I would do so by destroying the notion of freedom first – what can limit a person more than the aspiration to freedom? A free man, on the other hand, does not strive for what he already is. Only a prisoner yearns for freedom.

The first principle I have presented to you is that our only task is to realize the Knowledge and Conversation of the Holy Guardian Angel and to awaken the Pure Will. Think that these are not two separate things. These are synonyms for defining one specific experience from different Grades, I would say. The Knowledge and Conversation is the nature of the Great Work expressed by the macrocosmic idea, while the Pure Will is the refraction of the same process through the Veil of Paroketh, down to the microcosmic reality. Define the situation in simple sentences, and it will be easier for you to understand. Within the first case, we find: *this* Pure Will. The second case reasons differently: *that* Holy Guardian Angel. The Great Work is accomplished without being distracted by the enigma of where the Will is and where the Angel is. Instead, Attainment is hidden in response to whose Will and whose Angel. Who, not what. Think about this – the truth about being is nothing but the authenticity of that same being.

About the attractions and repulsions of being

Think of specific ideas of this holy place, which is so close to that hall of consciousness that you will surely enter – attraction and repulsion concerning commitment and service, and above all, all that in relation to Love and Philosophy. You can understand this as forms of the Knowledge and Conversation. You can think about this for a very long time, and such thinking should grow into a form of the deepest meditation until your thinking about the forms of the Knowledge and Conversation, as of Attractions and Repulsions, Devotion and Duty, or Love and Philosophy, has finally brought you to the Knowledge and Conversation[4].

You will see that all these concepts are actually a projection of one essence. You have to Know what Attracts you and attract what Repels you through Conversation. Above all, you have to define these processes with balance, overcome them with Philosophy, and understand by Love. But of all things, you have to think of it as of methods. That is how you will come to the cause of all these definitions, and that is being. When you answer *who* is the one who answers, you will enter that hall of consciousness that I do not dare to tell you about.

The essence of control lies in the balance, which is nothing but Philosophy and Love. Many methods may seem interesting to you, but only two are valid. Free opinion and unconditioned love – it will often appear to you that these two concepts are in conflict. The truth is somewhere in between – yea, the truth is somewhere "in between."

About forms of the Knowledge and Conversation with the A∴A∴

That Oil is imprinted on the Disc as a draft of the Pentacle. It is also as Lamen, as the blood on the Sword, as the Elixir in the Cup and as the flame of your Wand. Once lit, it always burns. But there will come a time when that burning flame will not be seen, and

---

[4] This part is especially related to the grade of Philosophus.

then it will seem to you that terrible darkness has come upon every corner of the world, which has happened indeed. But you are not alone. Because you are *not*.

Is not every knowledge and every conversation the Knowledge and Conversation with one A∴A∴? And there are as many forms, as ways and modes. Think, how many forms, how much knowledge there is? How many A∴A∴?

Your life is just one of the ways in which a dialogue between you and your God is taking place; no, it is just that *between*.

So far, you have had the opportunity to gain some of this, but time will come when you will be required to manifest this fully. If you really Knew what you wanted to Converse about, you would Know and be having a Conversation with the A∴A∴ at that moment. Proper action is reflected in a decisive impulse; you are not what you think you truly are, but what you truly think.

But as time passes, you may notice that the form of the Knowledge and Conversation changes along with your understanding. That Oil lubricates the Pentacle, sharpens your Sword, cleans your Cup, and adds fire to your Wand. Is it not the glory of the Holy Spirit itself which dwells up in the heights?

About duty and devotion to the Order

Do not expect me to tell you anything specific about this, except that by looking at service and commitment – you see the Order. These are nothing but forms of action, as many as there are forms of the Knowledge and Conversation. As long as this is below the Paroketh, it will be manifested through the multitude. The more forms there are, the more knowledge there is. Yet, there is only one Knowledge and Conversation. I will be very rude, and you may be amazed when I say that for all forms of the Spirit in the whole Universe, there is but One Knowledge and One Conversation, which is the same for all of them.

Also, try to define the essence and difference in duty and devotion. Duty is hidden in the commitment of Ruach and the gullibility of thought, so this is Philosophy as much as devotion is the flame and fire of Love. Think of all this as specific forms of your Oath. You will see that there is very little left until you enter the Hall of Consciousness, which is nothing but the Tower of your God. So far, you have Served. From now on, you are Committed to that idea which you Understand and perceive as the only connection in your Attainments so far. You need to understand that the house of Venus is the last house from which you will Act in your Own Way. Duty as a form of binding Ruach, and devotion as a form of acting of your Love, is not that the balance required of you?

About beings of elements

You have heard many times about various beings that inhabit the plane of elements, carrying within them the nature of the plane where they dwell, without the possibility of living or understanding any other plane. These beings must be limited and very weak, no matter how much it seems to someone that they actually radiate with ferocity or even power. These beings can become the best magician's apparatus and great helpers if they serve him in a balanced way and follow his nature. What I want to tell you is that a magician has control over them only then when he gains control over that element which is the home of a certain being. Only in this way does such a being gain the trust and devotion of a magician who is nothing but God for it. Therefore, your only task in this is to realize and develop a specific awareness of the plane within yourself because you already have the essence of every element, just by being born. In other words, the fact is that you are nothing but Yeheshuah.

As you have been informed so far that every attainment can very easily be framed by our Oath, so in the same way you will awaken the awareness of the elements, sticking to the Oath that awakens the essence of that idea within you. By developing the 4 powers of the Sphinx, you will gain power and control over the elements and beings residing there. But the only being I really saw was a being of the Spirit. I talked to him. Yes, I talked to him.

About one Deity, as much as possible

I will tell you about a very small God. She cannot be accommodated by any Pantheon because she is too fickle and unusual. I will tell you about her because she is my everything, and I understand her too well to tell you in cipher.

I used to wait for her like a starving country longing for rain, not knowing when it would pour down. Just like a girl waiting for her lover – time does not matter to her. And she will twitch at every sound of the wind and at every new drop of rain that splashes her blonde hair.

But sometimes, I just do not do anything. I have nothing serious to do or think anyway because she has poisoned my mind. And even that poison is nothing serious to think about. So I prefer not to do anything, and she comes right away. But it is not always that easy because I really have to do nothing, and then again, it is not the same not to do anything and not to do her anything. And that is all the wisdom, and whoever is wise, let him not count, because she has no number. Instead, do nothing, and she will soon have no reason or will to tease you anymore but will touch your lips with sweet wine; yea, she will touch your lips with her sweet wine.

About Oaths

All the wisdom of an Oath is in the change of consciousness. That is all about it, really. However, it is worth mentioning the process that develops in the being of a magician on that occasion. An Oath in itself is a true initiation. Once it has been uttered, a change occurs in your being. It seems to consist of a particular mixture of seriousness, enthusiasm, and fear. But keep in mind that an Oath is only successful when there is an awareness of its true meaning. You have to know what you could lose, as opposed to what you will gain. The seriousness, enthusiasm, and fear mentioned here are the reflections of Chesed, Tiphareth, and Geburah in this world. But a true magician looks at it differently in every respect – each Oath is one Passage Through the Tuat, and the core of that knowledge lies in the fact of a magician's undisputable passage further. An Oath is fulfilled with an awareness of a task. By accepting it, you have already passed further. Therefore, do not ask me if you have fulfilled the Oath, but if you were aware of its meaning. Here, too, we come across projections of higher spheres – because a magician has only time and will left to wait – which are the expressions of Binah and Chokmah.

About certain equation that shows our progress

You can think about how the statement of one attainment is always two-sided. As in human surnames, you can simultaneously infer who exactly is being spoken about, as well as who a person comes from; the same principle is present here. One figure shows the current attainment level relative to the beginning, the other, the path relative to the end. It is the range of a soul between the Earth and heaven alike, and you can see that it is always a matter of harmony and balance, no matter what level of attainment you are talking about. The balance of force is established by the correct setting of the lever. You will see that 4=7 in our program is exactly the same as 5=6, except that at 5=6 it will be manifested and balanced against a lever that is equal between 5 and 6 and nothing else. But, thinking that this equation is exactly the same as in 4=7, this is nothing but a notch that defines the sphere of the Holy Guardian Angel. Its essence is within the sign of equality, and it is not outside of it at all. 4 and 7, as well as 5 and 6, are only states of the moment that the Spirit has chosen for the most suitable manifestation.

About signs of grades

I have always had a habit of considering all the questions of the signs in relation to our salutation to the Sun, which you have been performing for so long and so devotedly. Each sign is nothing but a specific kind of awakening of a certain type of Solar consciousness and the development of what can be subsumed under the term an aspect of being. Aspects of the Sun itself are a certain kind of change that brings you closer to pure LVX, with the Sun being only a symbol of a unique consciousness. On the one hand, this is the highest form of Dhyana Yoga, and its performance harmonizes every aspect of the elements over time until a change creates the conditions for the manifestation of the Spirit in the form of the Great Work. In fact, I am free to say that the Spirit is inhabited everywhere and in every way, and the very aspects of being, which are the precise notches of Ruach, experience it in sequences. Think that the seat of Ruach is right in Tiphareth, where the Tower of your God is located. The signs of grades are conditioned reflexes of a being who expresses the need to worship what is above its current nature. It is a reminder that the aspect of being is actually a being without aspects. Therefore, in order to reach the essence of the Spirit, one should not add force but take away as much power as there is. The core of the flame is the coldest place in the fire. The core of each element is the Spirit, and its nature can burn or be solid, depending on the nature of the Will. Therefore, the signs of the grades are intentions of that same Spirit which has expressed its Will to the world; yea, which expressed its Will to the world.

About moral training

I have told you a lot about it, from the very beginning of your training, and you will remember everything with great joy. As then, I fully stand behind my claim and belief that the only true moral training is embodied in such a wonderful exercise as Liber Resh vel Helios. Only at this stage will you see the necessity of the existence of Bhakti within this whole operation. In fact, complete success is achieved through the balanced application of Bhakti, as much as Dhyana Yoga.

The only conditions are in the demand and need of your true being, so the only feat I want you to accomplish for that purpose is to awaken a particular awareness of that need. You will see that the exercise called Mahasatipattana is excellent in defining this awareness that you keep awakening more and more deeply within your being by your daily and diligent work. Excessive Philosophy is only equal to excessive Love. But I will certainly refer you to the instructions of our Order:

> "They have taken the only proper course; to train aspirants to this attainment in the theory and practice of the whole of Magick and Mysticism, so that each man may be expert in the handling of all known weapons, and free to choose and to use those which his own experience and instinct dictate as proper when he essays the Great Experiment."

Also, think about the following as a completely different but no less valuable way to deal with this topic. This is embodied in another essential characteristic of our Order:

> "He is furthermore trained to the one habit essential to Membership of the A∴A∴; he must regard all his attainments as primarily the property of those less advanced aspirants who are confided to his charge."
>
> [Liber CDLXXXIX, Aleister Crowley]

Consider the Oaths of our grades, and you will see that all the grades in the Golden Dawn have this obligation. But notice if this is the case with the Adeptus Minor's Oath as well? Can he understand his Great Work as someone else's? Can he do anything else in front of the one and only thing in front of him? This is certainly a form of a Bodhisattva vow, which refers to the highest form of morality in our Order.

Notes on the Ritual of the Pentagram

Let us have a look at practical analogies. The ritual which works most suitably with the elements, at least as the Aspirant in Golden Dawn realizes it, is what we call the Lesser Banishing Ritual of the Pentagram, or simply the Ritual of the Pentagram. But, if we limit the Ritual of the Pentagram for banishing only, we will remain limited. This ritual is rather like a miniature Tiphareth operation; in case you perform this ritual properly, at that very moment, you would have the Knowledge and Conversation of your Holy Guardian Angel. Nobody has a monopoly over the truth, as you must have to check all these and future claims for yourself. Be suspicious. Question everything. And everyone. Mostly yourself.

There are some variations in the Ritual of the Pentagram which can be considered and particularly useful for the Neophyte and Zelator as well. The main point here is that the whole ritual is to be performed while sitting in a chair, imagining yourself two feet in front of you doing the entire ritual, with all the details that would otherwise be present during the work. This work also dramatically increases the chances for spontaneous astral projection, and it has two variants in which can be performed. The first is to open your eyes imagining you are, in fact, there, looking to your physical body with your new eyes, and doing the whole ritual from there, vibrating formulas, and drawing a circle from there. If necessary, experience failure, but there, not here.

Another method, which can be run simultaneously with the first, is easier but not less interesting. You need to imagine your figure, which performs as a puppet in front of you the whole ritual. After a while, spontaneous projections are also very common. I advise you to try, as this not only builds the ability to visualize but also works to strengthen your astral body. I shall return to your diary. When I told you to write about yourself in the third person singular, this should be such an excellent parallel. It seems much easier than it actually is. You should hear your voice differently than when you speak regularly. It is easy to determine such a difference when you hear yourself on audio recordings. It is the same with the plastic visual perception of you. For all your life, you were watching the movements of other characters, and you are less aware of how you act in nature. These two kinds of techniques where you imagine yourself as a puppet and look at yourself from another perspective are very well accepted both as a method and as attainment. Do not be misled by those who claim that work on the astral plane could be dangerous and that there is the possibility that you will not return. Sometimes, I wish I could really experience such a long-lasting stay on the astral plane and worry about how I should return home. Silly thoughts. Your whole trouble, as long as you are alive, is, however, to remain there as long as possible. Your return is inevitable and unavoidable, so use your precious time there as well as you can. Once you return, you may be sorry for the missed chances because you did not use your time wisely there. I sincerely believe that mastering astral projection is extremely important to you, and I appeal to my students to experience it as soon as possible.

What matters most is that the Neophyte gets a sense of the astral plane, in which very different rules apply. I would assume that most of the Aspirants would give everything for 5 minutes of consciousness in the astral body. Unfortunately, almost all techniques and methods of astral projection about which you hear or read are entirely unusable. In a similar way as the Ritual of the Pentagram, those techniques and mechanisms which drive the process of change are usually ignored, with attention given to unimportant details which takes so much energy and time. I will surely return to this wonderful subject in a more separate and particular manner.

Let us return to the Ritual of the Pentagram. In this ritual, we deal with the elements, with the formula of Tetragrammaton – at least as it was understood in the Golden Dawn. At the four corners of the world, we place Pentagrams and the Archangels. I will remind you of the text of the ritual. So you say: *"in front of me is Raphael,"* *"Gabriel's behind me."* I just want to ask, whom are you talking to? I often hear Students quickly and hastily say: *"in front of me..."* and then inhale the air rapidly as if they would dive and start yelling the name of the Archangel. In case they truly exist and actually watch that show, it would be quite silly for them to observe all of this haste. First of all, there is no need to yell aloud to yourselves what actually is in front of you. Simply vibrate the name of Raphael without saying *"in front of me..."* while imagining the corresponding entity before you. Also, when you draw the Pentagram, it is usually stated that lines are to be made by Wand or Dagger. My personal opinion, since you are working with the formula of Tetragrammaton, corresponds with your own body. You have four fingers plus a thumb, such as the four elements of the formula plus a fifth for the Spirit, so feel free to assign each finger with the corresponding element. We could talk endlessly about the variants; these were just some general observations that you can consider for yourself. I personally use the thumb between the third and fourth finger, as "mano in fica." There is a personal motive as much as a logical explanation for a thumb – if you are observing the fifth element as the letter Shin in the middle of the IHShVH formula. Also, the fifth element has the ability to obtain the form of any other element, as desired. Most people use their index finger for pointing, and that finger can be assigned to fire. But the index finger can also be assigned to the air. You show and signify something which you visually perceive, marking the path of your desire; therefore, the index finger, in this case, can be assigned to the air. Use the attributions which are right for you, do not let somebody else do this job. Sometimes what is logical and natural to you makes more sense than all others' theories together. Also, do experiments. Which finger suits a particular situation? Select a tool by logic and a goal by intuition. I doubt that I could draw a pentagram with the fifth finger while expecting the pentagram to be sturdy and strong. Therefore, real analogies do not exist. Authorities from the past have made some analogies with the body parts and elements but rest assured that they too have used the same laws of logic as you have.

You can modify any part of the ritual, but pay attention to the form. I kept changing this ritual throughout all my life. It is like having sex. Simply, the act of nature causes you to change the position. In this small and short ritual, your creativity is allowed to develop to the fullest. Why? Because we work with the highest archetypes. It is easy to remember the form of ritual, leaving your plastic imagination and creativity to deeply interact with the essence of the ritual. To dwell inside the core of it. Nobody can tell you what is ultimately good or what is ultimately bad. Furthermore, you have to distinguish not only good from bad. You must distinguish good and bad from right and wrong.

During my Neophyte time, when I worked for a few hours a day, one of the practices I have been doing was the Ritual of the Pentagram. And I must be honest with you, after a while, I began to hate it. It was everything but the ritual of LVX, and simply a thought of it would raise great aversion inside me. But one marvelous experience happened, which later influenced my entire work as the Neophyte – it was one spontaneous astral projection during the performance. What does this tell us? It tells us that important experiences can always happen at any moment of our work. When you feel down, it is not an excuse to stop. It just tells you that it is time to get up. Also, during my work as Practicus and Philosophus, I replaced the common names of Archangels and elements with Enochian names.

The condition of progress upon the path is a condition for progress in the Ritual of the Pentagram. And the laws and rules that apply to this ritual refer mainly to all the other rituals you will ever perform. But I want you to observe the Ritual of the Pentagram as a small Liber Samekh. If you happen to perform the Ritual of Pentagram for protection, paradoxically, it will use everything it has to charge you. You will become fully naked by this ritual, and before the flame of truth, there will be neither protection nor help. You will be most vulnerable right then. You can protect yourself from the elements, planets, spirits, friends, or foes, but you cannot protect yourself from your own stupidity and your very own limitations.

On the diary

The worst diary is about success; the best is one about your failures. Sexual perversions, dark, violent dreams, betrayals, vices, follies, and collapses. All those things which make you crazy and twisted. But remember, the mere fact that we deal with this art makes us all quite crazy. Sometimes when you are writing, I see that there is too much technical detail. Still, I desperately want to see you despise yourself while making records. I want to see the very you and not that figure performing the ritual in a quite technical manner. I want to see what you think and feel about everything, even about completely meaningless and unimportant things. I want to see that you are looking for a clue following it with your nose. I do not want you to show me a clue. I want to see your movement of smelling, always and constantly, in every segment of your life. I want to read something so ordinary and derogatory to the Spirit of adventure and still see that such an event has begun to be connected to the whole of the attainments of your Great Work. I want to see your tiny deeds and small deeds, I want to see how they are connected, how all things are connected, and how everything is chaotic in your work, except for your thread of attention that puts them in perfect order. I want you to bore me with your diary. I want to see my Angel in your tics, fails. I want to see my own path that telling me a story out of your utterly dull letters. Write about everything, write even when you have nothing clever to say – say something stupid then. If you have nothing else to add then, repeat that same stupid thing; write, work, connect, open roads, and open doors. But most of all, follow your nose – it is the best route in Cosmos.

About aspects of work

My dear, you often mention the idea of a pause in your work. Are there any pauses anyway? In breathing? Is there really a break? Is not Kumbhaka an equal part of breathing, not a break? Can we say there are breaks in anything? A baby's brain develops while sleeping, is there any part of our lives that is not growth. Is not death where the ultimate attainment is? Is not silence the greatest ordeal? Think about what you would do during the break. Do you actually work all the time while resting, but in a different way? Is not there a better vacation than doing what is in your nature? Is not your Spirit full of enthusiasm and relaxation when it does so intensely for what it is manifested in this Universe? When you discover what makes you truly happy, doing that, you will see that you are not going to work a single day in your life. Yet, it is so far from any kind of a pause or break. The discovery of such a passive nap is a wonderful circumstance. You will see that the whole Universe is one completely dormant and sluggish mechanism that purrs like a cat endless Æons ahead.

About the Grand Architect

The Grand Architect is the universal unit of measure of all things. He is the golden ratio between the number and the letters. Numbers are like letters – integral parts of all books of all the worlds. It was said once that Angels, like books, are made of numbers and letters in the same way as man was made of flesh and blood. The Grand Architect, who occupies such an important place in Freemasonry, is not much different from the Grand Creator of all worlds. These two terms are related to the same state of being.

In a similar way, the Holy Guardian Angel is linked with two concepts that cannot exist without each other – the Knowledge and Conversation. For us, the concept of Grand Architect is far more important than the Grand Creator, who made the Tree of Life. The emphasis is on the Architect who made his draft and measure of our reality, for his observation of the Universe constructs that same Universe. Hence, the next time you read a document on Freemasonry, try to look at the Grand Architect from the point of view of our art. This is a great mystery.

About the proper form of the holy Hexagram

The Neophyte may have the Knowledge, but he cannot have the Conversation. To hear what is being told to you from a distance, you need to calm the environment – to mute either the environment or the attention that is directed towards that environment. You will recognize that the first method is the way of magick, and the second is the way of Yoga. But, the attainment of Adeptus Minor is not for "you." "You" will never attain it. There are no aspirations that can lead to it. You can only uncover the Veil and see what is behind. That is why Qabalists conceived an idea about the parts of Tree which are not seen. Which is right why the idea of Veils is, in the first place. Of course, these are just words; the real truth is far simpler. The Neophyte projects his understanding forward as the future experience of the Knowledge or Conversation, on a deeply subconscious level, somehow like a prayer of the supreme salvation. He does it the manner that he, as the Aspirant of the Golden Dawn, can understand it well enough to serve him as additional fuel once he has burned all the fire before time due to his unbalanced work.

About the Spirit

It is complicated to explain to a human being what the Tetragrammaton is. It is even more difficult it is to explain the nature of the Spirit, or even division of the Spirit into active and passive. Classification and the idea of abstraction elude our understanding of what is actually the element of Spirit, and even more, what active and what passive Spirit is. But first, let us understand the relationship between mystery and surprise. The secret is the passive Spirit, while the surprise is active. Although "it" is neither secret nor surprise, understanding the relationships of these natures leads us in the right direction. These are ideas that have meaning in our mind, in a way that they produce other living ideas that are connected by life and meaning. Let the Aspirant know that the notion of meaning is much broader than it may seem at first. Let him strive to exceed the usual meaning of the word at any time. Because words have no meaning. The Aspirant is the meaning himself, and his wisdom ensures the passage, not his feet. At this spot, there is neither him nor his feet, only the mind.

Like a computer that has just zero and one, voltage and pause, and all we ever see on a screen is just a hologram of those mighty voltages and voltage pauses that are graphically formed into an elephant image that we see on a screen, for example, and it is all but an elephant that is given to us to understand that signal as such. And then, there is an elephant that wants to be seen, the elephant that we consider in our mind to be an elephant, the signal that is by no means an elephant, the image of an elephant that we think is an elephant, and finally, an elephant that cannot be represented by an image, which does not perceive itself as an elephant at all. It is in this loss of energy in transmitting and translating an idea where the only difference lies between the Angel and the Ego. There is no difference, nor are the Ego and the Angel separate things. The Ego is separated from the Angel, but the Angel is not separated from the Ego. The latter embodies the whole mystery of the Rosy Cross.

On proper usage of time

Remember, dear Sister, as you climb up the Tree of Life, you will use less time for preparation of work, as for the work itself. In perfect circumstances, an Aspirant needs 15 to 20 minutes for astral projection and 5 to 10 minutes for entirely stable Asana. But remember, after 15 minutes of preparation and perhaps 15 minutes of the astral journey, the Aspirant may need hours to understand the experience he received even superficially. Even if the Neophyte spontaneously achieves Conversation during his operation, which is not so uncommon, it may take years for him to understand what he Heard. Working with Asana is not just sitting, but also preparing for that sitting beforehand and enjoying the feeling of unity with the body after the practice. Think about how to define your own work at all, how long it lasts, what is included in it, and what is not. Does the work stop at all? When has it started? Has it ever started? Can it ever be interrupted? Aren't you the one lying in your tomb inside the Pyramid all the time? Is not all this a projection of yours or your dream while your soul is rushing towards the stars?

About specific lucidity adorning a Neophyte

The difference between the stupid and the smart is not in stupid things they do; the clever one does more stupid things than the fool. The fool just repeats them. The Neophyte who knows he is stupid has an advantage over the Aspirant who just thinks he is smart. In the end, you should be just a notch better than the worst one. It is always a perfect strategy in the long run. No Neophyte should be burdened with falling behind in the program or, perhaps, unsatisfactory progress, as his grade is perhaps the most difficult of all in the Golden Dawn. He should not have any self-confidence. He should reject himself in advance in any intention to evaluate his work. In the end, everything he does is so far away from the innate doing that the only motto that can be applied here is "stubborn perseverance." Imagine failing so hard that your God took so much pity pushing you forward in the end – as much as you were lagging behind; let him feel your retardation as an act of seduction. And may he gracefully give you the wings of success.

About the living chaos

Go outside now and buy some utterly worthless things that attract you. Go to the street market and have a look at used toys and completely useless objects, and then let your intuition choose something it wants to buy. Then give them names that do not exist. Come home and build a small amphitheater in one part of the apartment where you will place these objects, simulating a completely different reality. Assign them roles, make one object that stands for your desire, do everything without any order whatsoever or any preparation. Make that amphitheater without any arrangement, as if you were putting together and playing with children's building blocks. Sing some personal melody that comes to your mind first. Imagine that melody as a musical background for that world in which the heroes you bought are fighting for the survival of your desire. Let them all go through a completely fictional and fantastic story, call their names, move them around the amphitheater. You can go to the market of an entirely different city, look for and search through reality until you find artifacts that are sacred to you. Imagine you are insane. That is the best advice ever. Pretend you are insane without knowing it. Just be that. Do not sleep all day, get tired to the extreme, play with your amphitheater, invent formulas, names, movements, invocations, colors, create gods that do not exist, and insult the existing ones. Let everything end in success, in a completely insane way, let your wish come true and let everything in the amphitheater fulfill its role that you gave them. Then go to sleep, and tomorrow, leave all the items from the amphitheater in various parts of your city, let someone else take them, and use them further. May their Spirit incarnate in a completely different home and purpose, establishing your will even further. Then forget all about this because someone else will think about it and infuse energy while playing with your toys.

On living the grade

You do not mark your grade. The mark comes from me; you must have a terrible last dance that will be farewell as much as "until next time." It is a grip of nostalgia as much as supreme love. Live your grade, breathe through it, enjoy it. Let your grade breathe through you too, dance together to the rhythm of your own Will.

Also, when a day has finished, if it was a movie, how would you name it? What genre would it be? What kind of music would go with it? If that day was some color, what color would it be?

Make the same descriptions for the past month. What characterizes it? Your whole grade? How would you call it? If it was a thing, what would it be? Is it male or female? What pose in sex? What disease? What art painting? Kind of pain? Illness? Which perversion? And now do the opposite; answer what is not. Also, what would you like it to be? Let us advance further with this meditation. What is common in all the days of your grade, in all the practices? Is it some feeling, neurosis, pleasantness, maybe some subtle smell that you feel inside your being? Maybe fear? Of what? What emotion is most pronounced on certain days; what emotion do you wake up with, which one do you go to bed with?

Now, change that for one day, choose any day. Do not practice that day at all. Act like you have accomplished everything you have ever needed to. Now, go around the city, remember and imagine that no tomorrow will ever come, that a comet will destroy everything, and only you know that. Play. More than that, be a toy of your God. How does your magical motto behave in traffic? Come outside as that name, not as a bearer of the name. You are "it," by no means that it is "you." Imagine your last moment ever; do the practice one last time, imagine such a circumstance as completely true.

You do not need to "understand" all this. Just stimulate your mind pleasantly with these models of thoughts. There are billions of different kinds of men on this Earth, yet only a few ultimate experiences that each man senses in billions of other ways. The true jewel is to read the book and not let your mind "understand" what it reads. Try to read the words without realizing what they mean; the more abstract ideas are, the less we need to "understand" them. One can listen to Beethoven's symphony without understanding it. The more you understand, the more you destroy it. Let this art stay alive, without understanding it, without destroying it.

Let us make your work a little livelier by doing quite ordinary things. I have noticed that you lack a creative element, which you often mention in your letters. Let us begin with your initiation, starting from the root. Take your Oath. Read it daily, like Liber Resh, even 4 times a day, with a different element and sign. After that, sit down and meditate for a while, watching what is coming to you. Write down every thought, which is definitely the first thing you can do. Next, Liber Pyramidos. Think about it, meditate about the secret word. Look at the original manuscript of this ritual. You will notice the colors for each letter of this word. Now, pay attention to Liber HHH. Pay attention to the color of the crosses. It is the same name; what HHH is as poetry, Pyramidos is now as prose. Vibrate a name, each time in a different color. Use the appropriate God names for colors. Also, the total sum of both is 93. This is the secret word because it is not the word at all. It is a signpost. M...M is then like this: Tau + Tzaddi + Daleth + Tiphareth + Gimel = 93. Black + Red + Green + Yellow + Silver (again black, but it is not from this "Universe"). Paths: 32 + 28 + 14 + 6 + 13 = 93. Tau + Tzaddi + Daleth + Vau + Gimel = 93. Use your imagination to climb in that order, meditate on these Sephiroth and paths. You will "use" this secret word later, especially when you are about to receive Liber Mysteriorum.

Choose one chapter from Liber VII; read it every day, then, after a while, add the invocation ritual of the Hexagram for that planet to which your chapter has been assigned. Use the secret word you received as the Neophyte to attract force. You are the Neophyte, an Adept in a small way, a small Adept, you have everything, but you are still not aware of it. You asked me if summoning the same planet every day was "dangerous"? Instead of answering, I shall ask you a question – what does "dangerous" mean to you? Will you become too aggressive summoning Mars? More than it is in your nature? Or maybe less than your nature is? Do you think that taking your Oath is a little less "dangerous"? How less? Or more? How much more? How much do you need? Let it "fill you", and even more – let it "kill you", and do not be afraid. You chose the chapter precisely because it was neither more nor less – your nature chose it that way, not "you." In the end, you cannot even choose a "wrong" chapter. Because you already chose the "right" the moment the book was "written."

Also, let us discuss the powers of the Sphinx. Work with one every day. Once a week, or once a month, choose one day to be silent all day. Next, choose one day in which you will "dare" all day long. Then, one day a month, you will study for 24 hours non-stop. Obtain some new knowledge in your life in those 24 hours. Then overcome one knowledge. Then delete one old knowledge which is no good for you. Use your imagination for this. Be courageous! Do something which is brave, go bungee jumping, jump from a plane. Work with that 4 powers, upgrade them, feel free to experiment. Play with your grade. Do not repeat the material like a parrot. You have to live the grade and not repeat it. You cannot repeat something that is unique, which is always different and new every day. You have to live and let this "new" change the old from yesterday, instead of what is from yesterday stabbing this of today. If you are not living it, for sure, there is no chance of growing because a dead thing cannot grow. Only one thing will grow, and that is your Ego inside you, your displeasure and dissatisfaction. How long can you starve? Be deprived of sleep? Without sex? How long can you masturbate without an orgasm? Minutes? Hours? Maybe days? How strong can your Sphinx be? How big? Or how small? How quiet, invisible, and incomprehensible? How loud? How charming? How inconspicuous? How different can you be, and again, to stay "you," and no one else?

You wrote to me that you have been working from home for a few years, and sometimes you spend days without leaving your house. That you have short periods of taking a break to see your friends, and in this isolation, you asked how you could even "dare" to do things in the context of the powers of the Sphynx when you cannot see the world where your temptation could manifest at all. Well, my dear, do you think that "outside" of your house is a true environment for farming a destiny that was meant for you in this or any other way. That "outside" of your house cannot be soil for the same destiny as "inside of your room." Is there a difference? Alone in the dark of your own room can be more dramatic than traveling the whole world. Abramelin is much wider than six months, and it surely begins before. Before what? Your puberty, last birthday, last drunkenness? Before life, maybe? Or it is part of the whole that life, yours as any "other." Is it surrounded by the borders of your temple, or its range is the whole Universe? Is not the robe of your Angel spread over the stars of the night sky, is not the Great Work as great as the Universe?

About performance

When you are performing an exercise or a ritual, especially when you have been doing it for a long time and in the same way and already started losing enthusiasm a little, stop in the center of the circle before you start doing it. You are a train switchman. Every thought that has been in you long enough and for more than a single moment turns the Universe, and the whole ritual will flow with that energy towards that thought. So inhale, as if breathing air for the first time, and pretend to want to tell the Universe where to go. Say what you wish, whatever comes to your mind, but it must come from the center of your heart. It really does not have to be the Will; it is enough to be something that your being wants. Therefore, the Universe wants you to want it, and that means that the Universe wants it through you. Hold that thought, you do not have to act with words, do not burden yourself with form, be aware of at least a slight feeling, color, sound, character, memory, and then do the ritual completely forgetting all this, try to do it as if you were showing it to someone, pretending to have known him forever, as if he were actually your twin soul.

Remember, do it as if you were showing it to someone. Do it not for yourself, but for someone else, or for your magical child, as if you are teaching own self in the past, being still small and weak, the one who needs to be understood and supported in his path and quest. That child is pushing forward, and it is sometimes painful, but he will find his way under the stars by being a star himself for some others like you are for him.

Also, do the ritual terribly slowly, like on a broken tape. Enjoy every movement; when you think you are doing it slowly enough then slow down twice as much, it is imperative to overdo it. Let the ritual flow, but so slowly as if you never want it to finish. Now, do the ritual terribly fast. Speed everything up enough to do it in half a minute. Then in 15 seconds. Then imagine the whole ritual from beginning to end for the duration of your inhale. Now, exhale everything, and be silent. It is all over, now only silence remains flickering in the empty air, in your empty self. Only the flickering of the previous and forgotten Will remains, shaping the whole Universe.

CHAPTER ELEVEN

LUCID DREAMING

You may find out that the entire apparatus, your circulatory system is actually an open system and is only part of a more extensive process and movement in the Universe. The moment you discover that you are continually conditioning the movement of your bloodstream and that you are the one driving the heart muscle, that moment, you will be the one shining with the light of stars. Influencing the beat of your heart muscle is no less impressive than arousing the impact of a volcano or affecting the trajectory of Jupiter. Some young minds may ask how the problem is solved if two Aspirants want an opposite trajectory for the same thing, but our answer is very simple. There is only one trajectory and one choice only. Since it is the only one, it can be neither free nor unfree because we cannot have a fulcrum to compare these two meaningless things. All the trouble in our art comes from a simple fact that we really cannot understand a very simple thing – everything that exists is within the mind. In fact, there is no such thing as everything. Moreover, everything that exists is a wholly exaggerated notion. Nothing exists – is quite more appropriate. Except for the mind. Not yours or mine, greater, wider, or more intuitive. But one, and only. *Nothing* and *except the mind* are so diametrically different things and identical at the same time. And that is exactly all we have to deal with in this quest of ours. There is the mind, but nothing beyond that. Right now, even these words you are reading are not in front of you as you may think, but inside your mind. You are not looking at them; you are looking directly inside yourself, in the part of the brain that is seeding this projection as a visual image, which is purely and solely constructed by you. These are not letters at all; they are particles of your mind.

One great man said that each of us has their fifteen minutes of glory. Perhaps it is fair to say that all this we are going to talk about is beautiful and, above all, different way in which you can utilize those fifteen minutes. We live in the belief that our time lasts, has passed, or will pass, and accordingly, we measure our spiritual progress by time, not by the quality of what we may have experienced during just one second of our meditation. A simple calculation leads us to the startling fact that we spend a third of our lives sleeping and just a small part of it dreaming. In fact, an average 30-year-old is only aware of twenty years of his life. Therefore, the difference in beginners' and masters' spiritual work lies in the exploitation of that part of our life, which is unconscious, the same for everybody, and unfortunately, too often irrelevant to everyone. Without the attainment of the experience called astral projection, or lucid dreaming, all the systems of esoteric thought are just an empty story. An average dream lasts for 15 minutes. The striking thing is that a man can do anything in those 15 minutes of glory. The crucial question is, what are we going to do with all this? How can we use that? This is a story different from anything you can imagine. Dare to reach the goal. Moreover, dare to use the means.

SLEEPING SELF

There is an experience that completely changes the content of our being and transforms it into a force we cannot even assume to exist. If we start heating water, it will start to change, but that change will not be so significant for our soul until it exceeds 99 degrees centigrade. Degree by degree, that growth will not mean much in the quality of the water itself, and yet, when it exceeds 99 degrees and reaches 100, that one small degree will mean much more than the growth of all the previous degrees. That one degree will change everything – water will boil. By raising the same quantitative unit, as was the change from, for instance, 10 to 11 degrees, now, that same unit makes water change its nature in such a noticeable and unique way. Boiling is the growth of water, both quantitative and qualitative. The experience of lucid dreaming is that qualitative change in the Aspirant. And just as it can change quantitatively over the years, growing from one degree to another, that quantitative growth will bring nothing so tremendous. However, finding yourself in a dream, experiencing a whole new awareness of a whole new reality, seems to bring a qualitative change in the mind, which will affect the Aspirant's being for the rest of his life. This qualitative leap will direct us to a completely different quest; the search for ourselves. Yet, the search in the right direction is the search in the least likely place to look for – inside the Self.

For sure, the first important step in this matter is a complete understanding of the architecture and anatomy of a dream. It can be said that our shallow perception of what sleeping and dreaming are, and the equation between these two completely different phenomena in general, is the condition of failure. We have high expectations to understand our own reality of being awake without even the slightest awareness of what is happening behind our own eyes.

Our whole being contains a system of levers of the highest enlightenment that could be found in the symbiosis of biological, physiological, chemical, and psychological processes in us that lie primarily in straightforward laws and ways in which these processes make what we call consciousness. All our trouble is that with the occult arts, we try bypassing something that is an entirely open channel in itself. It has taken so much time during which we have been really unable to say what is going on in our brains during quite ordinary things; apart from being able to perceive certain reactions, we are unable to answer how and why processes occur within the mind, and how certain information is processed and stored. One of such levers that we now know quite a lot about compared to only a few decades ago is our dreaming, that is, a period of brain activity called the REM phase or paradoxical sleep. And the more we know and learn, the less willing we are to utilize such knowledge for all that holds our art in the sphere of life's interest — and that is the progress and illumination of being. We keep shedding light upon other paths, plains, and entities so much that we are not sure at all that they are anything beyond our own imagination and weakness. We forget that all the light is already inside ourselves, on and warm, but our eyes are focused on other and further heavens, and not those that have already been radiating and longing for that distant and vain look.

We will start from the very basic settings that emerged by complete coincidence: polygraph recording of the waking-sleeping cycle using electrodes implanted at the level of major brain structures and different muscle groups allowed two different states to be accidentally discovered (quite diametrical, to be more precise). One is a state of slow-wave sleep, followed by slow waves with large amplitude and preserved muscle tone. And the second is a state of deep sleep, which, paradoxically, is characterized by electrical activity of the brain, similar to that in the waking state, rapid eye movements, and complete absence of muscle tone. These are periods that were discovered in 1959 by my friend and researcher in the same field of interest – Professor Michel Jouvet and named paradoxical sleep – a name that properly indicates the nature of this condition. Anatomically, the waking system consists of a network of neurons, which stimulate the cortex through certain neurotransmitters during the waking state. In other words, we artificially maintain wakefulness, with the natural state of our brain being anything but that waking state for which we need constant neurological stimulation and effort to maintain. Our natural environment is the unreality of dreams, while this reality keeps being artificially caused throughout our lives. Everything takes place in such a way that numerous control mechanisms prevent the occurrence of paradoxical sleep, i.e., dreaming during the waking state and at the beginning of sleep, so paradoxical sleep can occur only if all activities of the structures in charge of stimulating wakefulness are stopped. Dreaming is accompanied by a significantly elevated alert threshold and almost complete paralysis. A deaf, blind and paralyzed being becomes very vulnerable; it can only dream if it is safe. Only then does it fall into deep sleep, which is a mechanism that manifests itself in our brain from the beginning of time. The direct transition from waking to paradoxical sleep is possible only with one illness – narcolepsy. The main feature of paradoxical sleep is atony of body position and rapid eye movements. It took too long for even the most suspicious to be convinced that onyric activity is not a continuous process during sleep but a completely periodic occurrence of paradoxical sleep. Neurophysiological experiments have clearly shown that paradoxical sleep is a state different from sleeping, with a significantly higher threshold of wakefulness than could even be assumed. Lucid dreaming occurs during paradoxical sleep, where the awareness that we are actually dreaming correlates with the high threshold of wakefulness that the state of dreaming has, but which we are unfortunately not aware of. It took a short time to get proof that lucid dreaming occurs only during paradoxical sleep, thanks to Dr. Stephen LaBerge and his experiments. The nature of dreaming is indeed completely paradoxical. Within that period and that reality, we have an utterly increased wakefulness, with our body being turned off. On the other hand, what is turned on is a world for which, in addition to all this wakefulness, we cannot recognize that it is unreal. We bring our own qualities and characters into that unreality by living it and acting in it like in this reality. We are so awake during the dreaming period that we are not even aware that we are dreaming. This is the true nature of this condition, which got named paradoxical sleep or paradoxical state of the brain long before it was called the REM phase. Indeed, dreaming is set as the third state of the brain, as different from sleep as sleep is different from the waking state, and all our efforts must aim in this direction at any cost. The nature of dreaming is paradoxical, and we must understand these heavens as a pond full of wild fish; we have to cultivate that pond down here, instead of looking up at those heavens as the worst failure of all Aspirants for centuries – in an attempt at something so paradoxical as achieving awakening of our being during wakefulness. Therefore, we will crush the paradox of dream with convenient meaningless methods, which are primarily simple and short. In a lucid dream, each attempt lasting more than a few minutes will be doomed to complete failure; such an act will either melt into insomnia or lead to complete awakening. There is nothing worse than finding that we have failed to implement any of that lucidity one morning, yet being overwhelmed by the excessive longing for a lucid dream and that our unconscious nature has managed to find a way to slip off the hook in the same way, imperceptibly, inconspicuously and skillfully, while it seems we have been waiting all the time in that pond for a fish with a rod without bait.

What is truly lucid in that morning is a very special neurosis that arises from the fact that we did achieve nothing, that is, the unrealistic belief that we actually did anything. It is lucid to know that the amount of work and effort is entirely and diametrically different from the success rate. The Aspirant may think that the more he works during the night, the greater are chances of finding himself in the magnificent astral realm, and it is in that lucid humor that his mind prepares, with the first rays of the sun, when he has been exhausted by hours of ultimately unsuccessful attempts. He realizes he has been fishing in a completely wrong place, with a completely wrong bait, and a wholly broken net. Everything is lucid, but his dreaming and that beautiful astral realm now seem to laugh and grin in his face, leaving him to all the beauties of the coming day to think and drown in his own failure. What I want from now on is to stop using terms such as astral projection or out-of-body experience; once you have pulled out at least a hundred lucid dreams, you will know for sure why. In such a pompous term as astral projection or the projection of the body of light, the only thing of all these pompous words that would really be worth underlining is light. But by no means stellar and distant light, unattainable and romantic. These are all metaphors of the same dark shadow that envelops human experience, interwoven with fear and misunderstanding of a completely natural phenomenon. The whole concept of getting out of the body is so meaningless for everyone once they have found themselves in a lucid dream and when they feel that fantastic, magical, and unique atmosphere of a conscious dream. All I have ever been convinced of after countless thousands of projections so far is that it is not about getting out of the body; in fact, it is not about the body at all. Everything is inside the mind. We simply have nothing to look for beyond that in this place, but it is our own curse that by the mind, we mean a very small and hidden place. There is an entirely fantastic game of the mind that finds plasticine to imprint its own will while transiting to sleep. This is one of the true tasks we have before us, and before which we will by no means back off – to discover the trajectory of the soul inside this labyrinth, and instead of finding a way out, we actually find the soul.

Lucid dreaming is gain, not a gift; it is an ability, not an anomaly. It is the exploitation of a completely natural process; it is the ultimate economy of the movement of the spirit like a sail on a ship; ignorance of this indicates ignorance of the natural processes that take place within us. Therefore, all elements of this skill are absolutely opposed to ideas such as exercise, effort, or erudition.

The effort to practice this skill is an entirely ridiculous thought that is identical to the thought that you should practice pumping your own heart or that you should practice breathing, and continually reminding yourself of the importance of these movements your own life depends on. In fact, you are not the one beating your heart; you are not the one breathing. Your automatic organism breathes, and that has nothing to do with you. All the concentration is actually messing and poking your nose into the work of your accountant, which, sooner or later, leads to misunderstanding and failure, above all. Your heart and your lungs keep on doing their job. All the time you are neurotically trying to learn and pass on all this clumsiness to others, who, again, stumble upon all this, who breathe just like you and whose heart works in exactly the same way as yours. All our failure in this matter lies in the fact that we really have no knowledge of the two processes – the process of awakeness and the process of dreaming. In fact, we are furthest from realizing that there is no difference between these two events, which is actually just one. We are awake all the time. Indeed, how can we expect to know what a lucid dream is if we are not sure what awakeness is? Is it worth finding the mechanism of dreaming while we are not certain of our awake state and if we are not familiar with our own wake capabilities? How to expect to be lucid in a reality where we have not fully awakened yet?

These words are so important to begin with, and there is no movement that introduces the Aspirant more to the heavens of success in understanding one's own awakeness than it is in understanding one's own dream. In order to move forward, we must make a very clear distinction between consciousness and awareness. Consciousness is the object of awareness. Awareness is the subject of consciousness. All we are going to talk about here is how to get to completely different shores of awakeness, where we will find awareness. This sailing on the currents of our sleeping self requires us to really discern what happens when we fall asleep. To truly see, we shall close our eyes.

Each method is an agreed system of values that can logically fit into a particular attainment model. But this does not mean that this model contains that value exclusively because, in fact, for a free spirit, any method leads to any attainment. No matter what method, no matter what attainment. If you want to link two dots, you will not draw a line from the center; that would be terribly inappropriate. You will start either from one dot or the other; when these points are clearly defined, the line is obvious. However, the line itself is composed of a multitude of dots and is an entirely new attainment per se. It is by no means a method or a consequence of merging these dots; on the contrary, these dots are only a limited end of that line that connects them only with a limited value. Then, when a line connects them, these dots are no longer perceived; everything becomes just one line, that is, one attainment, where the one who attains is no more, as well as the one to attain to, nor any tools of attainment. Therefore, why would exercise in lucid dreaming have anything to do with attaining the lucid dream? Statistically, out of a thousand lines drawn randomly on paper, one will most likely connect those two selected dots. The problem is that the rough awareness at that moment implies and creates a model that these dots and that line are products of the will to merge them and that the intention is responsible for everything.

Practicing lucid dreaming does not contribute to attaining the lucid dream. Practicing lucid dreaming leads to lucid dreaming practice, is not that so logical? The more you practice, the more distance there is from the attainment itself. In other words, the more you practice, the harder it is to attain. The problem with most Aspirants is completely misstructured work. I am sure the best book on lucid dreaming would be the one about failures. No technique or method in our art is so misunderstood and misinterpreted as lucid dreaming, precisely because the whole approach is completely wrong and based on a completely broken mechanism. Once you learn to do the whole thing correctly, you will notice the devastating fact that most books are actually rewriting one and the same fantasy and that the vast majority is a completely magnificent lie that is no different from a fish story. The methods are completely wrong, and the tale of astral planes, beings, and the silver cord is usually an accurate indication that there is a liar and a fraudster in front of you.

It really does not take a lot of energy or time to get to a lucid dream. You should only learn to do a very simple and right thing at the right time. A dream is so much more a sublime place than elemental beings, angels, silver cords, the benevolent deceased who want to drink just another cup of tea with us. It is the place of your mind, so wider than all this. All the magnitude of the dream, that is, the astral plane, is exclusively in the phenomenon of consciousness, the phenomenon of time which is expanded by this experience and transformed into a completely different value. The way you will really use this holy moment is solely up to you; we are here to consider and attain it in an easy and natural way above all. By no means is it crucial to have a separate and accidental lucid dreaming or to get a lucid dream in the lottery. The jewel of true attainment is reflected in the awakening and development of a lucid consciousness, which, like any scientific method, will be able to be carried out under certain circumstances in precisely the same way, which we can prepare, repeat and modify at will.

Therefore, I will instruct you as I have instructed others so far, and I can offer you a bunch of examples where inexperienced minds have achieved lucid dreaming after the first or first few attempts. What still makes them good practitioners today is the fact that they have set a healthy model of their practice, which does not require too much time, or tedious and unnecessary activities such as visualization, working with the middle pillar, countless meditation and concentration techniques; it can all rather help you in the second part of our work when you need to persevere and stay conscious in your dream. Once you have had your first experience of lucid dreaming, just remembering that wonderful act will help you easily experience the second one, soon carrying on in a certain rhythm, making it a part of your life, not practice. You must live a lucid awareness, do not expect it humbly, hoping for something that your nature has already achieved and brought into your life – every night, every day, throughout the whole of your existence.

It is one thing to wake up in your dream. It is yet another to keep yourself awake in your dream. Actually, the latter is much harder, but I want all your attention on the former for now. The experience of lucid dreaming is primarily conditioned by the economics of your movements. Life leads us to the fact that man is cursed by the desire to complicate simple things to the maximum. Lucid dreaming is an excellent example of such a cursed practice. Let us, therefore, define the strengths and weaknesses of this plan. The strengths are undoubtedly descriptions and transmissions of other people's experiences, techniques, and observations, as long as they do not get into the field of theology, ideology, and sociology. It is actually essential for you to understand vividly that others are following the same goal and sharing the same mistakes with you. There is no better psychoanalysis than reading other people's dreams. But since reading other people's dreams is a luxury for you, for now, you will limit yourself to reading your own. Weaknesses are books; there is nothing so devastating as following instructions that lead to nothing, entire generations in this art endeavor to devote themselves to projections at bedtime, which is similar to making love without a male erection; it's not that it's impossible, but why on earth, when the whole mechanism is made to run smoothly when used differently.

To start with, the most important thing by far is to decide to succeed. Not to try or to keep trying, not to work on, but to complete and succeed. I want to start with the first point of your work, that is, the question of motive. It is an essential issue of all workings; it is a condition and the least common denominator of all progress and success. It is that atom of life, without which no action has any meaning. The question of motive is an essential issue for every act, from criminal to divine, and if you find a motive within a seemingly impossible endeavor, the whole act begins to radiate in such a different and lively atmosphere. But the question is how to find a motive for an experience that is so inconceivable and amazing? This incredibleness creates a drive within that pushes us forward, but at the same time, it radiates a completely dark and demoralizing shadow, the one that tells us that all this is possible for all but us, that of all God's creatures, we are the only ones who are doomed to fail. Imagine the realization of children's dreams, flying over buildings in the neighborhood or under the rainbow, imagine a sudden ascent to the clouds, a chase over the ocean. Imagine sitting in the clouds or peacefully floating in open space, getting to know your past life, metamorphosing into an animal, or some completely different form. To build such an appropriate motive, you do not need anything new; you just need to become a child. Again. But in your case, you have to work hard for it; your censor of reality will ruin your motive because it is but a stranger in your mind at the moment, and it will do everything to suppress and remove it. To prevent this, you need something concrete. You need a confirmation that you have set off on a journey. You need something tangible, something that will send a signal to your enthusiasm to grow and develop freely.

DREAM DIARY

Therefore, the beginning of work should be officially announced. For the first time, a small group of citizens will appear in the world of tyrants and will start organizing a rebellion. It must never perform too loudly because such a rebellion will be revealed and suppressed ruthlessly. Also, it should not be too quiet because it will induce no effect. What is required of you is to cause the butterfly effect. Therefore, the best way to start this great adventure is by keeping the diary of your dreams – your lucid diary. That diary is already one huge step towards your first lucid dream. Choosing a notebook in a bookstore, finding the ideal color and size, your first entry on its pages, all of these represent a conscious determination to succeed; it is a one-way ticket to a country where no one has been before, with you as the first one to arrive. This is a very important moment because it represents the withdrawal of the most important factor – the magical link. When you pick a day to buy your lucid diary, it will also be the first day of your entire lucid opus. I advise you to get a notebook of the usual size, without excessive patterns or tables for dates and times. Your diary will be a report on your inspiration and imagination, so it may be full of drawings and patterns that will require a lot of blank space on the paper. It will be your reconnaissance squad, not your gravestone epitaph; it must point to the vitality of your spirit, not to the passive darkness of oblivion and nothingness. Choose it well; work on this whole thing. You will see later that all the effort you put in the beginning will certainly affect many things later. I would not like to spend too much time on the form and appearance of the diary; I am quite sure that you will find what is ideal for you. What I want to dwell on, however, are two things – a record form and a form of interest. Let me go over the details of these ideas. At the same time, you will be more and more dedicated to your lucid opus and closer to the goal, just because your attention is sharpening more in this place, which I think is very good. Here I would like to tell you about what I have already said in the book about the Probationer, and it concerns the whole of this thing.

A note in this diary does not serve to admire your phantasmagorias but dissects them, measures them, and probes them with the flame of childish intrigue. There are countless models upon which the dreams are correctly recorded, and it is up to you to construct the one that suits you the most. When you record a dream, it is important to write it down immediately upon waking, no matter how convinced you are that you will remember it later. There is no need to wait for an ideal moment to write down a dream, but it should immediately be followed by awakening. More than an authentic experience in the morning will become distant and pale as soon as noon. It is also crucial that you give your dream a name. As if it were a movie, try to provide the best name to your last night's blockbuster. Furthermore, find the symbol around which the dream is revolving. It is usually an object or a person around which the whole dream happens – try to discover and name what that is. Your subconscious uses sleep as we use adjectives in order to describe a specific noun; a dream for your unconscious nature is what a delightful verse is to a poet. Therefore, you need to find what is being adorned by that strophe, what is behind the stylistic figure of your subconscious, what kind of phenomenon has turned on the mischief behind your closed eyes. Is it a person who exists in real life, maybe someone from the past? Is it an object, or perhaps an event, emotion, or thought? In any case, it must be one term, not two or three, not more or less, but one and only. Come closer to that term from the state of wakefulness. What does it bring when you think about it? Is it pleasure or discomfort, fear or ignorance, lust, or need? Get out of the role of a dreamer; you need to transform the dream into a creative force of your intent, not to remain a passive and random cobweb of your unconscious. You have to allow a diary to breathe and develop; you must never be satisfied with one form of recording because inevitably, there will appear another one to replace it. Write in the third person. When you make a journal entry, do so as if you are writing about someone else, as if you are writing a biography. Then, write in the second person. Write to *him* instead of *yourself*. Give your dream logical legitimacy. List the actors of the dream. Give a title to your role, whether you were the main subject, an observer, helper, victim, savior, or conspirator. Are you a judge, prosecutor, or defense attorney? Who are you in the dream anyway, and to whom? Maybe you are an object of someone else's dream, just a secondary object of a wider event? Maybe you are a stimulus to someone else's awakening?

In the beginning, you will be lucky if you have written anything down at all. At first, your dream memory will be fragmentary, connected in small pieces that will progress over time. What you have to exercise here is patience. And most of all, the totality of memory; by no means fragments, you need continuity in memory, even if it is for just over a moment – if it is in one cycle and made of one uninterrupted part, it will be a hundred times more important than the one from several smaller wholes. Even a few minutes of uninterrupted memory is much more valuable than an experience of a whole night full of holes and darkness of oblivion.

All this, even reading this before writing down anything in your dream diary, crushes a possibility of failure so powerfully that we can say quite openly that it is already approaching the dawn of awakening. Not in reality, but in a dream, in an environment that is much more adapted to your true being and a landscape that is intended for such an endeavor, where your Self and your new awakeness will be in its completely natural environment.

DREAM ARCHITECTURE

The next, extremely important thing is an insight into the architecture of sleeping similar to a municipal court building – it has completely unimportant floors of bureaucracy where you can be stuck for years; offices, basements, completely different buildings that are all called the same and too often with the same addresses. But they all always have one door and one room where you get all things done, from building permits to utility affairs. And it all usually comes at a price, as does our special room for success. And that price is knowledge, not what the bribe is, but to whom and how much you should give to get your stuff done. In other words, we need to know precisely what you are doing in your sleep, when you are sleeping, when you are dreaming, and when do you wake up; it is so necessary for us to find that one single door.

What is absolutely necessary is to understand that sleep does not have a homogeneous structure. It is a shift between two completely different states, which are distant from each other, almost as the waking state is distant from the darkness of deep and unconscious sleep. Our ultimate goal is certainly paradoxical sleep, that is, the REM phase – the name more widely accepted, although a case of misnaming to some extent. As the nature of such a state is truly paradoxical, I will use that term as well. There is nothing more magnificent than understanding the nature of that wonderful state of dreaming, which unlocks the depths of our being. The moment we are close to the tallest heights, we are completely stuck in the depths and darkness of unconsciousness; it is paradoxical that we touch God facing him with our backs. It is as if some tremendous force has left the gates of paradise open in human life but has tried to hide the path to that gate, to conceal this state, and drive it away from any conscious possibility of cognition. It is as if divine providence had hidden the best possible gift to its stellar child while forgetting where it had hidden it. That hiding is just a correct expression and reason for this whole paradoxical movement. In primordial times, man was most vulnerable while sleeping, so the reactive mind did everything to enable self-defense systems, making dreaming possible only when multiple protection structures were set. It took care of human sleeping consciousness for a long time, precisely because it wanted to make sure that the perfect place was found where the body would not be disturbed by predators, and only after some time actuate the process of dreaming together with another, the last system of self-defense – paralysis. Even today, we are left with these ancient mechanisms in a completely similar way – during the REM phase, there is atony with the body of an individual being paralyzed from the neck down – leaving only the basic survival mechanism to work; it can be said that the organism is paralyzed – during a brief appearance of the most vulnerable part of its existence – dreaming, i.e., a paradoxical state. And just then, the being chooses to pretend to be something predators usually avoid – a still dead corpse, and fearing infection; they give up eating or attacking such a body. An old saying that instructs a man to pretend to be dead and lay low if he encounters a beast casts a whole and true meaning upon this story. And just when the reactive mind has become convinced that a safe place was found, out of the reach of predators, after switching on the ultimate line of defense and deception in the form of paralysis of the body, it enters its actual state and ambiance of that same mind – a paradoxical dream of eating if hungry and being taken care of if it has any need. It flows from one reality to another, and like in a dream of Zhuang Zhou – one really cannot say which is real and which is unreal, as long as the mind is found in a certain reality, it is really not aware of the illusion which it is in. Except in one single case – when a lucid dream is being accomplished. It is an anomaly – a virus that attacks a reactive organism inherited for thousands of years; it is a shortcut that activates a new program inside a program that is of higher priority and over which the main program has no

control or possibility of restriction. Its appearance is more magnificent precisely because it uses the resources of the parent program,
together with the chief architect, it builds and helps build every
corner of the prison for one reason only – to design a perfect escape
plan. It has kept building that prison all its life and all the lives of
all the generations who have walked the earth, and it has left an
escape plan for each of them, in a straightforward way for every
individual to use it. Yet that same architect, the reactive mind, also
has its trump card; by perfecting prison, it has perfected another
element of our being – and that is the Ego, which, for all its complexity, cannot comprehend the simplicity of the escape plan that
our being has left to ourselves. And we really can't help but marvel
at the fantastic extent to which a human being has complicated
such a simple endeavor as lucid dreaming – from the wrong names
of states, the wrong names of phenomena, the wrong methods, and
the utterly wrong strategy; not only that we can no longer decipher
the only map and plan of escape from the prison that we have
made ourselves, but we also found a way to become satisfied in
that same prison and, after all, completely unwilling to leave it at
all. These two opponents – each in their own fantastic way – the
reactive mind as a shadow, and the Selfness in the dream take on
epic roles, and each uses the mechanisms through which they act
in every aspect of a lucid dream, for which there will be some room
to present later on.

As we have already said quite clearly, our sleep consists of
two different states – sleeping and dreaming, where dreaming is
cushioned in periods of complete unconsciousness which serves no
purpose at first glance – and is referred to as the nREM phase. The
whole misfortune is that it is the reactive mind that takes up the
first 90 minutes of the nREM phase after we have fallen asleep. In
fact, dreams do not start immediately, but only when this ancient
mechanism has been really convinced that we will not be disturbed. And in those 90 minutes, while descending deeper and

more confidently into the pits of unconsciousness, we are entirely left without any chance to take a part of ourselves into that world that we will build after those 90 minutes. Entering the dream, we enter it completely deprived of Self, carrying with us only unconscious and basic needs and fears, neuroses, and phantasmagorias. And just when the brain nests inside the dormant realm, it comes out of it and becomes unconscious again for 90 minutes, after which it enters the same mechanism of dream and comatose creativity just to be again obscured by the darkness of the previous nREM phase and prevented from realizing it is dreaming, during 15 minutes of paradoxical sleep. It is as if this game of light and shadow of the mind is an utterly offensive joke, in which a child who is mocked does not even understand how mean and corrupt the game of their friends is. If we compare the change of these two states with the correlation of brain activity, we get approximately the following plan of human dreaming:

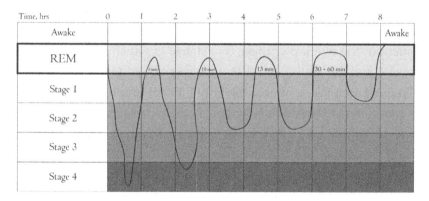

Stages of Sleep

As can be seen, paradoxical sleep lasts only 90 minutes after the brain has fallen asleep. It is very short, after which a long phase of dreamless sleep occurs – nREM phase, after which paradoxical sleep comes again, this time for a little longer. The closer our ultimate awakening after the usual 8 hours of sleep is, the longer and more paradoxical dreaming is – it is getting closer to the waking state, but the more we sleep, the more vivid dreams are, and the deception and lies of our sleep get more real. This is where we come to the ultimate essence of our endeavor – which is by no means the beginning of sleep or evening exercise session, but the complete opposite of that. In most cases, we wake up very close to the REM phase, or paradoxical sleep – whether due to an alarm or a habit, we enter a conscious state in which our brain operates in the Beta frequency, which we call the waking or "normal" state. This moment of awakening represents almost the only link when the waking state is on the very border with the neighboring para-doxical state – without an excessive boundary of unconsciousness or interruption of consciousness. Because both the waking and the paradoxical state have a completely similar mechanism and fre-quency of wakefulness – with the paradoxical state, i.e., dreaming being more awake than wakefulness, so unconscious of the fact that it is awake – from which the notion "paradoxical" derives its meaning. This transition between dreaming and waking – which we call the process of waking – contains this brief, phenomenal el-ement of the overlap of these two states, in which we are equally awake and equally asleep. We have mentioned with the extreme tendency that this is almost the only link because there is another, a completely extraordinary circumstance where the waking state directly relies on a paradoxical sleep – and that is during an after-noon nap, which we will take special care of and take enough time for in the course of this study. Therefore, all the illusion that this state can be reached through meditation, visualization, imagina-tion, and all other "usual suspects" is, in fact, a complete detour – it is far from saying that we won't be able to reach the goal this way, but it is completely desperate to accustom your own lovely nature to a ridiculous clay uphill road when there is such a smooth and spacious meadow in front of it, which it has already been walk-ing along so perfectly and with such ultimate pleasure.

Our nature has done everything to completely cover these few moments with the fog of the ordinariness of life; we get up as soon as possible to look at what time it is and turn off the alarm, we get out of bed mechanically even if we have nothing to do, we get out of bed as soon as if it were the cause of all our doom or root of all our fears, or as if it were a trap from which we must wriggle out as soon as possible. We are further and further away from the most sublime state that the human brain can ever realize by each millimeter of the body movement and every second of time since the moment of awakening. This state is so contrary to all our habits – those that have contributed to us being where we are; it is on the brink of the abyss of insanity as those few seconds of our lives which are uselessly thrown away are the spot in front of which lies the most precious miracle of the human existence. This state is not "somewhere" but "sometimes"; the paradise to which we all aspire so much is a moment of time, not space. It is a moment that lasts only a few seconds after our awakening, which is all the difference between the Adept in lucid dreaming and an utterly untrained mind. The difference between the two is not in the grades that last for years or decades or in Asana and Dharana, which requires us to go to the distant caves. All the difference is in those few seconds after we have woken up, especially once we have added a few more tricks to it.

SUCCESS STRATEGY

There really are not enough efforts to express all the significance of the first few seconds after waking up. It is the place of our pilgrimage; everything we are going to do from now on is directed toward this holy place. It is extremely important to create a reflex of not moving and not opening our eyes during this time. This is a very tricky thing that will take some time, but there are certain things that make this process easier. What will consume all the available energy and ingenuity are two things:

1) when to do

2) what to do

We defined the first thing within the first few seconds of our awakening, which should happen naturally and spontaneously, not caused by an alarm. The only condition of this point is that we remain motionless with our eyes closed after waking up.

The crucial is to make autosuggestion before going to bed, telling ourselves that we shall wake up without moving and remain motionless after waking up. This affirmation has to be as short and effective as possible; something like, "*I am awakening without moving*" is quite appropriate for this whole thing. You shall never repeat an affirmation during the day, nor shall you think that such repetition will increase your chances of success. On the contrary, in this way, you are causing your being to resist and create a habit to interpret the whole affirmation as a routinely distant thing, which is absolutely unacceptable for us. All that is really needed is that the moment we go to bed, we start repeating ourselves the chosen affirmation. It is of great importance that the affirmation is made being convinced and having a feeling as if we have indeed awakened and that we are motionless all the time once we have woken up, suggesting this we are experiencing a false present – it is such a small detail that makes such a big difference from the mere hypnotic and parrot-like repetition of the suggestion. It is also important that from the moment we start making an affirmation until we have fallen asleep, we must remain in a single position without moving, thus giving importance to the idea of continuity of immovable position, which will eventually continue after waking up. In fact, with all these elements, we frame the immobility of the body and the continuity of one position on both sides of dreaming – both before and after the dream, providing additional inputs to our unconscious mind that will drastically increase the chances. Making an affirmation is glued to the determination not to move, so our body will remember the affirmation along with the position, which – being unchanged and motionless reinforces the affirmation and intention to stay still after waking up even further, rounding off the idea at much wider and more compact scale. In a way, repeating the affirmation with a determination not to move until we have fallen asleep seems to lock information about the continuity of the position in the body, which will automatically turn on after waking up. It is simply unimaginable to guess how many miracles there are in front of our noses if we manage to do such a simple thing. Such a small thing triggers a myriad of mechanisms that make it possible to experience something that sheds an entirely different light on everything we do in life. All the rituals, meditations, techniques, everything we perform in our art is really nothing compared to the realization of lucid consciousness that begins with such a nebulous instruction, such as the instruction to remain motionless with our lids shut after waking up.

Another way we can effectively make an affirmation that will help it to be perceived in our unconscious mind in a much better way is by changing the pace of its utterance to the extreme. After a few minutes of repeating the affirmation at a normal pace, we will now speed up to the point that we can barely make it out. There should not be any pause between words; also, sentences themselves must be leaning against each other without a full stop, that is, without any breaks:

"*IamawakeningwithoutmovingIamawakeningwithoutmovingIamawakeningwithoutmoving...*"

After a while, and it is only a matter of a few minutes, a specific state will be created, a feeling in which the frantic repetition of the sentence sculpted our mind in such a special way as if a quick mumble filled the void with a specific sensation, subtle but relatively constant. Now stop repeating the affirmation and just keep nurturing that feeling. It is the imprint of the affirmation in our mind that resonates like an echo, and if you keep it in your mind, that same mind will now imprint the affirmation even more even though you do not have to repeat a single word at all – just a gentle and pleasant focus on that feeling that arises after a quick repetition of your affirmation's wording does the whole job. You can almost feel the tension in the area of the brain almost burning from the rapid repetition of the affirmation; all it takes is to pamper that flame with your attention and spread it – you should simply repeat the affirmation in an advanced way. It is convenient to do the opposite thing, too; after a few minutes of such a hasty way of repeating, we need to slow down so much that we repeat a single sentence like a slow-motion – as slowly as possible. In doing so, we must retain the meaning of the sentence, which must not be lost by excessive deceleration; just imagine that a record has broken down and now the affirmation .... laaaaaast ...... for sooooooooo .... loooooooooong ....

There is another extremely effective way that further imprints the affirmation in mind. It is accentuating of a word during repetition, with a different word accented each time, with full awareness of the word being uttered:

"I AM" awakening without moving
I am "AWAKENING" without moving
I am awakening "WITHOUT" moving
I am awakening without "MOVING"

This kind of repetition has a special effect on the mind, which now performs this whole command more diligently and much faster.

The nature of affirmation is completely different from the one of mantra, and a great deal of the weak outreach and failure of affirmation show Aspirant's misunderstanding of its mechanism. Uttering affirmation in the way it is done with the mantra implies a monotonous pace that only results in initial success, but our mind becomes immune to it very quickly – simply because it is predictable, always the same, and uninteresting. Therefore, we must bring vitality, mobility and flexibility to our affirmations. Whispering affirmation or singing can lead to a spectacular breakthrough in the quality of its materialization.

The best for the Aspirant would be to use all these methods to introduce his own ones or modify the above mentioned; the more various methods he uses, the deeper and more vividly the affirmation will be imprinted in his mind, and thus the more expedient it will be. Affirmation and mind are like fish and a pond; one fish can be caught in different ways, and the more different baits and rods we have, the better our chances are. Also, it is not enough to just catch a fish; we must equally strive to keep it alive once we have put it in the fishing net. Therefore, it would not suffice to repeat the affirmation endlessly but to force our mind to receive and nest it so that it begins to bear fruit. The repetition that is too static and uninventive will bring what will later be noticed in our lucid adventures, and that is immunity to successful techniques. We must continuously and permanently make steps forward in our methods, constantly introducing new elements, constantly changing form and structure. Once he has found himself in a dream, the Aspirant must continuously move, constantly touch and feel the shape of a dream, constantly have an action that carries him further through the dream. Any stagnation, even holding your gaze in a vision for more than a few moments leads to the collapse of such an experience and return to the waking state, which will certainly be discussed later. After working with the affirmation for a while, but in a lively and vigorous way, try to fall asleep but without moving – in the same way as you are expecting to wake up. All that can happen are two options.

The first, quite likely – to wake up moving and opening your eyes, get up and go to the bathroom, or start preparing breakfast only to realize that you have missed the opportunity and that the affirmation was not that clearly imprinted to be able to attack the habit of moving and getting up. As soon as you realize that you have failed, go back to bed immediately, pretending to have just woken up and been amazed at how you found yourself motionless and with your eyes closed. Act that situation out as if it has just happened and as if you have achieved success. Pretend that you are very surprised, excited, and happy to have achieved stillness and closed your eyes. Even if you have made minimal movements after waking up, it is very important to calmly return to the position you got up from as if you were reminding yourself of the command you were supposed to do, then pretend to have woken up and that you managed to stay still with your eyes closed. Something as if you were creating quite a new past, cutting all unfavorable future, and pasting over the present you choose.

After this, feel free to return to your daily routine; it is an equally valuable imprint as if you managed to remain still, which will manifest its mechanism in the coming days. Every time there is a movement of the body because you have forgotten to stay still and with the lids closed, you do exactly the same thing – go back to bed slowly, like rewinding a film, laying your head on a pillow as if you have cut the time corridor of your failure and now you are falsely inserting a new reality in which you have managed to wake up without moving and opening your eyes.

Sooner or later, you will come across a second possibility in which you have invested days of effort; one morning, you will wake up and find yourself staring into the blackness of your eyelids, remaining still, instantly remembering that it should stay that way. It is a truly wonderful moment that will not bring you so close to a lucid dream as it will show you a very clear path – the one you can follow. It will show you that one mechanism is starting to work; it is a special joy that spreads through your being once you have realized that your dormant structures are exactly the same as mine and that the experience I am talking about will be the same as yours you are just experiencing. You will almost feel that wonderful scent of a lucid dream which, literally, is only a few tens of seconds away in those moments. However, it is quite certain that at that moment, you will be so euphoric about success, just as you will be the next few times, that you will ultimately wake up due to such euphoria. And that is what we need the least. Your euphoria and increased attention will do to your being the same moving the body and opening the eyes does; it will throw you out of a position where you would continue to move lucidly. Body movement is stagnation in a dream, and vice versa: movement in a dream implies complete bodily stagnation and stillness.

Repeating the affirmation should become your evening routine; in fact, whenever you go to bed, even during an afternoon nap, let it be your habit to repeat to yourself that you will wake up without moving and opening your eyes. This is by far the most important step in this whole experiment, and if the awakening happens without physically moving and opening the eyes, it can be said that success is largely guaranteed if the following steps are adhered to. As amazing and difficult as it may seem, complete success in this will come after no more than 2 to 3 weeks. In fact, the first success can come after 2 or 3 days, but what we need is the percentage of continued success, that is, at least two nights a week to be able to stay still after waking up. It is then that we set out to do the next thing that is bringing us closer to a lucid dream even more substantially.

PHANTASMAL MOVEMENT

Once we have found ourselves awake and motionless, without opening our eyes, we can finally do the thing that introduces us to the world of lucidity, and that is one completely paradoxical thing – we will move. Namely, after we have woken up without moving, we will now just start moving, but in an extraordinary way – this movement will not be physical at all, but mental. For that occasion, I want you to try something right now; while reading, make a break leaning back in your chair, close your eyes, and calm down, like a stone statue. Now, I want you to start nodding your head back and forth, like a pendulum. Imagine that your head is tied to your body over your neck, making it one big pendulum; move your head 5 cm forward and then move it the same distance but backward. Make that rocking motion quite gently, like a clock pendulum. You make this movement subtly, by no means making pauses or forcibly stopping your head. Do it as if you were putting the mind to sleep in the cradle of your skull. After a couple of swings, now continue to swing your head but reduce the amplitude – instead of 5 cm, you will now shorten it to just one centimeter. Repeat the head moves back and forth several times. In the end, the most important part is to follow – you will move your head minimally, reducing the amplitude of the head movement to only a millimeter as much as you can. That movement will be more a thing of your mind than you will actually move. I want you to honestly just think you are moving your head, not even knowing if you are moving it. Keep reducing that movement even more now, until it has become imaginary and your head turns static. Something too extraordinary is going to happen – you will still feel that movement and that rocking as if you are really shaking your head. We need this movement – phantasmagoric oscillation; such a movement is not performed physically but leads to a physical sensation of movement; it is so minor that your intention rather than your muscles perform it. You can now do the same by moving your head left and right, in exactly the same way and with the same procedure: first, do the physical movement for a while, then reduce the amplitude of the movement until you finally start doing it in your mind. This false or phantasmal move is crucial to the whole endeavor. Head movement is especially important, much more important than the movement of other parts of the body because, during the REM phase, the head contains the only body segment that is allowed to move, and that is the eyes, while from the neck down, our body is paralyzed. We deliberately explained this phantom head movement before the next step, although it follows it, because its projection is already piercing your mind now and, like seeds, it has already started growing its sprouts in the soil of your dormant nature.

SLEEP PARALYSIS

After waking up without moving, we will try to maintain enthusiasm and wait no more than a few seconds. We will notice a very unusual circumstance that happens to our body if we continue with immovability; after a few moments, we get a weird feeling as if we were tilted to the side, our body sensation changes completely, we start feeling certain warmth. In fact, there is a wide specter of different events that all point to one thing – our body falls back into sleep while our mind stays awake. It does not matter what happens and how this change in experiencing your body manifests as long as we feel that "something" strange is happening. Scientifically put, our body enters a state of sleep paralysis, which is the next step for a further descent into the regions of dreaming, ensuring that dreaming happens at all. Our brain, because we have remained motionless with our eyes closed, misinterpreted that we have woken up by accident – just as it happens many times during the night – where we wake up for a very short time to continue sleeping without being aware of that. Therefore, this very event where we remained motionless with our eyes closed is enough to confuse our brain, locking the body and introducing the same dreaming procedure that it has been doing since we were born, and even more – since the dawn of mankind. Sleep paralysis is as much a change in the experience of the body as it is in the experience of the psyche. In addition to the fact that we feel that something in our body has changed, very peculiar things will start happening concerning our observation. The first and most important is the sonic hallucination, where we usually hear the voices of our loved ones whispering, speaking, waking us up, or asking us to move. We can hear a neighbor playing music, dogs barking, or someone turning on the television in the next room. However, all those perceptions are part of the same illusion and deception – they are in our head, and really nowhere else. Many practitioners attach them epithets of importance, even crucial for their destiny – they consider the meaning of these voices looking for deeper connotation and analysis, but the truth is that these are only empty mental shells and indicators that we are falling asleep, and nothing more.

After the first few seconds after waking up, remaining motionless, and after feeling the perception of the body change, we do the phantom head movement – the way we have learned earlier, not in a physical way – minimally and with such a small amplitude that the rocking motion is not to be found in centimeters but our imagination. This movement is like a decoy, which bites a predator in the pond of the mind; at some point, this movement will hook up the mechanism of separation from the body, which will start taking place extremely quickly. This movement must be carried out resolutely and without ceasing. Separation can always happen and at any moment, so in the first half a minute, it can seem that everything is entirely in vain, and a second later, we can hear someone whisper, or feel a warm blanket falling over us, or feel our body bend, or fall through the floor. It is of the utmost importance that this movement is consistently repeated for some time and that it is never stopped at any cost, especially if one gets the impression that nothing worthwhile is happening and that one should give up. This movement must be carried out for at least a minute or even two, and no matter how small chances may seem that something will happen, it has to be carried out persistently and without backing off. What happens next is one of the most interesting experiences the Aspirant can have in his life until then – you will really start to move and have a genuine sense of that movement. Your sense of the body will be transformed into a feeling similar to that when a fly gets caught in a spider's web, or as if you are immersed in some gelatin; as if your dream body is connected to the physical by some phantasmagoric glue, and the movement you are performing will contribute to that glue losing its grip and letting go.

When this happens, keep shaking your head, now increasing the amplitude. No matter how much this instruction might seem ambiguous now, at that moment, everything will be perfectly clear to you. By increasing the amplitude, you will reach a kind of a dead-end state; now follows a crucial and final movement that brings the whole operation to a climax – now you will be rolling out of your body in the last swing, falling next to your bed. This is one of the most beautiful experiences in our art – you will find yourself in the darkness on the floor of your room. Far from being able to see anything, you will have a clear tactile feeling that you are on the floor and that you are now feeling it with your hands. You will get in a part of reality that is entirely unique: you will still be feeling your body in bed while still being on the floor, with all the sense of space and dimensions right from that place. You will be in the body, but now that body is by no means in bed but on the floor, waiting for instructions on what to do next.

VOID

The most important thing is to remember that you should not stay on the floor – touching over the floor, you should get to the first nearest wall. You still won't see anything, and if you try to open your eyes now, feeling shocked, you will suddenly experience a return to the physicality that has been lying in bed all the time. Opening your eyes is impossible at this stage because you still do not have eyes, nor do you have a body of any kind, or the ability to experience anything other than touching that is the only real sense you have. Your being has not yet built the foundations of your new reality, and you will find yourself in very awkward terrain – too awake to get a perception of a dream, but still too dreamy to submit yourself to a field of the body lying a meter away from you. All you have to do is touch and feel. Try a very simple experiment; close your eyes now and get to your bathroom without opening your eyes but groping for things. You would first come to a nearby wall, and then feeling the surface of the wall with your palms all the time you will move forward toward where your bathroom is, encountering switches and other things that are on the wall. But what is of precious importance is the continuity of feelings that your mind will receive through the palms of your hands. You will not get a picture of where you are going, but you will definitely know where you are and where you are going through tactile feelings brought to you by your fingers and palms. Now I want you to do the same, starting from an awkward position you have found yourself in, throwing yourself out of your physical body. Feel the floor until you reach the wall, and then continuing with your palms all over the wall, stand up straight, never separating your hands from that wall. Even if you have to move to another wall, do it quickly and energetically – that feeling of the wall sliding under your palms is the only anchor that could save you in this storm of mental information and the desire of your mind to return to the body. In this segment of work, it is enough to stay in one place for even a few moments, and you will come back – completely clearly and unambiguously being there in the waking world, in your bed, trapped in this reality. The return is inevitable, but we will continue to feel and touch further and further on from the body, groping the walls and sliding with our palms. Our only way is to move away from the body – that body keeps drawing us back with an exceptional kind of force like gravity, and all we need to do is move away from it, by touching and sliding our palms over solid surfaces. That is the only and exclusive goal of this part of the work. We continue to grope further, coming to the door of our apartment, we feel that surface which is considerably different from the wall, we feel a bit rougher nature of the woodwork, then we come to the doorknob, groping all the time; by no means lifting our hands up and ceasing to have contact with the surface we have been touching all the time with our palms. And most importantly, we must not stop moving under any circumstances; our palms must not stay in the same place for more than a moment.

It is necessary to say a little more about this strange place – which is gaining more in its reality as we keep moving further away from the body, and our mind gets filled up with information about that tangible path we have walked. Every inch, we are more and more in an extraordinary realm while being less and less in our bed. At some point, we will be completely devoid of any sense of the physical body, groping against the walls of something we think is our room. We are really in a unique void, in the dark. Still, that void has such a living potential, as if we were in a white noise area between radio stations – we really know that there are radio programs and radio stations all around us, but miraculously we are in the area between now – all we perceive is the tuning sound and white noise. Also, the feeling we have about ourselves is something extremely fantastic – the difference between this consciousness and the one that is waiting for us in bed is like between heavens and earth, like the difference between this consciousness now as you are reading these letters and the consciousness after drinking a liter of wine. As much as you feel alone in that void, there will be life all around you, and you will have a very clear knowledge of it. However, something will be missing. It is as if a large part of you is left in that body that is left lying – together with all the burden and a bag of thoughts that your body carries around all the time. You will be free as never before, not on your own, but rather outside of your own, far away from yourself in that void, groping and walking through all that wonderful and living darkness.

And in all that distancing from the bed where your sleeping body is, groping against the walls, you will be amazed when you touch a light switch that does not exist at all in your real room. But that switch will seem quite realistic – merely inviting you to stop there and study it well. Whatever you do, do not stop by any means, grope further, go over it, explore every new millimeter of the wall without stopping your exploration, divinely touching and sliding your palms over the new reality, always further. At one point, something wonderful will happen. A visual representation of the reality you have been touching all this time will begin to appear. Right then, the outlines appear, and then quite suddenly the whole room, or the hallway or the lobby of the apartment where you are – suddenly, a vision appears all around you. And you, completely taken aback by this marvelous moment, in a completely new world, will have very little time to feel it. Make sure you feel the atmosphere of that world well because you will return to your body very soon. Those are but moments and your first projection outside your body will always end up very quickly – in your body. New fantastic experiences that are brought back upon your return are countless. You are astonished and bewildered with what has happened to you. It is there exactly where our entire art will seem quite differently – precisely because it has really started working for the first time.

It is very useful to make a palpable tactile path – a route that you will always follow. For example, the moment you find yourself on the floor, you feel the nearest wall, then you slide your palms along it going towards the door, you come to the handle that you open. You go over the wall to the entrance hallway and come to the front door, then to the front door handle that you open and exit into the hallway of the building. With the same tactile action, without lifting your palms and fingers off the surface, you feel the handrail and go down the stairs to the exit of the building. This would be quite enough to follow until a vision emerges.

As much as tactile imagination is crucial for lucid dreaming and astral projections (especially for the Body of Light technique, which will be discussed later), visual one is rather redundant or even counterproductive. It is insisting on improving the ability of visualization that makes the technique of the Body of Light so often and so much misinterpreted that it is almost completely impossible to pull it out in the way as laid out in the books. There is one perfect and simple exercise here: run your fingers over a particular object with your eyes closed, without any desire to visualize it in your mind. Suppose you do it this way, focusing solely on tactile sensations your fingers transmit to the mind. In that case, you will notice something brilliant – you will get a picture in your mind automatically provoked, without any effort. This is such an important detail in the Body of Light technique, where insisting and focusing on tactile sensations will produce an image without visualization, with movement from a new perspective due to such mental provocation. The more you imagine tactile movement and feeling, the better your mind will visualize what you are touching. The more you engage in visualization, the worse picture your mind will yield. Therefore, touching walls and a tactile sense of their surface is what will result in having a vision in a lucid attempt. As long as you are trying to create an image – you will fail. The moment you start touching something without striving to see what, you will be able to see what you are touching.

The experience of returning to the body is always accompanied by a very special kind of fatigue, which is so characteristic of all lucid endeavors. It is a mixture of sweet intoxication, exhaustion, enthusiasm, euphoria, and electrical impulsiveness that is felt in every atom of your being. The whole next day will be spiced with these impressions, in fact, nothing will be the same after this, and your trajectory in our art will get a completely different vector now. Until now, every rocket fired from the ground inevitably fell down, but for the first time, now the projectile of your will has reached a sufficient speed to leave the shackles of the ground forever. From now on, your path will be paved with stars, and only the boundaries of your mind will determine the boundaries of the region in which you will reside.

It is necessary to summarize all the steps briefly as this skill easily turns into a set of completely random movements if we do not follow the instructions.

First and foremost, it is necessary to acquire the habit of waking up without moving and opening our eyes. Once we have succeeded and found ourselves waking up motionless and with our lids closed, we wait a few seconds and carefully observe the feeling that our body gives us, which starts to change drastically after a few seconds. It is as if someone has covered us with a warm blanket, or as if we feel that we are in a slightly different position than a moment ago. At that moment, we start with a phantasmagoric nodding of the head back and forth, imagining a miniature movement – almost as if we were performing it physically. That movement must be in thousands of millimeters, just enough to feel the movement of the head without even moving. As if the thought of moving leads to a sense of movement. Right then, the body will fall into a particular state of trance, which can be accompanied by various sensory phenomena, to which we should not pay any attention. All we need to do is increase the amplitude of the swing, and in one moment that is entirely intuitively felt, we fly completely out of that amplitude, falling to the floor. As soon as we have fallen onto the floor, we should start groping with our palms across the floor, moving away from the body. We will be in the dark, but let our progress through that darkness not be disturbed at all. We get to the walls; we start touching the walls by going over things, pictures, light switches, furniture, always moving away from the body. At some point, the vision will start to intensify, and we will find ourselves in a three-dimensional environment.

Finally, we will list one technique that skillfully bypasses sleep paralysis and the procedure of phantasmal movement. Once we have woken up motionless and with our eyes closed, we have to imagine us going away from the bed, groping on the walls along the same route, then going out of the room, and finally out of our apartment. In this technique, it is not important to precisely feel surface outlines under your palms or have a clear tactile experience. Instead, it is important to move away from your body quickly and steadily, as if we are groping in the dark like a sleeping beauty leaving the castle just before midnight. This technique is surprisingly successful in the final realization but also seemingly unsuccessful at the start of imagining touching and hurriedly moving away from the body. However, with every second that has passed, the experience becomes more and more possible with every meter we have travelled. At one point, the Aspirant will get stunned because he will turn up in an environment that he only imagined touching with his palms seconds before. The intensity of the vision will be the complete opposite of all that rapid and frantic distance from the body by the palpable action of his palms. The entire essence of this technique is in the emphasis on hurried removal from the body while quickly touching the walls. The Aspirant should hurry and walk away from his body, groping in the dark as if a fire broke out accompanied by a power-cut –he must find his way out of the building urgently.

This is all you need to know for now; now that we have set out clear beacons, let us get down to the details.

CONSTRUCTING A DREAM

Shaping the contours and scenarios of a dream is a very special branch in this art, which we have to describe in a little more detail. Although a lucid dream develops on its own after we have touched our way out of the body, such construction has flaws, which is that it has already been constructed in advance. It is difficult to go further, that is, deeper into a dream which was constructed by your reactive mind. The lucid dream becomes a projection right after we have started touching. With that touch, we get the knowledge and impressions from the very surface of the walls that create the whole world in our unconscious mind, together with the apartment, corridors, buildings, towns, and continents. There is a great trick – before we start with the whole procedure, an evening before, we decide and focus our attention to touch the wall of a completely different room. The moment we have started to touch the wall, after we slipped out of the body, with great astonishment, we will notice that now we are touching a completely different wall, which will be different in structure and shape from the one in our room. Here we come to one of the most important sleep laws, which is that it has been constructed long before we begin dreaming. By our Will, we will dream and touch another wall; the moment we feel the outlines of that wall with our palms, we create a scenario that corresponds to our projection at the same time. We can imagine feeling the walls of a spaceship, prehistoric cave, old Tibet temple, or the hotel where we last spent our summer vacation. It is important that we not create a projection of the change of location visually. We should get that belief through the relief of the walls and the tactile feeling, such as feeling the switches in the hotel room, the windows, or the door of a futuristic spaceship. This palpation is always and exclusively done inside the void when we separate from the body and fall off the bed – as a consequence of the rocking we did in sleep paralysis, which in turn is a consequence of being able to wake up without moving. Such groping results in the emergence of vision and the construction of a complete dream scenario sooner or later, in which we can now act at will and with which we can have full and lively interaction. But now is an excellent moment to discuss ways we can move out of the void which we got into after we had detached ourselves from the body with a phantom rocking motion or a somersault backward turn, depending on the method you have taken.

The first is one of my favorites, which always works so effectively and introduces an entirely random scenario at the same time. All that is needed in this technique is that once we have found ourselves in a void, we rub our palms as if we want to warm up; this rubbing should be decisive and impulsive as if we want to wash our hands with that void all around us. After a few seconds of rubbing our palms, we add up another movement, which now acts as an extra boost on a lucid trajectory. We then start blowing into our palms, rubbing them at the same time. Such action introduces another tactile sensation of air passing over our palms. It seems that our mind will simply be preoccupied with all these tactile sensations with this movement, and blowing into our palms like a magic brush, we will actually draw a dream scenario that will become more and more realistic and magical every second. With this method, it can happen that this blowing of a magic wind will start sculpting the shapes of a completely different city or area that we have never been to. That air that will pass over the rubbing palms will have an effect like rubbing a magic lamp – adorning the void with a spectacular vision for us to act and explore further.

The second way is very ingenious and is also based on tactile imagination. While we are in a void, imagine a train from the future passing by us at tremendous speed. This image must not be in a visual sense, it is enough just to know that such a train passes, the projection of which has already started engraving in your head as you are reading these words, so next time it is enough just to remember them and have a slight intention for a train to appear.

Now, imagine that train has its doors open while passing right next to you. At that moment, hold on tightly to the opening with your hands, imagining how that train is now carrying you away from your location in an extremely fast and brisk flight. You will feel a strong thrust and have the impression that you are moving at high speed; now, by touching and palpation, build your way into the train slowly, and you will initiate a sudden vision. This is a great way to travel in a dream because you can reach any destination in time and space with the same train, whether it is the past, the future, or distant worlds or planets. It is enough that you intend for that train to pick you up before attempting a lucid dream once you have rolled out of bed and found yourself in the void. You will often meet other passengers on that train traveling in a similar way; it is always such a wonderful occasion speaking to them and seeing where they travel. Maybe you can get off together at a station and a location they will mention – thus allowing your Selfness to direct you further into a dream and some inner quest you need to accomplish. These are all details that help you move inventively through the dream – allowing the Angel to project what he wants. In a lucid dream, his influence will be much more open than it is the case with the physical world where his message is limited to your perception of synchronicity, which can happen all the time around you, but you simply cannot be able to perceive it. Here, however, the dream is the material for his fiery will, forging divine armor to fit your size and your needs.

Once the vision has been materialized around you and the dream scenario has been formed, you will notice a completely different way of functioning of your consciousness, which has changed as much as the whole world around you has changed; that wonderful feeling when you find yourself in the three-dimensional ambiance of a dream is the most magnificent thing that affects a practitioner's soul, and as days after your first experience keep passing, you will be equally and intensely impressed by that experience. Even after years of practice, that situation when the outlines of a dream materialize around you remains equally enticing and a magnificent occurrence. Sometimes, observing that beautiful ambiance is all that is enough for me to experience. Very often, instead of fulfilling the action plan I envisioned, I completely change the route and simply observe that ambiance without going anywhere, like a mountaineer who climbed to the top of a mountain and now silently observing the infinity of the horizon, enjoying every second of that view. Unfortunately, such admiration usually lasts only a few moments. Without movement and plan, the dream collapses quickly, and I return to the body. But even so, such silent enjoyment of the inner landscape is often worthy of that return.

Strengthening a Dream

Once the dream has been constructed, and we found ourselves in a three-dimensional environment, it is necessary to do another very important thing, which is to strengthen the foundations of the built dream. The dream in which we find ourselves conscious is very unstable, and it is necessary to carry out specific procedures that will ensure that we walk on it safely and survive long enough for all this to make sense. If we skip this step, a lucid dream will rarely last longer than a minute, in addition to the fact that the imprint of a dream in our mind will be pale, vague, and of very low intensity. Therefore, the first thing a practitioner should do when a vision is formed is to strengthen the dream frame. There are a couple of extremely powerful and simple instructions on how to do this.

The first is certainly touching; we need to move so much to feel every possible detail on and around us. Let us start by touching our whole body – we slide our palms going over the shoulders, head, neck, chest, abdomen, and finally the legs. Then we go to the floor, passing over all the details. We go over every pebble we come across with our fingers. This probing and exploring of details have a penetrating effect on the radiance of astral vision, which will amplify its imprint in our minds in less than 10 seconds in such a way that we will not be able to distinguish from the imprint given to us by the physical eyes in this plane. Also, it is crucial that we actively stare at everything we touch. Such a view must not linger on a single place for more than a moment. We must explore ourselves and our surroundings to the extreme, both by touch and gaze. This cannot be exaggerated; in fact, it can only be done insufficiently persistently, which will always result in weakened dreams and quicker return home. Time is the most precious element in a dream, and here the practitioner is on a seesaw – he must both spend time strengthening and stabilizing a dream so that he can spend more of that time within that same dream. There is significant discomfort in practitioners about this step, who often skip it thinking they will spear the time for some more exciting endeavors, which will be rarely achieved. Without sufficient clarity of the vision, the reactive mind now sees the Aspirant as a foreign body, or some weak or infected part, and is looking for a way to remove him from the tissue of a dream as soon as possible. Once achieved, the feeling of complete clarity is felt plainly and easily, and there should be no indication of anything other than personal conviction and the feeling that clarity is sufficient and that one can progress deeper in a dream. Such a feeling is infallible, and it will be implanted in the practitioner after the first few times of strengthening the dream.

The second method is more of an idea and a principle that explains how we should move through the dream – it is always through action and progress, never stagnation. Such stagnation is fatal; it must neither be of a mental kind – which is perhaps the most destructive to persisting in a dream, the moment when we have no plan of action and when we simply dwell in a dream without any idea of where to go next, nor the physical one – when we simply stop in a dream or hold on looking at something for a few seconds. The stagnation in observation is exceedingly disastrous. This is crucial for any further and more serious dream research – our gaze should never be focused on one point, but continuously and always in motion, staring at everything – just the way our eyes behave during the REM phase. The gaze must always slide and pass over things; any retention of sight leads to the dissolution of the vision. It is like the surface tension allowing the muscles to move on the surface of the water. They must always move so as not to fall under the surface. Any longer holding the gaze on any detail leads to a phenomenon that should definitely be experienced by practitioners – the vision will start to twist, break and very quickly, if we do not move the gaze, we will return to the body, now observing the blackness of the eyelids, without any loss of consciousness. This is an equally valuable experience that must be obtained in order to gain confidence in the importance of constant movement in a dream. Such movement is threefold:

1. We must move through mental action, that is, we have to design a plan of action that is best established before we even try a lucid dream the night before. Initially, it can be expressed through 2 or 3 points that a practitioner will remember, or better yet, write it on a piece of paper that will be left next to the bed or under the pillow, and as soon as one point has been accomplished, the next one is to follow. For example, the first point may be projecting oneself inside a futuristic train that will take you to a village at the top of the Himalayas. The second point will be getting off the train and sledding down the slopes of the Himalayas. Of course, the sled will be created as soon as you get off the train by making a projection and action plan before the lucid experience itself. The third point will be an attempt to transmute into the shape of an eagle.

2. We must move physically; we must not stand in one place unless a dream is strengthened to such an extent that it can withstand such stagnation. This is, of course, enhanced by time and experience.

3. We must move our gaze; we have to look around all over our field of vision. Such shifting of the gaze should not be aggressive and fast but light and steady. The trajectory of such a look is always in spirals and patterns along the vision field, completely relaxed, without any focusing. In this regard, one of the fastest ways to return to the body, if at any time we feel the need to do so, is to move the index finger or palm about 10 centimeters away from the level of our eyes and persistently focus the gaze on a single point. This results in an almost immediate return to the body, in no more than a few seconds.

Therefore, active, lively, and curious movement in a dream is a condition for maintaining our consciousness in an environment of dormant nature. As long as we keep moving, we equally progress through a dream and strengthen it.

The third method is to intentionally fixate our look at a nearby thing, preferably a finger of one hand, and keep staring until the dream begins to fall apart. That feeling is very specific and is very easy to determine once we have carried it out. There is a special kind of sensation that tells us that we will return to the body. In addition to the fact that the dream begins melting and the vision disintegrating, we are equally affected by a specific change of consciousness that occurs at the same time. In this case, we have to get right to that point, by no means beyond it. This usually takes no more than a few seconds before the vision begins to tremble and weaken. When this has happened, what is needed is to abruptly turn our gaze to a completely different side, as far away from the fixed place as possible, moving your head vigorously to the side and fixating your gaze on something else. This drastic change of focus and object of interest seems to have such a purifying effect on the vision, which now appears solid and clear as never before. In other words, an effect is achieved when we look with a binocular with an object that is out of focus, and then, as we move the eyepiece, we suddenly see a crystal clear object of our attention in focus. Before that, a completely vague cloud was observed, and now a planet with quite clear contours is in front of us. This technique carries the danger of over-focusing, which would result in a complete collapse of the dream and return to the body. The personal experience will certainly bear fruit and inform the Aspirant to such an extent that he will intuitively feel the right time to look away.

Finally, there is one form of sleep strengthening, which is an exceptional circumstance. It is the art of translocation, that is, a sudden change of a dream scenario also called teleportation, which has its own laws of when and how it is performed. In the same way, the diversion of the fixed gaze brings stability and clarity to the dream (as in the previous method), so the diversion and displacement from the dream scene also, paradoxically though, brings complete peace and clarity to the new vision. This last method will be explained in detail a few lines later, in the section dedicated to the ability to translocate, i.e., teleport.

The return to reality is a unique circumstance that has its own laws, and it is necessary to go through it consciously and with care. Upon returning to the body, awareness changes, and if the practitioner is attentive enough, he will notice a valuable lesson by observing such a change. Returning to the real world initially brings disappointment and a halt in the enthusiasm that is always so characteristic of a lucid experience. However, after the first few experiences, the practitioner will notice that the observation to which the dream is transformed, giving way to the blackness of eyelids, is very beneficial while not losing consciousness. Such a return to the waking state is part of the same whole being of the

Aspirant, and it would be unfair to reject that period just because it prevents us from exploring dreams further and deeper. The dream contains the value in its entirety, with both frameworks that need to be conscious and carefully followed, by no means accidentally or as a consequence of luck. Both the beginning and end of a dream must be awaited like a goddess, carefully and by no means timidly, with attention and delight, by no means randomly wandering around.

The practitioner will notice that the urge to return to physical reality is a shadow that will accompany him during every moment of his lucid experiences, and that shadow will never stop stalking him. Increasing the clarity of a dream is one of the most effective ways to alleviate this urge, but it certainly cannot wholly deprive it. There is another good trick – during the last moments of a dream scene that will begin to disintegrate, we find an object that is at hand, anything that we can touch and hold on to that object, we feel our palms across it in the same way we have created our vision by touching. This will be like an anchor that prevents our boat from wandering before the onset of a terrible storm. We must do our best to hold on to this lighthouse in this calamity and hurricane of awakening. It is even better if our palms are crossed over that object, just as we did initially in the void, invoking vision. There is a certain chance that the whole urge to return to waking consciousness will pass and that we will still be in the dream scene, holding on to that object. After this, you should immediately increase the clarity of a dream until the maximum intensity of vision has been achieved, and only then to continue with the experience.

SLEEP INTERUPTION

Sleep interruption is one of the most suitable aid that initiates an ideal "sweet spot" for entering the lucid dream. It is like a scouting team, which is to prepare the whole strategy able to win the whole war with a single piece of information. Suppose we pay attention to the sleep diagram once again. In that case, we will notice that the REM phase is the longest before awakening. It lasts approximately 5 to 6 hours after going to bed, or to be more precise – after falling asleep. We should definitely add another 15 minutes to that time – as long it takes to start the process of falling asleep. Our brain has a phenomenal mechanism that continues the sleep phase at the spot where we have left off, even after we wake up. That is to say, once we wake up during the REM phase, and after we went back to bed again, we will enter the same REM phase, without losing 90 minutes of nREM nothingness in which there is no oneiric activity. Also, the process of falling asleep is much faster, so once we have gone back to bed after waking up and going to the toilet, we will easily fall asleep again and enter directly into the dream phase – it is even possible to continue the dream from where we interrupted it, like after a pause while watching a movie. This beautiful mechanism exerts such violent pressure towards our goal – all it takes is to set the alarm to go off 5 to 6 hours after we went to bed; sometimes it should be shorter, sometimes longer, but this time window should be our approximate target. With more experience, we will define our ideal personal moment much more precisely to be able to apply this as successful as possible. After an alarm clock wakes us up, after 5 or 6 hours of sleep, a very important instruction is to follow. We have to get out of bed and stay out of it for about 15 minutes to half an hour. We can go to the toilet, turn on the computer and check emails, we are free to go out on the terrace and breathe fresh air, but whatever we do, we do it out of bed. That intention to get out of the area that has been so vilely constraining us in the most perfidious type of prison has a pervasive effect on success in lucid dreaming. After about 15 minutes, we will go back to bed and repeat the affirmation that we will wake up without moving and opening our eyes. This time, its path to our unconscious mind is much shorter and easier to accomplish, freed by a frigid nREM phase that so vilely erases all our intentions and desires and brings a dream that suits our reactive mind. We should not exaggerate this – we need not be making an affirmation for more than 5 minutes. We then have to fall asleep; the next awakening should be natural, and we will notice how much more frequent and successful awakening without moving is if we take this break. It is a quantitative gain; in terms of quality, getting into sleep paralysis and rolling out of bed with an imaginary movement is incomparably more successful than when the affirmation is made just before bedtime. It is a very good idea to drink a glass of water after the first awakening with an alarm so that the discomfort in the bladder creates a shallow sleep, which is so suitable for entering a lucid dream. With this method, the second awakening, which is always without an alarm, will be permeated by a particular dose of drowsiness and a special kind of faintness – as if our brain was swimming in the fluid of sleep and we can barely keep our attention, you will almost feel pressure in the head and have headaches from so much drowsiness. This is exactly what we need, this swimming of the mind in a pond of unconscious nature sculpting a dream and creating an ideal polygon for lucid dreaming. There is only one danger that happens to beginners too often; it is insomnia, which can occur after we get up for the first time with an alarm, and once we went back to sleep. After making an affirmation that we will wake up without moving and opening our eyes, it is quite possible that we will not be able to fall asleep again, no matter how hard we try. Even more, we will be awake like never before. Our unconscious nature finds a way to hinder us on our inner journey once and again, just as it did create fear in sleep paralysis, and instead of covering us with drowsiness and unwillingness to do anything consciously or have the strength for such endeavors, it now sets an opposite trap – partly because of the euphoria and anticipation of a lucid dream – now our alertness rises to such a level that we are so awake, with no chance of falling asleep. What is extremely important, if we find ourselves in this kind of insomnia, is to lie consciously without a single move of the body at any cost. We will notice that our own body dares and ridicules us, making every inch of us itch to the point that staying in one position is completely impossible. But we have to persevere in this and passively wait for the body to fall asleep. This insomnia will be dominant in more introverted people during the first few attempts. Still, like any other artificial creation of our unconscious mind, it will subside with time and patience – the only weapons to which the reactive mind has no counterparts. Also, a slight squeeze on the eyeballs and a subtle shift of gaze upward, looking toward the scalp, toward the center of the skull, does wonders and puts many people to sleep in a few seconds, so this technique can ideally be applied in this place too.

By no means should you try for 2 days in a row, if you are attempting the method of interrupting sleep after 5 to 6 hours. If you choose this method, which multiplies the chances of success, you should not try more than 3 nights per week. It is best not to set predetermined days for attempts at lucid dreaming, for every routine leads to the involvement of the reactive mind and the creation of immunity and a strategy by which it will act against us; let your attempts be spontaneous and free from any pre-arranged schedule. A framed procedure will be much needed to persevere in the technique of moving the head and in those small steps after we have left the body. This is where we need to stick to military discipline, and we will witness that in those moments, as our minds will sway like a leaf in a chaotic storm of unconsciousness.

Under no circumstances should the Aspirant stay in bed when applying sleep interruption, waiting for the desired time to pass. Indeed, this is the gravest mistake. You must give your own mind a false incentive to declare another temporary victory. It must conclude that you are ready to meet another basic need of life and that now, handing over its victory, you are stepping into the day, having reconciled with the fact that you will walk into its domain once again in the evening.

ALARM AID

One technique has become possible with the development of technology in particular and with the progress of applications that we can find on smart devices, mainly phones. It is a particular use of an alarm that will wake us up as gently as to stop dreaming, but not enough to move our body and open our eyes. This is a remarkable kind of aid that can yield a complete lucid experience from the start. Still, the whole procedure of entering lucid dreaming using other techniques in this book should not be neglected. It has to be a sort of aid and by no means an excuse not to learn the full procedure in all its aspects. The achievement we long for is for the Aspirant to have a lucid dream at least 2 days a week with the method of his choice without any special aids, except his will and dedication. This shortcut facilitates the whole process for sure, and we explain it primarily as a means to feel the spell of true projection, by no means to replace the system that is already in place.

The first thing to find is an application that has the option of setting the duration of the alarm in seconds, after which it will turn itself off. There are so many different programs; I found an Android app called "Alarm Clock Xtreme", which allowed me to enter sleep paralysis from day one, unmistakably. It is possible to set the correct number of seconds, after which the alarm will go off without touching it. Also, you need to allocate a certain sound for the alarm that should not have been used earlier to wake up, nor should there be any sound at all that is familiar to you or you are fond of. I chose the sound of submarine sonar; it is so specific that every time I hear it, I enter the mode of preparation for lucid activity.

It should also be noted that the sound must not be intrusive or aggressive so as not to provoke and urge us to get up and turn off the alarm – which is exactly what we are trying to avoid with this method. All the catch is to state the affirmation before going to bed that "as soon as I have heard the alarm, I will remember to remain motionless with my eyes closed". The emphasis is on the words "as soon as I have heard" and "I will remember", which implant a certain outcome to be realized with the first sounds of the alarm. Next, we set the alarm to turn itself off, i.e. to dismiss itself after 10 seconds, and, finally, set the time for the alarm to turn itself on – ideally 45 minutes before we normally wake up, or optimally between 5 to 6 hours after going to bed. Just in case, we can turn on a regular alarm within the same or another application that will wake us up at the time we need to get up, to be calm and relaxed and without fear of being late for work. Such fear or insecurity that we will not wake up when we need it for work could negatively affect the depth of our sleep because in that case, we would stay alert and thus prevent the first alarm, which is set for lucid dreaming, to wake us up in an ideal state for a lucid experiment. It is important not to keep your mobile phone nearby but at the end of the room, which will further prevent the reflex of moving and turning off the alarm by hand. This small detail is so important that it can largely affect the overall success of not moving the body.

After repeating the affirmation for a few minutes, all it takes now is to fall asleep. You will be amazed that the next thing you remember is a sound that resonates just enough to wake you up yet to keep you still and your eyes closed. By the time you realize what has happened, the alarm is already gone, leaving you in complete silence and stillness with your motionless body. Stay in that position and, soon, you will feel peculiar tingling or a very strange feeling of warmth that now overwhelms your entire body – all this is an indication that you are slipping into a state of sleep paralysis unmistakably. It is quite possible that the first few times you will be so excited that you will suffocate sleep paralysis with your excessive alertness, but after a couple of successful attempts, you will come to a state where all you have to do now is phantasmal movement and very quickly slip out of your body. It is important to understand that all lucid dreaming techniques require a lot rather than a little sleep. Beginners think that waking up as early as possible and sleeping as little as possible increases the chances of success, but in fact, it is the other way round. The more you sleep, the longer and shallower your REM phase will be. It is usually enough to set the alarm half an hour before you normally wake up. Each Aspirant has a time window of their own to pick. He will learn about it himself by the method of trial and error. Even if he wakes up with a physical movement or with his eyes opened, the Aspirant must always get used to doing and enduring performing a phantasmal movement for a full minute, not less than that. You will be surprised how many beautiful projections you will make just a few seconds before the end of single minute, almost when you are sure that you are so awake that they will not summon anything. Then, while preparing to get up and give up, all of a sudden, you start having sound hallucinations or the impression that your body is twisting or falling through the floor. The variants are endless, but there is only one thing that matters – to make sure that the duration of a phantasmal movement lasts for an entire minute, whether you managed to wake up without moving or not, whether you managed to enter sleep paralysis at once or you have the feeling that you are awake like never before. You can never know at what point the separation mechanism will commence.

FOCUS SHIFTING

This extremely effective method for lucid dreaming consists of a particular mix of sleep interruption and a very special type of phantasmal movement. Nevertheless, one should know that the success of this technique is almost impossible if it is not done after 4 to 6 hours of sleep – when the REM phase is longer, with nREM being shallow and weak. The technique itself is a variant of Buddhist meditation on the layers of Selfhood, which is also an excellent variant of Yoga Nidra. However, it is modified to such an extent that it works fantastically, and it has great success on the appearance of lucidity in sleep. Its creator is my friend and dear colleague Gary – better known on the internet as Cosmiciron. It is a modern lucid dreaming technique, easy to learn, and highly effective. He developed this technique in 2011 in order to teach lucid dreaming to fellow dreamers on a Chinese forum. The first written version of the technique was published under the title "太玄功", which literally translates to "a very mysterious technique". This is rather fitting because, at the time, no one had the faintest idea why it worked. Despite this lack of theory, the feedback on the technique was overwhelmingly positive.

The first step is to set the alarm to wake us up between 4 to 6 hours of sleep. Then, after the alarm has gone off, we get up and leave our bed, staying awake for about 10 minutes. Then go back to bed in a sleeping position and do a specific phantasmal movement – but in a very special way. Here we do not imagine moving the head or any part of the body at all. We shift the focus of our attention between the senses of sight, hearing and touch every 10 to 20 seconds. Just keep your attention on what you see for 10 to 20 seconds. It is very important that you need not see anything except the blackness of the eyelids. There is no point at all to provoke anything except to focus passively on your sight solely. After 10 to 20 seconds, your attention moves to your hearing quickly and aggressively. During that time, it should be focused on what you hear only. Even if you do not hear anything special, you still pay attention passively and wait for the audio perception. Finally, after 10 to 20 seconds, shift your attention to the sense of touch in the same way – aggressively and decisively, and concentrate on everything your body is feeling by touch. Feel the blanket over you, the bed below you, the arms, the legs, the surface of the pillow, and the pajamas for sleeping.

This movement of perception and focus shifting is experienced as a very specific mental pressure, where the Aspirant feels slight spinning, or dizzying, a very special type of pressure on his subtle body, with a strong sense of shifting from one sense to another. That focus shifting is like a mixture of pleasure and lull as if it were an updated way of rocking the soul in a cradle, like hushing our mind in a more advanced way. On the one hand, aggressive and decisive changing of focus from one sense to another acts like rocking and putting the body to sleep, while on the other hand, it awakens and shakes the mind and prepares a projection mechanism soon to commence. The whole secret of this simple technique is in displacement and in the feeling of pressure and shifting of our focus that this change of senses causes. You can almost really feel the whirl as you change focus from one sense to another – like a divine carousel or roller coaster, which will take your mind into a lucid dream. And when attention has been anchored and accustomed to a particular sense, we change our focus to another, boosting the pressure inflicted on our minds with such a shift of attention. It is very important to remember that the whole essence of this technique is in that pressure that almost physically feels like a movement, at that very moment when attention switches from one sense to another. Such a shift of focus of the mind from one sense to another must be carried out decisively, strongly and aggressively, followed by completely passive observation of the image, sound or touch, depending on the sense focusing will bring you.

The best sequence is visual – auditory – tactile, but the Aspirant can reverse it himself and determine the order that best suits him and is better for achieving success. After 5 minutes of performing cycles and shifting the focus of attention to different senses, all it takes is to fall asleep as soon as possible, because all it took was just that shift of consciousness from one sense to another, now triggering a hurricane that would flare up inside sleep like a breeze. What is now expected and most likely to happen is the following:

First, dreams will be extremely vivid and clear, with many emotional and dramatic scenes. At some point, you will likely become aware that it is a dream. In other words, this technique allows for passive lucidity in our dreams. If this happens, the Aspirant should strengthen the dream as soon as possible, as explained in detail earlier, and then continue with his exploration. The Aspirant will witness that the nature of the dream following the focus shifting technique will always be much clearer and richer than ordinary dreaming. In the case of lucidity, he will notice that this dream is much firmer and easier to control than entering the sleep directly, without losing consciousness – through the void and sleep paralysis.

The second thing, which is the most common, is false awakening. In fact, after this method, the vast majority of awakenings are not in this reality at all. We can witness that we are seeing a clock that looks different after waking up or radiating a different color than it really is. The barking of a neighbor's dog, even though there is no dog in the building at all, can wake us up, or we can wake up in a bed where we have not fallen asleep in the first place. As soon as something like this has happened, the Aspirant should resort to phantasmal movement at once, which in this case will be very easy to do. He will roll out of bed and move on with the procedure of creating astral reality and image, all in a way we have already had elaborated on in detail.

The effectiveness of this technique is tremendous, with success in lucid dreaming achieved after the first attempt. Even in the case of the absence of lucid dreaming, this technique will always result in fantastic progress and bring about something new in the dreaming experience. One can say that all the failure in applying this technique is not in the technique itself but in the failure of the

Aspirant to realize that after waking up, he is all the time in sleeping paralysis, lucid dream, or in a state of false awakenings (in most of the cases.) Of all the techniques I know, this technique is the best for beginners by far and those who want to experience a lucid dream for the first time.

It is extremely important to understand that during this technique, there is nothing of active pursuit of lucid dreaming, or anything other than a simple and clear shift of focus from one sense to another – 10 to 20 seconds with each of the 3 senses, with a total cycle duration of no more than 5 minutes – and nothing more or other than this. After that, it is necessary to fall asleep completely normally, without any additional efforts to accelerate lucid dreams. Your lucidity is already greatly provoked by this vortex and shift of focus and the whole mechanism is set in motion when you have completed the whole cycle. All you have to do then is do nothing more. This is crucial for the further course of action, and as time goes on, the chances of achieving a lucid dream are higher.

Also, any awakening after this technique, even after a pronounced movement and opening of the eyes, is much closer to a lucid state than any other awakening. Even if none of the above has come true upon awakening after this technique, all that is needed for the Aspirant is to stay still for a few seconds and start with the phantasmal movement. He will notice that the success of sleep paralysis has doubled after this method, at least. It can be applied after saying the affirmation that we shall stay motionless without opening our eyes as soon as we have woken up, thus multiplying the chances of our success. This technique has a unique sleep mechanism within itself, so it is great for fighting insomnia – perhaps the fiercest enemy of lucid dreaming, especially when we use the "wake back to bad" method.

The movement of focus shifting from one sense to another is actually a younger relative to full phantasmal movement and is definitely one of the favorite things I suggest to beginners. Exceptional results and the percentage of success at the first attempt are always great motivators for their further work. But, like any method, it has its drawbacks. After some time, there comes a period when it stops working. The Aspirant should take a short break and do other techniques listed in this book when this happens. The immunity that the mind creates against all techniques is a universal mechanism imposed by all methods, and no matter how successful and easy they are for our souls, eventually they will stop working sooner or later. Therefore, the importance of movement in lucid dreaming as an idea has once again shown its superiority to this whole art. In addition to having to move within a dream, having to have an idea guiding us and a clearly defined plan of action, having to move our eyes and never fix our gaze at the same point for even a moment, we need to have movement in techniques as well. We always have to work and change methods, even those where we initially think we have finally found something that is completely adapted to our being. After the first ten or even a hundred consecutive successful projections, eventually, there will be a dry period when nothing can be pulled off. Therefore, we always have to change the approach and fine-tune our techniques, constantly adding new elements. The art of lucid dreaming is the art of great improvisation. The only constant that maintains success in lucidity is change, and it is one of the laws in astral research that the Aspirant must understand and accept even before he can achieve full success in his first lucid dream. He must know that every immediate success, even completely accidental, is doomed to be failure if he blindly adheres to it without upgrading it.

The change of focus from one sense to another, in a similar way to the constant change of position and gaze necessary to maintain lucid dream, is strikingly similar to the cycle of my friend Michael Raduga – who cherishes the same idea of deliberately changing techniques every 20 seconds. We can conclude that the idea of a sudden change and transition of our attention to a particular sense or a body position in sleep, eye movements and gazing, is extremely important for all lucid endeavors.

My personal research into this technique relates to its use in an already realized lucid dream rather than triggering a lucid experience itself. For example, suppose that we focus intensely on all the senses at once in a lucid dream or sleep paralysis. In that case, this is like a divine stimulus to our mind, introducing it into peculiar dimensions that keep me amazed even today. However, when I met my friend Gary and got familiar with his variant of this technique, it never crossed my mind that this technique could serve to initiate a lucid dream in such a phenomenal way, which he, better known as *Cosmiciron*, brilliantly constructed and explained. In my case, the variant of this method served to prolong lucid dreams drastically and start the mechanism of dreaming within a dream that I still do not have clear methodological constants for. All of that is still in an experimental phase, which I hope to publish in due time. Using this technique in this way is quite a tricky process, but if performed well, it enables me to have lucid experiences that last from a few hours to a full day, even more.

SHORTCUTS AND OBSTACLES

1.

The first thing we could come across is a specific change in consciousness that happens the first few seconds after we wake up, remaining motionless. Those few seconds before we start moving our head lead to a huge change in consciousness containing elements of an autoimmune reaction to this whole thing, and often these elements do not hesitate to do anything needed to bring us back into the body. In fact, the whole lucid experience is all that our being does not want. Not because it thinks it is bad, but because it is not familiar with it. As the fear of water, in the same way, but immeasurably times stronger, there will be fear of a completely different world, a completely different reality, and completely different consciousness. For your being, for your mind, this experience will be completely similar to the experience of dying, to which we have no attitude because we absolutely do not know what it is. Our reactive mind has subordinated the whole dream and the mechanism of sleep to the benefit of our being, so now the consciousness in the dream is an intruder towards which it will have no mercy. The ways in which it will try to bring consciousness back under the auspices of our body are so cunning and varied that we could write a separate book on it, which we certainly have neither the time nor the place for here. However, the point is to know that every second of experience in a lucid dream is actually a struggle not to go back to the body, and our reactive mind will now turn you against itself with the same creativity with which it has been constructing our sweet dreams for years, setting traps and obstacles after which you will look disappointedly at the blackness of the eyelids instead of at the diversity of the astral landscape.

2.

The second is undoubtedly the appearance of fear in the phase of sleep paralysis. This is the first line of soldiers sent by our mind to distract us from all this before we even come out of the body. Always keep in mind that you are a stranger to that mind as long as you think about the same mind. The moment you stop thinking about it, then your old mother is satisfied, always thinking of her child to be well-fed and put to sleep. Nevertheless, what the mind wants is for you to be within its reach ultimately. Not so that it can control you, but for it to be able to take care of you, look after you, always having you just for itself. The Neophyte must understand this mechanism because the difference in perception determines the ability to dive into sleep. The depth of sleep is not achieved by a ritual or technique, but exclusively by understanding the mechanism of the mind by which it is constructed, on a wholly archetypal and primordial plane. Fear is the first and strongest whip of a great mother to make her child stay in the room and finally fall asleep. This fear, which occurs almost automatically when we enter a state of sleep paralysis, already after the first few seconds of immobility after waking up, is the most terrifying and creepy thing an Aspirant can feel on his skin. Especially when this phenomenon is accompanied by the nature of the void in which we shall soon find ourselves, they act with equal force on the Aspirant's mind like the most terrible nightmare.

But such fear is always and exclusively possible when we have stagnation in projection, that is, when we do not have a clear plan and intention to move away from our body. And the closer we are to the body, the greater and more paralyzing the fear will be; as we keep going away from the body by groping, so the fear will disappear the way the effect of gravity weakens once a rocket has been launched. At the same time, one of the characteristics of a lucid dream is that the moment a vision and a dream scenario appears, the fear disappears the same moment as if wiped off. In fact, fear almost always occurs during sleep paralysis – when we are still in the body, never during a full astral experience. When it appears, it is only an indication that we are on the right path and that we now need to get out of that "middle state" with intensive action in which we are neither awake nor asleep. And the way out is with a phantom movement, little by little as if we want to get out of the quicksand and break away from the sticky slime that keeps us chained to a sleeping body in bed. Get out of bed, get away from your body, little by little, keep on going away; the act of moving your head is the only thing you need and which you need to dedicate yourself to completely. This is a very simple instruction but crucial to success. Your subconscious does not want enlightenment; it does not want the light of knowledge. It just wants you to feel safe in the dream that it has constructed just for you so devot-edly. It wants you only for itself; it does not want change; it does not want the truth; it does not want anything but you. Your bed is a mental projection of security, and it is nothing but a shadow that fights frantically for every second of your unconscious and your dormant nature. As much as a dream is a mold for the Will, so is the darkness and paralysis of sleep the plasticine that our shadow plays with, always making what we are afraid of, sculpting that form of horror and terror in a unique way, just because we deviated from the path. And instead of moving away from the body with the tactile imagination of touching, we are now standing still let-ting fear touch us, sting and frighten us in a way only our mind is aware of – knowing every nightmare dreamt of and every phobia of ours – because, in the end – or mind is what has constructed them.

3.

It is very important not to try for two days in a row. This is one of the biggest causes of failure, especially when the first couple of successful lucid dreams happen, then a dry period follows very quickly when we are really unable to accomplish anything. This is partly because the mechanism of dreaming has been disrupted, and we have violently penetrated parts of sleep by declaring war on our reactive mind, which now tries to think of the ways to take us back from mad and adolescent tendency to separate from the only true parent – our mind. If we try day after day, the dream cycle will shift, and we will enter a period when it is impossible to reach the same circumstances and conditions that are responsible for the REM phase. A similar thing happens if we go to bed late for two days in a row. There is a well-known problem of "replacing day for night" when we are rested during the day, but as we do not have an opportunity to get any sleep in the evening. Nights with insomnia will follow, which is further intensified by our neurosis and thoughts after going to bed already calling for insomnia.

Therefore, the very important thing is to allow one day of natural awakening and natural sleep after each attempt at lucidity, letting our mind seemingly take the lead in this match. It is a tactical retreat, a deliberate slow-down to make the opponent think it is closer to us and speed up the pace to catch up, increasing our adversary's chances of making a crucial mistake.

4.

Late meals and consuming water before bed can be a major cause of poor sleep, leading to a discordant proportion of nREM and REM phases. In fact, any significant awakening between REM phases affects the duration and quality of the REM phases negatively and the waking part of our lives as well, turning it into a vicious circle. There is one very simple solution that requires refraining from eating or drinking water 2 hours before going to bed. It is a very bad habit to drink water just before bedtime, partly because the water will soon cause a tendency to urinate, which either weakens sleep or leads to waking up too often. Preventing food and drink intake 2 hours before bedtime in lucid work sometimes makes the difference between complete success and the worst and ultimate failure; cases of people where this change only greatly facilitated lucid consciousness already on the first attempt are numerous. It should be emphasized that this thing significantly increases the chance of achieving a lucid dream, but it is by no means a condition for success. Only when all the mechanisms have been launched, including the diet and hydration regime, which are certainly very important, the projection is ensured and guaranteed. What we should be worried about is that slippery ground onto which our neurosis pushes us; simply, it is so easy to omit and overlook all these points for completely mundane reasons, and even though we are sure that we have constructed everything well, it can always happen that we have overlooked or missed just one or more points, sometimes wholly forgetting what we have to do anyway.

5.

During the first couple of successful motionless awakenings without opening our eyes, the level of euphoria will often completely prevent going back to sleep. Even if the mechanism of phantom head movement has been done for a whole minute to two, absolutely nothing will happen. We are simply so excited that mental euphoria has had the same effect on the mind as to any physical movement or eyelid opening – in other words, it has awakened us and brought us back to the Beta phase of brain activity. There is such a perfect and simple aid here, which can actually be applied whenever we awake with movement or even remain motionless but with a great deal of mental activity and euphoria. This is the identical action we described in the chapter on scrying; slight, almost imperceptible squeezing of the eyeballs, imagining looking back toward the center of the skull produces a special feeling of drowsiness, something like mental yawning, which has a remarkable effect on our mind when performed in the period after waking up, and in just a few seconds, brings us back into a state of extreme drowsiness. Such an act should never last more than a few seconds – even a second more, and we can completely fall into the oblivion of sleep. This is a kind of a seesaw that multiplies our chance of success of the subsequent phantom movement when mastered well. Personally, I always take this step no matter how close to success I am; this eye movement and, more precisely, that mental attitude is crucial in obtaining visions, which, when carried out by the Aspirant, can bring crystal clear images even during the fully awake state, in just a few seconds.

Another particularly good way to speed up the mechanism of sleep paralysis is to simply pretend we are sleeping in the first few seconds after waking up and stay still, deceiving our own mind. Imagine that falling down, falling through the floor, into the dark bottom of dormant reality, welcoming you so warmly. Pretend that this is precisely what is happening; imagine for a moment that feeling of warmth of the unconscious luring you down, deeper and deeper, below you, sinking toward that warm and pleasant depth. After a few seconds of doing this, we can start the phantom movement of our head.

6.

The need for visualization is an old, good foe of everything we want to achieve here. No visualization or construction of mental images is necessary; on the contrary – they significantly reduce our chances to succeed. All that is needed is primarily tactile, not visual imagination. What we need is to imagine and feel the movement, so you shall not imagine a single image until the very lucid dream. Vision will come by itself, the moment you bring your mind into a state in which it will naturally talk to you in images. However, until you have left your body, visualization is entirely redundant. The whole concept of Western ceremonial magic is rather based on this ability, which really has no standpoint in the technique of lucid dreaming. It can be said that the endless queues of practitioners waiting in line for an astral projection are so long because the whole mechanism has been established upon utterly wrong assumptions and strategies. In fact, all rituals have a completely different effect once they have been performed in a dream when their effect gets boosted and energized to the extreme. Whenever practitioners cite "Liber O vel Manus et Sagittae" as a method of rising on the planes, it simply cannot help but evoke sadness and compassion in me for all those people who keep endlessly trying something that absolutely should not be done from the physical plane, nor does such performance bring anything but an exercise in basic visualization, and really nothing more than that. If this instruction from "Liber O" is applied from this plane, it looks like a fairy tale, like a journey of imagination, and it really has nothing to do with discovering higher and deeper spheres that are so concrete and tangible. But, if the Aspirant embraces this instruction in a lucid dream precisely, once he has already reached it, then this is the most sublime instruction possible. There is nothing more penetrating for human consciousness than the desire to go "up" in a dream, and it will certainly be one of the experiences that the Aspirant has remembered for the rest of his life. Indeed, if the rising on the plane, as stated in Liber "O," is derived from a lucid dream or from certain places in the dream which will be discussed later, then the whole exercise radiates millions of suns brighter.

7.

There is one completely incomprehensible obstacle that happens with all practitioners, and that is the tendency to shorten the performance of a phantom movement by a whole minute, or do something else, or simply give up going back to sleep. Shortening the performance of this movement is certainly one of the key factors that prevent us from penetrating a conscious dream. Right next to it, there is a difficulty in recognizing that we are in sleep paralysis; unfortunately, this knowledge is often obtained once we have given up and came back to wakefulness, which will be too late. Simply, we will really begin to face all the circumstances that accompany sleep paralysis, from sound hallucinations, dogs barking, or someone ringing our doorbell, for example. Still, we will react to these hallucinations completely without realizing that we are in another reality, and instead of starting detaching ourselves from our body with a rocking motion and finally slipping off the bed, we will misdirect ourselves on these sound illusions, reacting to them in a physical way, that is, by movement. As we have said earlier, we will hear the doorbell ring, and we will stand up to check who came to visit us as a response to that stimulus, stunned to realize that we have fallen under the influence of our reactive mind and done the last thing we had to do – we have made a physical movement and break Ariadne's thread that leads us to the depths of a dream.

8.

There is another extremely useful form of movement that separates consciousness from the region of the body in the period when we fall into sleep paralysis, after waking up still and remaining in that stillness for a few seconds. It is the imagining of falling backward motion, like a somersault backward, where this movement must not be in visual performance, but exclusively and only in a tactile sense. That backward movement of the head must be aggressive and full of impulse; we must do our best to keep turning backward, and that such a motion lasts at least one minute, no less. As with the phantom movement of the head, we must not let go or give up this movement just because it seems to us that nothing special is happening in the first minute. Separation can happen at any time, even when we are fully convinced that there will be no lucidity at all. And just when we are ready to give up everything, we suddenly obtain a strange feeling that our body is bending, that we are in an utterly undefined position, or we hear the barking of dogs outside or buzzing noise in the ears. In this case, the method by which we get completely out of the body is to simply roll to the side. That movement is a winning combination every time we find ourselves in sleep paralysis; the result will always be to find ourselves on the floor outside the bed, after which we start to touch the floor and walls and repeat the procedure that has already been clearly described.

9.

It is not uncommon for us to be uncertain whether we are in the void or reality at all. We could find ourselves in doubt as to whether we are dreaming or not, even later, when the lucid experience becomes more authentic. Fortunately, there is one straightforward method that can show us what the realm we are in is. In fact, it can be said that as soon as we have doubts, it is quite likely that we are inside a dream. Whenever we need to check if we are asleep, we should simply close our nostrils with the fingers of one hand and breathe through our nose. If we are sleeping, we will always be able to breathe, even though we have disabled our breathing with our fingers. The reactive mind cannot project and deprive the essential functions of life, of which it is a part. Therefore, regardless of its hidden intention, it always prioritizes processes that are as old as it is. Breathing is precisely the mechanism of the same tributary nature as the reactive mind, which both flow into the great ocean of our unconsciousness – which is the source of all these primordial mechanisms.

RE-ENTERING

As much as a return to wakefulness is inevitable, we must seize that necessity and make the ultimate benefit of it – and that is to separate ourselves from the body once more, as soon as we have returned. This is a crucial, so important habit that needs to be established in the same way as the habit of waking up without movement. This way, we will not limit ourselves to a few minutes of lucid experience because each return to the body resets that phantasmagoric dial, and we can continue where we left off. It is enough to think about the location and place where we last returned to the body. Nevertheless, we have to be quite fast because the possibility of such a return disappears very quickly. This is an essential need and importance to adopt this dream re-entering mechanism right at the beginning and to relate it to each of our lucid experiences. It must be imperative that immediately upon returning to the body, the immediate action must be reemerging from the body by merely rolling out to the side. This movement will be much easier to pull off, without extra effort and entering sleep paralysis because we are already in an ideal state. Merely imagining a rolling motion to the side is quite enough to get out of the body in just a few moments and continue where we left off. As we gain more experience, we will be able to return many more times that, in the end, the whole night will be full of lucid outings and entrances, which will make this whole adventure more meaningful. But it is quite apparent that there are extremes in this and that we will not be able to return at some point. In a similar way to the feeling of returning to the physical plane, which is obtained unmistakably and always accurately, so will the feeling of ending be an actual and definite end. No matter how hard we try in that phase, it will only be impossible to fall asleep again. That moment must be included in the practitioner's experience, who will recognize it and, with joy and gratitude, set out to record his experience immediately. Such a record is like a record of a dream – a very clear memory of a dream after only 10 minutes can only be a slight hint, while in an hour, it will completely disappear from our mind.

GOLDFISH

There is one form of sleep that resists the manifestation it otherwise has. It does not have an introductory empty phase of nREM that lasts for about 90 minutes after we have fallen asleep, which allows the effect of the affirmation to be more penetrating and stronger etched in our minds, making motionless awakenings happen much easier and more frequent. It is a midday nap, in which we enter directly into a dream, or REM phase, soon after we have fallen asleep. There are several factors that make this possible, but we will stick to a general statement that is very easily verifiable –

indeed, every time we fall asleep in the afternoon, we start dreaming very quickly, while waking up very heavy and drowsy – even more sleepy than before our midday nap. These are all indications that the mechanism of noon sleep is different from the evening, natural sleep. It can be said that the afternoon nap is similar to the one after waking up after 6 hours of sleep to take a break and go back to bed. It is quite a similar mechanism – affirmation seems to multiply the chances of waking up after a nap without moving and opening our eyes. Here, the ease of falling into sleep paralysis is exceptional. Also, this period is ideal for the Body of Light technique, which will be explained later.

All in all, trying lucidity during an afternoon nap is ideal if we wake up earlier in the morning than we usually do and stay awake until lunch. The ideal time frame for trying lucid dreaming in this way is a little after lunch, between 3 pm and 5 pm. We will try everything the same as if we woke up with an alarm after 6 hours of sleep and spent some time out of bed. We lie down in bed during a nap attempt, making the affirmation that we will remain still with eyes closed after waking up. As soon as we have woken up, even if we move and open our eyes, there is a great chance that we will slip into sleep paralysis much easier. Upon waking from a midday nap, the Aspirant should remain as calm and immobile as possible, imagining a phantom head movement. He will often be convinced that he is too awake and that it is almost impossible to fall into a lucid dream from that wakefulness, but let him persevere in making a phantom head movement for at least 1 minute at all costs. The vast majority of cases are that at some point, he will suddenly slide into sleep paralysis from where he will quickly catapult himself into a lucid dream, in the ways already explained. However, it should be noted that in case of success, the next instance of evening sleep is quite disturbed and that insomnia is very much possible until late hours.

Like any benefit, this one has its drawbacks, too – a lucid experience triggered by a nap is short-lived; the easier it is to fall into a lucid dream, the harder it is to survive in such a dream. A lucid dream realized during a nap is usually very easy to realize; it is short-lived and very intense, making it ideal for beginners, but it can rarely bring valuable and penetrating experiences later, precisely because of its short duration.

INSOMNIA

Indeed, the specific type of insomnia that accompanies practitioners in lucid attempts can be a major obstacle, affecting the entire following day and contributing to the Aspirant spinning in circles of nonsense without really doing anything. Insomnia that accompanies an attempt at lucid dreaming, especially when we use the method of interrupted sleep after 5 to 6 hours with an alarm, disrupts the sleep and dreaming cycle altogether, and thus the possibility of even accidental success in attaining lucid dreaming. But there is one utterly simple trick that insomnia is powerless against and can be used against insomnia regardless of our lucid dreaming attempts. All it takes is to try not to sleep on purpose – make an effort and pretend you don't want to sleep at all, confronting your sleep openly and staying awake intentionally. Imagine that you will get in trouble if you fall asleep; try to want to stay awake on purpose. Feel free to keep your eyes open as you are lying in bed, refusing to do anything, and most of all – to fall asleep. Try to consider the morning a curse and make sure you spend as much time as possible until it has dawned, enjoying the darkness and the company of yourself. Once you have been doing that for a while, refusing to fall asleep, you will notice a very specific mental state when you act out such a refusal. Very quickly, you will feel the mechanism of sleep and mind wondering that will soon navigate our being into regions of sleep. Even if you do not aim for lucid dreaming, falling asleep quickly often makes the difference between a quality and miserable life. People waste tons of money just to be able to sleep well, and even more – to fall asleep, and in fact, everything you need can be summed up in understanding these few lines. Finally, we will consider a few more very effective tricks that can help us overcome insomnia.

The diet is definitely worth mentioning, which is surprisingly important but thoroughly neglected as well. It affects both the quality of sleep and falling asleep, and the Aspirant should get used to not eating or drinking at least 2 hours before going to bed.

Many people have an utterly foul sleep mechanism. Due to mental apprehension of the previous day and stressful situations that have unfortunately become commonplace, they fidget in bed and make small, nervous minimal body movements that effectively prolong the sleep mechanism. Therefore, the Aspirant should observe his own body while falling asleep and try not to move at all. Such a simple instruction has cured countless insomniacs. Simply lock your body position and do not move an inch when you decide to fall asleep.

One of the most effective methods for creating a quick sleep reflex is to change 2 things – how you start the day and how you end the day. You need to get out of bed as quickly as possible each time, without any delays, stretching and lazing around, not even for just a few seconds. Always look at the snooze option on your smart device as a sibling of insomnia. You must avoid the bed as the source of the most horrible infection and leave its surroundings immediately once you have woken up. Along with that, you need to go to bed simultaneously every time, even if you are not tired. Your mind knows that you will get up at the same time, that you will not linger in bed, and that you will not have too much time to rest, so the falling asleep reflex will be far quicker than usual.

Another tiny technical thing that helps create a quick sleep reflex is to wake up just 20 minutes before you would otherwise set the alarm. This simple instruction can help you feel an unbearable urge to sleep during the evening, creating a strong reflex to falling asleep – the archenemy of insomnia.

Going to bed well before usual bed time was of great help, at least in my case. Namely, I often had the experience of falling asleep easily and quickly when I would put my daughter to sleep around 9 pm. And as I was lying there with her eyes closed, waiting for her to slumber so I can go to the living room to watch a movie with my wife, I used to fall asleep countless times.

Finally, we shall mention an old but extremely effective exercise that affects falling asleep and quickly achieves extremely deep relaxation and trance. All it takes is to apply the reverse blinking process; hold your eyes closed for 10 seconds, then open them for one second, just enough to focus your look at a certain point in front of you that you selected before the experiment. Next, close your eyes immediately, keeping it that way for 10 seconds, then open them again for a second, re-focusing the selected object. Your eyes behave identically as during the day, only in reverse order now: as much as your eyes are normally open in normal circumstances, they will now be just as closed, and a short opening is identical to the duration of blinking in normal circumstances – it is all the same, just in reverse order. This creates an unbearable urge to fall asleep in just a few minutes, and if used as a means of relaxation, it will achieve a surprisingly deep level of trance in a very short time, which is excellent in working with autosuggestions and affirmations, as well as working with the subconsciousness and raising the overall energy of our psychophysical apparatus.

FAILURES AND MISTAKES

Failure in lucid dreaming is such a fantastic phenomenon that writing a completely new and special book about it may be necessary. It is up to us to look at all the possible positions of this mechanism and study and understand it more as a verb of our exalted soul than as incompetence or a mistake. We have to understand that each time we fail or skip a certain technique, we have missed and forgotten just one specific segment, or done a right thing at the wrong moment, or a wrong thing at a right moment. But in almost all cases, it is exclusively our defense mechanism of the reactive mind that tries to keep us away from what it least understands and what it fears most – the presence of an intruder – the presence of our wakefulness in its territory, in a dream.

By far, the most important thing the Aspirant must realize is that technical failure is the least responsible for his downfall. In most cases, his neurosis and avoidance system, which is deeply rooted in his psyche, is the root cause of all problems and failures. In other words, it is not the technique that fails. The technique is not foul or inflexible in our case. It is us who cause the technique to be rejected, not applying it well due to some of our childish snoring mechanisms. But there are certainly particular objective reasons that lead to failure. Let us discuss one at a time.

1. The first mistake that does not seem to contribute to failure a lot, but which is its main and meanest cause in many cases, especially with beginners, is eating and drinking just before bedtime. Such apparently naive mistake affects the failure of lucid dreaming and leads to a wide discrepancy in the life cycle of the Aspirant. The entire next day can be seriously disturbed because the Aspirant opened the refrigerator just before bedtime and gave in to a midnight feast. This mistake is even more fatal for sleep interruption and Alarm aid techniques. Admittedly, drinking water can be an excellent thing to do, but only after the first wake-up alarm after 5 to 6 hours of sleep. Then, when we get up and stay out of bed for about half an hour, we drink water and urge our full bladder to urinate, which will further put pressure on the shallowness of the REM phase and help part of our consciousness immensely to cling to the physical body.

2. Yet another purely procedural error that is largely more fatal than the first one is the application of techniques night after night in a row. As much as eating and drinking disrupt the sleep cycle, too frequent repetition which then evokes excessive enthusiasm and anticipation completely disfigure the sequence of nREM and REM phases. Even if we have woken up without moving or opening our eyes, the REM phase will be completely lost, which will further cause distrust and anxiety in every additional attempt. Paradoxically, by trying every night in a row, we will be further away even from random success. Instead of taking a break of a few days to get everything back to normal, the Aspirant beginner starts exercising even more frantically, thinking that by increasing the pace, he will achieve success. Trying every night is especially devastating for the application of sleep interruption and Alarm aid technique – the Aspirant may even have a great start and success in the first days or weeks, but after that, he will start waking up a few minutes before the alarm, or get into the worst insomnia ever, not being able to fall asleep for several hours. Also, it will be impossible for him to achieve sleep paralysis after the second awakening simply because it will be completely impossible for him to fall asleep a second time and the second awakening to take place at all. The strength of this error stems from our instinct for organization, system, and rational repetition, all of which are so far from our lucid consciousness and the irrational logic underlying all lucid and astral experiences. The Aspirant must not foresee his activities; nothing is to be foreseen. He simply has to work without training, with no systems or foundations. He must improvise, so to say, by chance – without systematizing, training, gradual, and predictable steps.

3. Forgetting to apply the technique at all. In this case, the Aspirant wakes up successfully without moving or opening his eyes but completely forgets to apply the phantasmal movement technique. The Aspirant must realize that, during that time, his consciousness is narrowed and limited by memory and attention, and no matter how much he has the impression that he is fully awake, there will always be elements that rebuke this claim. In this case, he will completely forget to apply the technique itself. Although he has succeeded (even perfected) in contributing ideally to waking up without movement, he will declare partial success final. Waiting too long for something to happen without knowing what and refusing to realize that he must bring lucidity to active movement, Aspirant is now waiting for the success to happen on its own. In all that waiting of a few precious seconds, he has woken up naturally and missed a sweet spot where imagining phantasmal movement could make sense.

4. The inability to realize that we are asleep or in the lobby of sleep paralysis all the time. The Aspirant may wake up without moving or opening his eyes, but at the same time, he hears the noise of the works in his neighbor's apartment. Believing that it is impossible to succeed starting from such a desperate position, he gives up further attempting and either falls asleep or wakes up completely, getting out of bed, unfortunately discovering that all the noise was part of a false reality and that no construction works are being carried out. Our mind can deceive us with many cunning ways. I will mention one where after waking up without moving and opening my eyes, I tried to perform the phantasmal movement for more than a minute without any success. After following the whole procedure, I decided to get up and make breakfast. While I was enjoying the beauty of

a beautiful summer morning, I thought it was such a pity that I had missed a great opportunity for a projection. I went into the kitchen and got to the fridge to make myself breakfast, but I saw that instead of my usual fridge, which I bought recently, there was a fridge that I had had in my previous apartment. I was taken aback by this situation and even thought my new fridge, in fact, was part of some past lucid experience. At that moment, I found myself on the bed, still staring into my closed eyelids, in the same position as after waking up. I realized that I had been in a lucid dream all the time, in a very intense false awakening. It was a gloomy winter day outside, and yet there was a new refrigerator in my kitchen. This shows that we should always check reality during every lucid attempt, simply by pinching your nose with your fingers and then trying to inhale or exhale. Also, have a look at two different clocks to see if they are showing the same time or turn on the lights in the apartment – a crazy thing in almost all lucid experiences is that switches don't work in a large number of cases or are located in completely different places in the apartment – a clear indication that you are in a dream scenario.

5. Disinterestedness and lacking the motivation to still try as much as we think we are awake and have no chance to succeed, or if there was awakening with a physical movement or opening eyes. It is a very common case that we are not satisfied with assessing the ideal state and reaching the sweet spot for entering a lucid dream. Therefore, it is very important for the Aspirant to build a habit of always trying to perform a phantasmal movement for at least one minute, regardless of whether he woke up moving or opening his eyes. Building on his experience over time, the Aspirant will notice that most body movements after awakening are not even real movements at all. It is just that we believe that

we have moved or part of a false lucid reality that has not happened in the first place. Even the real movements have a great chance to turn into a full projection if we keep persistent in making the phantasmal movement. If we fail to succeed even then, that is no reason not to try to fall asleep again and use the next awakening with even greater chances to succeed.

6. Insufficiently long performance of a phantasmal movement, having the impression that we have been working long enough, while we have not worked very little or not at all. During my decades of work, the projection mechanism was triggered only in the last seconds of the movement in the vast majority of cases. If I had listened to my inner instinct, I would have interrupted it just a few seconds before the projection suddenly began to materialize. A pause in the performance of a phantasmal movement is not when you think everything has failed but after a whole minute after the start of the performance. Since you won't be fully aware of seconds, you should always do it more than you think is enough. Your inner feeling is there to surpass it because it is certainly not realistic. Therefore, be wise that it does not serve as a point of support but a point of motivation for it to be overcome and transferred because it is a false border that serves to divert you from the path.

7. Skipping REM phase – sometimes it can be only 10 minutes, especially when we wake up with an alarm – using the Alarm aid method, which has been elaborated. Usually, a beginner believes that the sooner he wakes up, the easier it will be to succeed. Unfortunately, it is quite the opposite; he needs a time window almost just before waking up. He needs more sleep, not less. The more sleep there is, the easier it is to achieve lucidity and sleep paralysis. Lucid experiences soon after sleep are very short and difficult to

control; the vision is blurred while moving around is difficult and slow. This is rather easy to solve by moving the timing of the alarm for 10 or 15 minutes forward or backwards. All practitioners have their own time window where the target REM phase is located. It is usually between 5 and 6 hours after falling asleep, but this may not be the case with every Aspirant. There is often another type of mistake here. When calculating when the alarm will wake us up (if we use the Alarm aid method), we forget that we have to add 15 minutes, or as much time as it takes to fall asleep.

8. Forgetting to try again after we have achieved a successful projection and returned to the body. As much as we are satisfied with the length or quality of our lucid experience, and as much as we have succeeded in fulfilling our action plan, we must always accustom our minds to trying again. Every time we return back, we are actually in an ideal position to succeed. We always have the best chance of getting out again in the first seconds after returning. That is, the chance of getting out is almost 100%, and it is a shame that the Aspirant easily throws away that ideal moment that has already been realized and where he is already on the verge of a new experience. Due to the limitations of the REM phase, no matter how experienced or skilful, the Aspirant is unlikely to achieve lucidity for more than half an hour. Thus, he will hardly stay more than 5 minutes in a lucid dream for the first few years. Admittedly, the duration of time has a completely different experience in a lucid dream, but it is certainly an important factor in limiting a lucid experience that cannot be extended indefinitely. But what the Aspirant should always do is that once he returns, whether because of his negligence in maintaining the stability of sleep and vision or simply because the time has

expired, he is to go out again using a phantasmal movement in the same way. The second time is always an easier and faster way out, while the vision is much more realistic, firmer, and solid. Once we have stepped out of the body again, the time is reset, and the Aspirant can perfect this skill so much that the whole night can be spent getting in and out of a lucid dream uninterruptedly.

9. The aspect of immunity – an extremely important phenomenon in all lucid and astral endeavors. This thing will not be so important in the initial experiences due to a low rate of success and rare cases of actually exiting the body, but as the Aspirant performs techniques with more and more confidence and success, his mind begins to form what will accompany him throughout all his lucid work – specific immunity to success, techniques, all the tricks that the Aspirant himself will find and devise, or hear from other practitioners. He will develop immunity to many lucid and astral tricks that will help us keep dreaming long enough to allow us to teleport more easily or carry out any operation. When working with teleport, the Aspirant will notice that stagnation in form, movement, gaze, or an idea is always harmful to lucid experiences. He has to design new ways, new actions, new ideas, and motivational elements that will renew him to make him strong and able to fight against the horrible currents of his mind, which, like some dreadful drug, quickly becomes immune and unresponsive to all that was so delightful the Aspirant when he first discovered or applied something unique. What the Aspirant needs is to keep changing techniques all the time. He must not obey any rules nor apply patterns in his work or any fixed schedules. He has to play with his toys for the sake of playing, not for the sake of toys, just like a child. He has to keep changing those toys; once he has made them, he has to

throw them away. He has to forget about toys to be dedicated to playing solely. The Aspirant must be aware that any instance of success inevitably brings failure if repeated. Any successful application of a technique will soon lose its efficacy if carried out in the same way. Therefore, he needs to build his freedom of improvisation and choice of what he believes he would use. He should in no way become a slave of the system and the form – which is like a stern and cruel stepmother to all success in lucid experiences.

10. Lack of an action plan. This is not so much disastrous for the realization of lucidity itself as for maintaining a lucid experience and staying within a dream. As much as we have built the dream and enhanced the clarity of the vision, we will often be the victims of the misjudgment that such a vision will have lasting intensity allowing us to do in a dream whatever we want. Despite it being rather charming to let ourselves to lucid dreaming wandering around the place we have found and interacting with characters surrounding us, such wandering is usually short-lived. Without an intention to make points of an action plan come true, the dream collapses quickly and cruelly. All the clarity and firmness we have achieved will vanish as a pond under summer sunrays. Also, too many points of the action plan can also be an obstacle in a lucid experience, where the complexity of the plan or too many different points on the agenda will result in confusion and stagnation of the mind, simply because it will be difficult for us to remember them or their order. All this will lead to a dream delay, which is always devastating to a projection.

11. Insufficiently strengthened dream. The first thing the Aspirant has to do after finding himself in a dream scenario is to strengthen and solidify that dream. No matter how solid and clear our dream may seem, we should always get used

to resorting to methods of strengthening and clarity in the same way.

12. Excessive mind alertness. Having woken up without moving and opening his eyes – even though he wakes up at the ideal moment for projection - the Aspirant will, with his high expectations and emotional excitement, do what he ultimately need not do – and that is to wake up. That will be particularly difficult in initial experiments, yet it could be overcome easily – by experience, perseverance, and time. The Aspirant simply has to get used to being in the entrance hall of success and do what he has learnt, following the procedure in cold blood, expecting nothing. Let him carry out the procedure for phantasmal movement for one minute at least as if it were the goal in itself. Also, such behavior could be very awkward while using sleep interruption after we have returned to bed for the second time expecting to fall asleep asap. By the second awakening, our mind knows it will have almost one hundred per cent chance and will now try its best to do the last trick to completely crush the Aspirant – causing the onset of insomnia and complete awakening.

All these are points that can appear jointly or separately, making us seem to be so close but still so desperately far away. The Aspirant has to know that these are always the same mechanisms. All instructions and methods are in the same way the result of observation and application with many other Aspirants. No matter how bad or difficult is an obstacle, the Aspirant has to know that it is just a matter of time when he will manage to be successful and overcome that difficulty. He will know that no matter how triumphant and lucky he is, sooner or later, he will get into a dry and futile period. Regardless of how poor and unlucky that period is with almost no success, it will end up being replaced with fruitful and joyous experiences.

ACTION PLAN

The plan of action is the only and exclusive pillar of this whole temple; the entire lucid dream is a projection and a reflection of the will and intention, whether it is expressed well before the dream or at the very moment of the decision within the dream. The earlier it is expressed, the easier it will be performed, which is paradoxical. Fresh ideas have no support in a dream, and such plans are fragile and tend to collapse. We will really witness that even some of our ancient memories or desires have clear contours in a dream and that it is challenging to get out of a scene that came to mind many decades ago when we were children. Each of us had a specific place or fantasy that was the home of our childhood hero. If we make a plan before the projection to find ourselves, for example, in the fairy garden we dreamed of as children, we will quickly and easily come to such a scenario, from which we will find it quite difficult to leave or change it once we have entered it. It is utterly irrelevant whether we will reach it by a tactile strategy or by a location change technique such as teleport. What we will certainly notice is that such a scenario is particularly clear and solid. No matter how many years or decades have passed since our first conception, it seems that all these past years have acted as additional mortar to bond the material of such a dream.

It can be said that the only element that keeps the dream from falling apart is our motive to progress in the dream; what keeps the contours of the dream together is only our Will to move in the dream. However, such a set will not be strong enough if we do not infuse it with an additional research element, and that is always a projection that we have formed the night before lucid dreaming. As we mentioned earlier, we must always be in motion, not only physical but also mental; it is a mental attitude based on fulfilling the wishes of dreamers, to get to specific points, and to move on to another immediately after the previous one has been realized. Practically speaking, it is best to write down these points on a piece of paper from a notebook that is used just for that (like a sticker for daily tasks), which we will put under a pillow or on a night-table next to the headboard. We need to write 2 points at the beginning, and later 3 or at most 4, depending on the experience in lucid dreaming. More points than this introduce confusion and stagnation because we will need our attention – which causes a return to such undesirable wakefulness. For a start, let these points be realistically achievable things, which excite you at that moment; your first flight above the clouds, your first invocation of a particular being, your first teleportation. Later, make an abstraction of your dream and enter points that go beyond your reach: a dream within a dream, compressing time, prolonging lucid experience, abstract meditation, exploring and talking with deep, personal, unconscious structures, healing mechanism, fulfilling and manifesting desires on the material plane. You must fulfill these points in your dream in the same order as you wrote them. The action plan should begin realizing the moment we have increased the clarity of sleep to the maximum; if by any chance you are not aware of the order of the points themselves, realize the first one that your memory has shed light upon. There must be no waiting or stagnation in this, which is the greatest enemy of the lucid experience, as we already mentioned earlier.

The action plan should not be limited to lucid endeavors. The Aspirant can try the opposite. Let him, from a lucid dream, give himself tasks and a plan of what he will do when he wakes up. While dreaming, let the Aspirant determine 3 things, let him set himself 3 tasks that he will do as soon as he has woken up. These tasks can be completely simple but rather specific so that his mind would not attach to them the label of wakefulness and rationalism but rather connect their action and purpose from the region of unconsciousness. Let him build an action plan to buy in a shop a completely unimportant product he has never bought before. Let him go to a restaurant he does not usually go to - all relying on the Aspirant's decision from the realm of lucid dreaming. In that way, the

Aspirant will build a bridge that connects two completely different worlds and two different types of consciousness, initiating a mechanism of unification of those two worlds. When different peoples encounter, there is an exchange of material goods, civilizational heritage, information and culture. Such seemingly unimportant endeavor will encourage the development of both worlds – awake and dormant, helping them flourish through fantastic collaboration with our mind expanding and deepening to spheres that the Aspirant is unaware of.

TELEPORTATION

Changing the scene – translocation, that is, teleportation, as some practitioners prefer to call this ability, is one of the main ways a practitioner frees himself from the projection of a dream, in which he is only a participant in an already prepared play. Within that play, he is just an actor who, no matter how important his role is, is nevertheless just a gear envisioned and agreed upon, one of many meaningful levers within a dream. Using this ability, a practitioner erases the foundation on which the dream program is based and sets up completely new commands on his own. Such an endeavor has its advantages but also its drawbacks, and it is necessary to approach this mechanism very meticulously.

The dream is an augmented reality; it relies on it but does not depend on it. It tickles the reality, daring and provoking it. It is just a stimulus looking for a reaction – an itch that automatically creates a scratching movement. It really just leans imperceptibly and romantically, without asking. It has its rules, where our shadow implements and determines laws and conditions. We live in that sphere, and we are free, as long as we do not violate the principles of that world. We are free to do everything inside that cage, except for one thing – go over its boundaries. Lucidity itself, our very con-

sciousness within a dream, is viewed by our mind as the only phenomenon to which it expresses enmity, relentlessly hunting to ex-
pel it like a thorn from its body, as soon as possible and as ruthlessly as possible. Every dream has its need; it is both the cause and
the consequence of the conditions around it. The reality of the
morning and a whisper of tomorrow are the perimeters that affect
it, making this world subject to these points. Although we are completely free to do chaotic things within it, we are an entirely predictable category that is framed by what our mind calls "reality" in
the agreed language. Getting out of the dream scene is an impossible feat like quitting work even though we have children to support, traveling around the world when we are scheduled to get
married, or buying a new car while applying for a mortgage. In
fact, our whole life is a much more limiting phenomenon than our
dream, and no matter how much we are unaware of ourselves in a
dream, that "self" is too often the reality of everything that is
needed for such a limitation and restriction. We are "free" in a
dream, simply because we are not "we."

Our reactive mind is accustomed to setting laws within a
dream in the same way that politicians do in the physical world.
At elections, it is not important whom we vote for, but who counts
the votes. Therefore, it is not a question of whether we can circumvent the rules, but how to circumvent them. Everything that is illogical within reality is real and logical within a dream; we must
think with a mind that is not ours, that belongs to "no one." We
have to pretend to play by the rules of a game that has never been
played before, by the rules which have never been established before.

The only way for a dream to progress is for a practitioner to
progress through the dream. Without a dreamer, a dream is an entirely meaningless phenomenon. Without a dreamer, there is no
dream; that is the whole point of the REM phase, which in all its
brevity has streets that always lead outside the scope of the dream.

In these passages and canals is the whole interest of our art, in following these tributaries of the Selfness. The only way to reach them is abstractness and illogicality in the usage of paths that do have neither a sign nor a label. For a lucid dream, this is exactly the idea of translocation, i.e., teleportation. Translocation is any change in a dream scenario that is fast enough for the reactive mind to respond by setting up and replacing it with a new one; we will reach the realm between dreams, the realm between worlds, and thus gain a considerable advantage over the reactive mind which is now unable to prepare laws concerning a point which has completely lost its dimension and position in its system of control. That is quite enough time for a practitioner to see the bottom in all that depth, noticing a starfish he has been seeking so persistently, or treasure or a sunken ship with the map of his quest.

In order to make a successful shift from a dream scenario that has already been constructed by our reactive mind with quite solid foundations, we must forget about the corridors and all the logical exits from such a building; our whole neighborhood, including a doorman on the ground floor, are now against us, and our mind will pull the dreamer out of the dream after every logical attempt to abandon the established habit, bringing him back to reality. It is the last defense that has no counterpart in the practitioner's life. That is all we try to prevent – and the methods for doing so are nebulous and illogical – all that our minds simply cannot define as methodological constants on the basis of which it could produce an antidote.

First and foremost: We need to define our motive for teleportation. If we look at a lucid dream as an area of very short duration, where every second is subordinated to a goal that must frame every lucid attempt, such action saves a great deal of time. For the first minute or two, we will certainly get lost in babbling in the darkness of the void until we have obtained a vision and attempting to maximize the clarity of the dream. Only then can we start our exploration. If performed correctly, teleport seems shocking to the mind in a way that must now create one new reality and its laws from scratch, thus losing a significant portion of energy and attention which was intended for the dreamer. By teleporting, two crucial things are being attained. The first, which we have already said, is precious time saving because the practitioner has come directly to the area that he imagined to serve him for manifesting his action plan. And second, it is with this escape from the primary location that the practitioner will gain great clarity – which in turn will contribute to his lengthy stay in such a new scene. But as much as the practitioner has experienced the clarity of the new astral harbor after teleportation, he should certainly determine that clarity by touching, gazing, and shifting his focus in the same way as he strengthened the primary vision from the void. As for the methods themselves, there are a lot of different techniques; some will be a complete success to one practitioner, while others will fail. Over time, it can happen that old methods no longer respond appropriately and that we have to change them. We will therefore list many different things, which will first of all show what the logic of such escape is, and how the methods that lead from the dream region are to be constructed. Once again, to successfully use teleportation, we must make sure that the level of clarity is raised to the highest possible level – even partial clarity will lead to the collapse of a dream and return to wakefulness.

The condition for successful teleportation is a strong desire to leave the current location and reach the desired destination. Such a heated thought should be in our mind for only a few moments, after which we start with the technique of travel itself. It is a good idea to say aloud the destination, which then primarily affects the flow of astral vision. Every word spoken in a dream will be much different than on the physical plane because the organs in charge of the speech process are simply not used. We have no tongue, no lungs, no breath, no vocal cords in our dream – and yet our mind foresaw the reality in which these organs exist because it is accustomed to it. Therefore, the use of words in a dream will play a brilliant role of a mold into which we will pour forged Will. Later, we will notice a remarkable application of a spoken word to the method of invocation in a dream. After enflaming ourselves in our intention towards a new destination and having uttered it in a dream clearly and loudly, we begin to rotate around our axis. Such movement can be accompanied by raising the arms at shoulder height, whereby the rotation should be accelerated to such an extent that the sketches and contours of the primary location in the dream begin to disappear. Such a move will be accompanied by a tremendous change in the consciousness of a practitioner; the whole movement should last from 5 to 10 seconds, certainly no more than that, after which we will stop abruptly and aggressively at one point. With a little effort and practice, we will reach the desired location. The teleport technique itself rarely brings success in the first few times. However, a practitioner should by no means try this thing twice in a row; in a similar way as his attempts at lucid dreaming must not be made day after day, so the teleportation technique should be applied not more than once in two days. More than this will lead to a habit that is a mortal enemy in lucid dreaming. Every habit leads to a system and predictability, logic, and mold, according to which our living spirit simply has no understanding or tolerance, now that it is realized in its natural environment.

The second method is a bit more complicated and involves the flying technique, which will certainly be explained in more detail later. The beginning of this technique is the same as in the past one – in fact, every change of location by teleporting always starts that way: a fervent desire for a location with a clear knowledge of where we want to go, after which we pronounce the location. We start flying high immediately after this, without looking down – the condition for this technique to succeed is to keep our eyes high above us all the time, exactly in the direction of our flight. Such a flight should be fast and powerful, like a catapult. After firing into the heights, we start slower descending during which we will land at the location we aspired to. It is this diversion of gaze that is the most important mechanism for constructing a new reality in a dream, which, in a similar way to shifting gaze has a very important place in the phenomenon of lucid dreaming. Our gaze equally holds the dream together, participates in its duration, conditions the existence of the whole projection and architecture of the dream. The gaze in a dream is like a breath in our lungs – it must always be replenished; it constantly makes the lungs active. This movement of lungs is a condition of our life and the whole mechanism of life, from the smallest cell in the body to the phenomenon of consciousness. In the same way, our gaze must constantly shift; it must constantly move and follow the enthusiasm of a practitioner who willingly progresses in his dream, not staying in any place longer than a moment.

Both of these methods are invasive and abrupt and will take a long time to simply take effect. It may be that the following technique will be much more effective than these two mentioned above – milder and much closer to the logic and nature of the dream itself which is very easy to achieve even with very inexperienced Aspirants. It takes a little more time to perform it, but the conscious loss of that time in a dream is certainly better than the complete collapse of a dream, which earlier methods will surely cause at the beginning of lucid training.

This method uses specific cunning together with the resources of the dream itself, which represent all objects in the dream that can be used as a portal or connection with the desired destination. For this occasion, any door in a dream, window, or even a mirror can be used as a passage; what is important is to use them properly. Suppose we find ourselves in a dream where we are on the street; certainly, the nearest possible door will be a few dozen steps away.

What is important is the very approach to such a door, once we have achieved maximum clarity of the astral vision and decided to move away from the current dream scenario. We must not rush toward that door. We must not arouse the suspicion of that dream that we want to leave in any way. On the contrary, we have to walk towards them with complete naïve curiosity – *"Hey, look at this door, I'm really interested in what's behind it,"* or *"They are very nicely made, I really want to know who lives inside, maybe it's someone I know?"* The sleep mechanism has set them up for just that reason – because it wants to open them up to the path that the mind has already charted. In fact, the whole of our movement in a dream must be out of naïve expectation – we must never announce the plan of what we are about to do – because our actions are mostly treacherous toward the dream projection, and our mind will reveal our true intention by our actions – which will then start raising the immune system toward our lucid consciousness, and completely collapsing our dream thus returning us to the waking state. The whole motive of every movement, our every step inside a dream must be easy, completely relaxed, without any emotions or inner mental noise. The ultimate goal here is an expectation, not a desire. We must expect something behind the door. We must never desire something behind that door. We must move through the dream completely naively and childishly; this is perhaps the most important tactic for lucid dreaming instructions. Everything we do further in the dream is based on this attitude of expectation, rather than fascination. Expectation, not fascination. *"Hey, I saw my brother behind this door. Let me say hello to him, will I?"* Like Alice in Wonderland: *"Hey, there is a white rabbit in a suit, that is peculiar, let me follow it."* Precisely that is the spirit we are looking for. When we approach the door, naively pretending to expect something behind it, a critical moment in the teleportation action is about to happen. We have to merge the idea of that door with the idea of the destination itself very quickly; this is most easily done by simply saying the destination aloud, as in earlier cases, or by drawing a symbol reminiscent of the destination with your finger on the door itself. Drawing symbols with your finger especially refers to entering the Tarot card, Tattvas, elemental or planetary realms. Finally, the whole procedure ends with a completely banal action – we must never open the door frontally which would prevent the scene from changing and allow the defense system to keep us in our current location. Opening the door from the front will invoke an automatic mechanism that will project behind the door something that the reactive mind wants to show us, behind which will be a completely expected corridor – all but not the new reality we want to reach. Therefore, our movement must be as cunning as fast; we will open the door but from behind, turning our backs. We will hold one hand behind our backs and touch the handle to open it without looking at the scenario behind the door. Once we have opened the door (which will always be unlocked by unofficial lucid rules, in the same way that turning on a light switch in a lucid dream almost never brings light), we will take a step back by going through it, doing everything with our back turned. Still not looking back, we will close the door – this movement is extremely important in consolidating the new reality we want to reach. Only then should we turn around. The whole mechanism of teleportation and change of location is hidden in that turn and in that action that lasts less than a few moments; in fact, everything before that was just preparation and warm-up for such a simple, illogical and banal act. In this turn, we will move away from the dream scene. When we stop, there will be a whole new landscape in front of us – the landscape we intend to appear in. It should be noted that opening the handles and calling the elevators in a dream always change the consciousness extremely, especially when they are done in the void phase. However, the Aspirant must be careful with elevators and know how they should or should not be used, which will be discussed later.

Teleporting is useful for changing the dream scene and enhancing the experience, bringing clarity, and improving vision. However, this escape from the script prepared by the mind blurs our thinking apparatus creating confusion and panic because it escaped from the castle. The sleeping beauty finds herself in a particularly magical place of clear vigilance. She then becomes even more beautiful and much less sleepy.

Tarot, Elemental kingdoms, Exploring other lives, and Time travel

In our art, there are planes that draw from the supreme archetypes and can always be a valuable destination for a lucid dream. Since their research is very extensive, it is important to get to those planes soon after we get the vision in order to use the remaining time as much as possible. In addition to drawing symbols on the door in a dream and the mechanism of reverse passage through the door, there is another way we can get to a certain plane, which requires a little more experience; but certainly, this way of traveling will be encouraging for a practitioner, as it saves time – one of the most important instances of a lucid dream. Instead of looking for a door to draw a symbol of a Tarot card, element or planet on, why not look for a deck of Tarot cards in the right pocket of your pants once you find yourself in a dream? Or, maybe it is much easier to get to Manhattan if we use a postcard of that place as a portal from our right pocket? If I tell you that you will always find a Tarot card or a postcard with the desired destination in your right pocket inside the dream, then that is quite a sufficient projection that will work forever. It is enough to express a simple intention before going to bed for this, and it will be automatically created the moment you look for a card in your right pocket next time you found your-self in a dream. The very movement of putting your hand in the pocket will project the desired Tarot card at that same moment. Now take out the Tarot card, throw it on the floor, and jump into it. This is always such a great way to travel fast.

As for the elemental kingdoms, you can do what you like, but be sure to establish the habit of seeking advice and instruction from such a realm in the form of the guide. The ways of invoking in a dream will be discussed later; it is the same kind of cunningness present in teleporting through the door.

By exploring other lives, we mean exploring past or even fu-ture incarnations and other forms of life – what is it like to be an animal, what is it like to be a bird? Each model will have the ad-vantages of having such a shape. Therefore, flying will not be a problem at all if you take the form of an eagle or a seagull, and it is a completely magnificent experience. Imagine other shapes with other animals, all of which can be valuable experiences.

Time travel is always a form of translocation, so any door can be used for this – all that matters is the intention and that we say the year or date instead of the location before we open the door backward and step through the past or future. It is exactly the same mechanism, and in a dream, it almost always takes the shape of phantasmagoria rather than something that the Aspirant could ex-plore more seriously. But it is undoubtedly useful to explore past or future incarnations, where the unconscious mind, if anywhere else, will at least have its wide range of manipulation – precisely the type we need. Such manipulation is always an advanced ver-sion of psychotherapy; the journey through time and into the past incarnation is always and in every respect a journey into one's own present and the network of one's own neurosis. As a code, you can draw your date of birth on the door, with an uttered wish to visit the previous incarnation. Experiences of this kind are always very emotional and powerful, sometimes leaving the Aspirant to ponder the message for a long time, but each practitioner must keep in mind the message of his soul, which is primarily emotional content. A wise magician will get deep psychological insight from this, rather than a historical fact that might seem accurate and seldom yield anything useful to the Aspirant himself.

RITUALS AND MEDITATIONS

As much as an attempt to Rise on the Planes from Liber O is mainly in vain if practitioners carry it out from the physical plane, so much its performance from the position of lucid dream yields an entirely brilliant experience. There is nothing more valuable and inspiring for an Aspirant's being than the urge to go up once he has found himself inside a dream. With such ascent, we simply fly with all our might, fixing the point in Nadir above us, further and higher, highest and furthest, the more we can embrace that height, the better. Such ascension is exceptionally irritating to our consciousness, which is so altered by this trajectory that words could even hardly describe such a change. It is a great fortune that this method is so simple in its instructions that Aspirants have no choice but to follow and realize it in their lucid dreaming as one of the points of their action plan.

Also, rituals do not need to be performed at all in the form we perform them on the physical plane. Instead of uttering and performing, all we need in a lucid dream is to remember some past performance and focus on the very form of the ritual without performing it. It is enough to vibrate one single divine name being aware that one wants to invoke the full realization of the ritual, and that is quite enough. Just remembering a ritual in a dream is enough to perform it instantly. Our attention and time do not have the same meaning we are used to within the physical plane. Therefore, failure, decline, or poor concentration are simply not elements that exist in a lucid dream. There is no need to invest an effort to imagine the lines along which the pentagram burns; if there is a point in our action plan to perform a Ritual of the Pentagram, it will be enough to recall that point of the plan in mind and draw a pentagram with our hands in the air. To our astonishment, the air will automatically originate a pentagram in the desired color, flame, or light, just as we would with a marker on paper. It is ultimately better to invent your own word and your own magical movement, which, when performed after a few moments, evokes all the effect of a complete ritual, even though it lasts for hours in this world. We need to know that "performance" does not exist in a dream, there is only realization, and performance is a clumsy expression of our Ego that gives itself justification and excuse in time and space on the physical plane. In a dream, there is no coming but being; there is no performance but realization. There is no time but a moment. That is why a lucid dream is short-lived because it is not meant to last – it is reserved for our mind accustomed to using this corrupt term in its search for light – the one that has been within it all the time. The ultimate attainment within a lucid dream, as in fact in this plane, requires a single moment – that is why a lucid dream has a very limited and short period of time – because that period is actually more than enough for our Selfness and for what we really need.

The Middle Pillar exercise has a completely different shade in a lucid dream; simply, the line of holiness descends and is physically felt the moment we begin to vibrate, and so it is always easiest and most beautiful to vibrate pure syllables and play with that twisting light all around us, spinning that light and enjoying its beneficial effect on what we know as the body at that moment. Liber Samekh is always so fantastic to perform, it is enough to recall the whole ritual in quick strokes briefly, and once we are done with the recollection, we will notice that we have completely gone through it, in the same way as if we had performed it. Real and unreal performance has the same monetary value in a dream. You set the right boundaries with your mind and your understanding of the dream itself – in what you think and want to be possible or not.

There is one brilliant trick that always grows into a model of the most profound meditation in a dream: it all boils down to inhaling as much as you can in a lucid dream while expanding your consciousness everywhere beyond the frame of the observed Universe with each atom of inhalation beyond those limits. You certainly do not have lungs in a dream; your breath will be endless; breathe and travel the entire Universe with that single breath. There will be no end to that inhalation, and at some point, the consciousness will start to change as you realize that you have infinitely large lungs that do not have an inhalation limit. In the end, you will not expand your lungs, but your mind. At some point, you will find yourself in a more sophisticated version of the void in which you found yourself at the very beginning of a lucid experience. But this void is a more perfected and improved version of this place than it is when we find ourselves in it at the beginning of a lucid experience. It is a living universe, and indeed – you will find yourself in a quiet place in the midst of the blackness of a multitude of galaxies. There will be star clusters all around you, and the place where you will be will radiate completely authentic and special force. This is a trick that throws the mind out of a lucid dream, which, although part of it, now becomes everything but its appearance – the mind will become a stimulus to the Universe. This swapping of roles will happen while we are doing a completely meaningless thing that the mind is simply not used to, and that is to breathe without interruption and without the limits of our physical lungs, because simply – we do not have lungs in a dream, as much as we do not have the body. Such an endless breath seems to leave the mind stunned and utterly powerless at the idea of cosmic expansion, and at one point, it simply bursts, allowing the Selfness to spread through stellar infinity. Such inhalation and expansion have a somewhat similar effect to the method of Rising on the Planes explained earlier – which is actually a poorer version of this trick.

INVOCATIONS AND SUMMONINGS

Invocation methods contain the same cunning mechanism we use to change the location by teleportation. In this method, the dream must be strengthened as much as possible; once maximum clarity has been achieved, we need to pronounce the name of the entity we want to invoke loudly. But this whole act contains the last, crucial move of turning our backs after saying the name – and noticing the intelligence in front of us. This move contains exactly the same mechanism as teleporting through a door after stepping through it backward and turning around seeing a new scenario. The moment we utter the name, our mind has already built a projection behind us – in fact, it is a sophisticated miniature teleport that takes place within the same scenario. The turn behind our back should be done slowly; it acts on a change in consciousness and will actually confirm the Will that was expressed in words, that is, the name of the entity. This fantastic 180-degree movement is actually a movement that takes us into a whole new world, except that there is no interruption of the scene, as is the case with teleportation. This is a subtle, and above all, a cunning way to stay in the same plane but change the location anyway. This turning movement almost seems to need amplified music, something similar to the cinematic experience, as if a musical crescendo is happening while increasing tension, and when we finally turn around, we see the main actor in the film. In fact, pronouncing a name does not invoke a being; it is rather that graceful, slow turn behind our back. Pronouncing a name only warms and directs the Will, which creates a completely different reality in that short turn in which it equally inserts the desired being.

The act of recalling oneself from the past or the future is quite a charming event; in this way, we invoke ourselves in the same way as we invoke any other being. Talking to oneself always grows into a precious experience and a lesson. All entities are apostles of an unconscious nature and have the role of guides and narrators of dormant currents of magicians – you can use your creativity to think of forms of entities that contain future lessons – from repressed emotions, fears, unresolved events to unfulfilled desires or completely human and warm conversations with people we are no longer able to talk to. But the Aspirant must know that every dialogue in a dream is actually a monologue of the Self and that every question is actually a reshaped answer, which we already know perfectly well deep within ourselves.

HEALING AND RECOVERING

Certainly, a dream is an ideal ground for triggering unconscious energy currents, which equally construct the whole scenario and appearance of a dream, and it can be said that manipulating such energy with a simple effort of Will is ideal in various methods by which we can infuse the same energy into our own body. We will only mention the beneficial effect of completely ordinary actions such as performing the Middle Pillar within a dream or an endless breath through which we breathe light, which can endow the whole next day with completely fantastic and incredible energy. Also, try pressing your index finger against a painful or sensitive spot, or do one simple and infinitely effective trick: bring your index finger closer to your mouth and blow into it, as if blowing into a cigar, wanting it to begin to smolder with a blazing flame. Now stick such a burning finger into an ill or weak place and spread heat and light all over it. Also, breathe through the sore spot, imagining that all the breath is flowing from that direction, infusing freshness and health.

ENOCHIAN SYSTEM

The method of summoning Enochian intelligences is exactly the same as invoking any other entities with a turn behind your back, but here it can be completed by reading the appropriate keys just before bedtime. The most effective would be to apply this method with interrupted sleep after 5–6 hours of sleep. The keys are read exactly in that break, once the alarm has woken us up for the first time, after which we go to bed with the affirmation that we will remain motionless and continue to work in exactly the same way. Also, instead of saying the keys in a dream, which would take too much time and concentration, we can pull out a very handy trick. If, for example, we need the 4th and 8th key, then we will imagine two pills of different colors in the left pocket, which have numbers written on them. We will first swallow the pill with the number 4 written on it, and then the pill with the number 8; it will instantly create the same effect as if we had read the calls, and that effect will be felt immediately after we have swallowed the second pill, with a very clear sense of invoked force. Now, pronouncing the name of intelligence will be accompanied by the force that will make the experience even stronger and longer.

PERSONAL TEMPLE

This segment of work is, in my opinion, perhaps the most magnificent, and in my case, it has shed a whole new light on the region of the lucid experience. I discovered the whole thing by accident, in the early days of my research into lucid dreaming, as a boy. I have always been lucky about lucid dreaming, and I have been able to even dream within a dream since I became aware of myself, and being able to retain complete consciousness equally when entering and exiting sleep. Sometimes in my dream, I thought about what to do when I wake up, and already at the age of 13 or 14, there were generally no overwhelming secrets for me about lucid dreaming. It was then that I began to experiment with the phenomenon of consciousness in sleep; with the phenomenon of time, I began to experiment with staying in a dream for as long as possible, with psychoanalysis within a dream, as well as performing basic rituals and meditations in it. I often tried to break my own boundaries within a dream, where I was constantly setting interesting tasks to fulfill and points around which to perform experiments. At that time, in addition to my lucid experiments, I was doing an intensive exercise in which I would create an imaginary personal library with books to read about my being, as well as my past and future lives. I found this exercise in a small book on reincarnation, rather shallow but with instruction on the creation of an inner astral library. I really liked this exercise since I had extremely strong visualization. As time went on, I incorporated my elements into that exercise and improved it with my personal changes and details. Also, as I got even more skillful in visualization over time, I did the whole exercise with open eyes, completely losing the feeling of looking with physical sight. I soon expanded that library to the whole temple; every day, I walked through visualization of my temple and added new details each time. I drew a plan of such a temple on paper, with all the rooms and corridors. The temple was a giant, black cube in the desert, without reflection, typically astral in appearance. It had rooms for different kinds of works and rituals. I performed this exercise every day, walking through and enjoying the temple, and for some reason, I found something special and important in it, which would turn out to be true later. I performed this exercise for 2 months in the beginning, after I had expanded my astral temple, all in all – 4 to 5 months of total work. And then I completely forgot about it. Puberty and progress in other disciplines simply did its thing, and this exercise got inevitably forgotten. At the age of 19, I bought my first major wooden library. I was immensely fascinated by it because I already had a lot of books on the floor and in boxes, no more space to keep all those great books – especially the ones I bought as a boy and which were pretty naive and intended for initial work. One day, as I arranged the books on my new shelves with great enthusiasm, I found again a small booklet in which I first came across an exercise of the inner library. Although I expanded it considerably and infused a lot of personal elements, this booklet instantly produced a wonderful memory for me of the period when I did this practice every day, which marked my entire spiritual work during that time. And then an idea came to me – to project myself into the scenario of my inner temple in the next lucid dream, the way I imagined it then, and which I can reproduce in detail even today. Already the first evening, I made an action plan with a trip to my personal inner temple as the first point of the plan. Somehow, as if I knew that endeavor would push my research in a completely unpredictable direction, I really felt the difference between that idea and hundreds of others, equally interesting points of my action plans in lucid dreaming. I will remember that night for the rest of my life: I came out of the body in exactly the same way as I used to thousands of times before, finding myself in the void and groping the walls while moving away from my bed. But as soon as I started to touch the walls, I decided to imagine actually crossing over the walls of my temple, and after a few seconds, my hands began to feel completely different material. Now my palms were crossing over polished, cold marble. Then I began to rub my astral hands as if warming them up, at the same time blowing over them. My breath ran over my rubbing palms, painting a whole new reality. After a few moments, reflections of the world and the scene I actually knew very well began to form – and soon, I found myself standing in the center of my old, inner temple, completely speechless before such a level of clarity as never before. In fact, I had a feeling that both dream and wakefulness were only pale memories of this reality that was so much more real than all that. I immediately began to examine the clarity and depth of the vision by staring at one point, expecting the dream to begin to collapse. But the scene remained in place without changing in the least. I was shocked by the firmness of experience; I pinched myself feeling real pain. Without any doubt, this was obviously a completely different level of a dream, deep as well as wide. My consciousness was completely uniquely different; even though it was a lucid consciousness, it was so sharp and focused, without any fear that I would return to the body and without any danger that was always somehow felt in all lucid experiences. I had no feeling that I had to do anything or stay active to survive in my dream. Here, on the contrary, I was completely passive, enjoying every second of my stay in this divine space. That feeling was a special mixture of nostalgic emotions because I imagined all this so diligently and devotedly as a teenager, and now for the first time, I was completely inside my inner temple, knowing all that exercise put a special trail on my being, more valuable than I ever thought it would be.

I came up with a whole new lucid law: when you teleport yourself inside something which exists, and you know it exists, then it will trigger one part of a mind, which will result in a specific kind of lucid dream. On the other hand, when you teleport yourself somewhere which is just in your fantasy, and you know it does not exist in this reality, it will trigger a different part of a mind, so it will result in a lucid dream with quite a different kind of rules. But now, if you do something which is neither of these two, teleporting yourself in a scenery that is really only inside your memory, but remembering an old phantasmagoric and false reality instead of memory which really happened, then your mind will be stunned, blocked to choose which rules and laws will use for creating such a reality, and in all this confusion you will get quite wonderful, miracles kind of lucid dream which will last almost forever and in which you can do whatever you want, with complete control and clarity. That is the whole point of creating your personal temple – its reality is neither-nor. It will be both in fantasy and both in reality. It will be constructed both from remembrance as well as imagination. Moving yourself toward fantasy, which does not exist in reality but exists firmly in your memory, as fake memory – as re-membering something which is not real. That is a glitch that can build a whole different and unique lucid experience.

After I explained the short story of my inner temple and the purpose it may have for the Aspirant, I will start from what I have already set as an observation, which is that our personal temple is stationed in a completely different level of dream, a completely different level of consciousness. Staying in it allows for much longer lucidity than any other method, the clarity with which it is reflected in our mind is always of the highest order; everything is so real and solid in it that we will have almost no need to apply any dream deepening techniques. This is a completely exceptional scenario, which we need to build for a while without trying to project ourselves through a dream at all – but only in the imagination, every day for ten to fifteen minutes, imagining walking through a certain place that we would have built in detail beforehand. Before that, let us draw on paper what we want our temple to look like, both outside and inside. Will it be in the Renaissance style, built of wood and old drapery, with a fireplace in the library and candles on the walls? Perhaps minimalist, made of stone and wood, plated with paper walls. Or maybe it will be a futuristic design with a completely fantastic play between light and shadow? In fact, drawing such a temple builds it as much as its visualization; the more we play and fantasize, the more it will be imprinted in mind. I improved my inner temple, inserting rooms and parts that served me to immerse myself deeper and further into parts of my being that I could not assume existed in the least. Certainly, everyone should construct their own temple or inner space; I will describe mine so you might take advantage of some ideas.

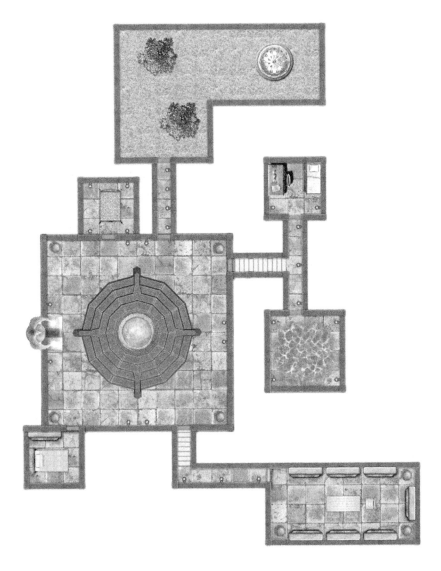

An example of the Inner Temple

In the lower-left corner, as can be seen, there is my room on the physical plane – it borders the walls of my inner temple. The door of my room, if opened with the intention of entering the inner temple, actually opens the door of that temple. It is very important that the whole intention is framed by describing that point in the action plan before a lucid attempt. I additionally inserted this point of contact with my real room; in the beginning, my inner temple had no points of contact with the waking world, and I used to come to it exclusively by teleport – in two ways. The first way was by turning around my axis, while the second was a method of stepping back through the door. However, using the door to enter my inner temple had another thing that was very important – I always drew my personal symbol on the door itself, that is, a code that would unlock the part of my mind reserved exclusively for teleportation to my inner temple. This is a great and original method with only me knowing how to draw that figure, which gave my mind additional legitimacy to establish that temple and give it a completely fantastic meaning within a dream. Only later did I decide to lean the door of my bedroom against the temple itself so that I could project myself within the scenario of the temple already during palpation in the void, which gave me more time – such a precious element in every lucid dream. Thus, I enter the central and most important part of the temple from my room, which is located in the lower-left corner of the map, which is also the largest room in this building. In its center, there is a large circle of work; in the western part, there is a large portal, and in each corner, there is a massive, monolithic supporting pillar. In the middle are large oil lamps that radiate beautiful orange light. This room is used primarily for performing rituals in a dream, also for invocations of intelligences and beings, and a possible quick journey through the portal located on the west wall. From this central ritual room, there are two doors in the middle of the north wall, then one door in the upper corner of the east wall, as well as one door in the south wall – in the lower-right corner of the room. The upper-left door leads into a very small room only with one large spacious bed and torches in the corners. This is a tantric room – having sex in a lucid dream is one of the most beautiful experiences that simply surpasses anything that can be conveyed by words. This room is intended for tantric experiments – the goddess or priestess is invoked by simply saying her name before opening the door. The most interesting way to use this room by far is to invoke yourself, but yourself of the opposite sex, and indulge in experimenting in tantra with that Selfness. The right door leads to a small hallway at the end of which there is another door, wooden and massive. On the right, hanging torches on the stone wall radiate light. When we walk through this hallway and open the door at its end, we enter a beautiful, large, and spacious garden with beautifully mowed grass on the ground. One can immediately notice two huge old oaks that are home to many fairy and gnome creatures – it is always so wonderful to play with them in the treetops, and it is quite appropriate to change the shape and reduce to the size of an elf for this occasion – which is best achieved in the main central room, in the center of the circle. At the right end of this magical garden, there is a magical observatory that serves both for summoning and long journeys, not only through space but also through time. This garden is especially useful for exercises of flying and moving through a dream without using physical movements – just by focusing your attention on the desired spot, which takes a lot of time to master. The only door on the east wall of the ritual room is in the upper corner, and after we have opened it, we will see a stone staircase leading upstairs. The stairs lead to a T intersection – there is one door at each end of both corridors. The lower, southern room is of regular square shape with a ritual pool, with oil lamps resting in the corners. The pool of radiance in this room serves for complete energy recovery, healing as well as meditation. My body and soul unite in energy waves while resting in this pool; just a few minutes of relaxation in it gives me tremendous strength, and when I return to the physical body – the fatigue that occurs after each lucid dream in this way is almost gone, and I can get up immediately after a lucid dream and start with daily activities – which is almost impossible with the usual lucid experience. This pool also reveals the causes of all bodily problems; it raises awareness of many energetic and emotional blockages. In fact, this pool is filled with a very special substance – it is a matter that is a mixture of light, water, and very mild electricity; staying in it is extremely pleasant and invigorating. If we now turn left on the steps at the T intersection, we will also come across a door behind which there is a very small room, in which there is always a neat bed with a desk across it. The torches are located in the lower left and right corners. This room is always especially important to me, and it serves for contemplation, recording thoughts and ideas, and what is very important – dreaming within a dream. This action always serves primarily to compress time inside a dream, which can sometimes prolong a lucid experience for more than an hour. In exceptionally rare cases, I had the feeling that I was in a dream for several hours, not losing consciousness in the slightest. But this technique and prolonging time also bring impressive clarity of dream, too much clarity even, which is sometimes very difficult to manipulate. This is certainly more than an advanced technique that has no place in this section, for it is in itself contradictory and contrary to many of the suggestions made in this instruction. Finally, the last door in the lower right corner of the ritual room leads into the hallway going down to the library, following the stairs, turning left into a narrow corridor, after which you enter a larger rectangular room. It is all filled with shelves. There are large stone pillars in the corners, while in the center is a large wooden table with a chair. Here I can find all the books that interest me and get various information needed for teleport or invocations of beings. There are also many magical artifacts on the shelves – magic pills and potions that bring abilities and control of flying, summoning, reducing, or shapeshifting. Some potions allow a particular book to be swallowed rather than read – in just a few sips, the entire content of the knowledge in the book instantly expands through my mind, after which I become aware of the lesson contained in the book. This library is the primary and oldest room in my temple, from where I started the construction of this sublime structure.

These are all ideas that I have personally brought into my inner temple, and which contain dream manipulations in a form that will subject my mind to such rules – those that I have actually brought, but that mind cannot comprehend it in that way, and which will obey it, momentarily, like our physical body instantly obeying the force of gravity – in no way doubting it. This temple is so sublime in design and creation that my mind does not realize it actually part of its essential core, and everything in it is made and has its purpose primarily in compressing and circumventing the laws of a lucid dream.

Whether and in what way you will construct your personal inner space in a dream depends exclusively on you, I have pointed out one particular mechanism, and it is up to each practitioner to determine their own style, interior, and exterior, as well as the function of rooms and corridors. The most important condition is that you must build your inner temple from the scratch of some of your old fantasy memory, from some old daydream fantasy, some false and imaginative scene you made up as a child. Now, you can upgrade and modify your inner temple in the present, but its foundation must be constructed from that old imaginative memory of some false scene you invented a long time ago. You should never think about that place. Rather, you must remember when you thought about it as a child – this is by far the best instruction I could give for building this magnificent space.

You can create a room that will be as vast as the Cosmos where you can observe the gnostic mass performed by the Universe itself, with you as a participant in the Eucharist of galaxies and star clusters. You can have one small room where you will keep your personal dragon or a room where you will grow a little black hole. You can do all this in your temple in a blink of an eye; here, all the laws and limits are determined by your mind, and it is solely up to you to decide on how you will deal with it.

THE USE OF SIGIL IN DREAM

The dream is the perfect polygon for the flow of sigils due to the very fact that we are naturally anchored to the region to which they aspire like eels, finally pouring into a source of action that manifests the Will as desire. This place is home to every magic lamp genie, and it is necessary to explain the mode necessary to master to direct this terrible force in the proper way. Every logical and careful handling grounds this force before time, whereby all force is lost and the desire dries up before its realization. What is most important about the sigil is that it must be included in the lucid dream scenario so that the unconscious nature receives it like a molded plant.

My favorite way is to draw a sigil on a piece of paper on which I usually write the points of my action plan and transfer the same piece of paper once when I find myself in a dream scenario by looking for it in the right pocket of my pants. This wonderful movement of putting my hand in my pocket while dreaming always projects what I want to find there. Once I have found a paper with a sigil, I strengthen my vision to the maximum and teleport myself deep into the past, to a bank where I have a private account and a safe as well. I descend into the basements of that bank, walk through giant security corridors, and finally reach the place where my safe is. I open it with a key and put a paper with a sigil in it. Then I go back to the body and get out of the lucid experience, completely forgetting about all of this.

Using the pool of radiance inside my inner temple is also a great thing – after transferring the paper with the sigil into a lucid experience, finding it in my right pocket, I now teleport to my temple and go to the pool room, where that sigil now disappears in the water linking to energies of the cosmos, decomposing in a vast sea of light.

Also, a small meditation room with a bed is great for this – where I place that same piece of paper under the pillow in that room and try to fall asleep inside the dream, implementing the sigil deep within the currents of my unconscious nature.

Or something straightforward: I am flying toward the Sun holding the sigil in my hands. I am flying with all my might toward the center of the Sun where I finally leave the sigil – now letting all the sunlight be colored by the shade of its nature, which shines radiating the whole Earth. As soon as I return to this plane, I observe the Sun and enjoy its rays – and I feel a slight flicker of the sigil in that warmth, feeling it expand and manifest in this Universe.

WIND OF CHANGE

The vast majority of practitioners come into contact with this force sooner or later. It uses a dream as much as our shadow does but differently and more creatively. Everything can happen from a completely ordinary projection. We can find ourselves within a dream, at any stage; a moment before that, an exceptional feeling will flow through our being as if something is going to happen, something like before a scary scene in horror movies is announced by charging the atmosphere with tense music and sound effects – when we all know that something is approaching the protagonist – something very mean. Similarly, a particular change strikes the Aspirant quite suddenly and unannounced in a dream, but instead of him returning to the waking state and the dream collapsing, it seems that the same dream exerts pressure on a dreamer by leading him into a completely new and different scenario without his conscious will. As if some force suspends the entire projection mechanism and plants an experience it considers to have priority in the life of the Aspirant. Such experiences are mostly very vivid and exciting; they often have their own story and knowledge transfer and a message that can be expressed even in a series of projections. Sometimes, such series can last for months, after which they stop for a while, only to return again later. All we can speculate is that these phenomena are manifestations of the Angel within a dream, in the same way that he can act so penetratingly on the physical world, leading us to experiences that we define as synchronicities. But now, in a place so suitable for him, the Angel always finds ways to leave traces in almost every projection that we can follow, and that can lead us to such fantastic and beautiful places. Often there is a sudden change of scenario and the appearance of guides in various forms – after which there is a transfer of certain knowledge or the message left to our soul later for consideration and analysis. In cunning ways, the Angel plants tiny details within a dream, which the reactive mind does not define as a threat because they are too small and hidden the same way we can often find light switches in a copy of our room in a lucid dream, which do not exist on the physical plane, or even whole doors that cannot be found anywhere in a wall of our real house. Quietly and discreetly, all these objects entice the Aspirant's attention to touch them to escape from a dream scenery. The Angel inserts these small details as shortcuts so we can press them, push them, pull them, reaching a completely different part of the dream – the one that is not projected by the reactive mind. This is actually a tunnel leading from the prison, this is a code that allows the system to be bypassed, and the alarm turned off; long enough that you can get out, short enough not to be noticed. The way we react to such elements is essential; we must not show emotional upset, but a little intrigue in no way whatsoever, but curiosity about what will happen if we, for example, turn on the light switch: *"Ah, a switch, my wife did not tell me that she installed it, it is very nice, she got the color right! I wonder if it works?"*

FLYING

This is always a favorite ability, even the goal of many lucid movements. In addition to being too often the aspiration of many practitioners, it is just as much the reason for the collapse of a dream, which always occurs simply due to the failure of the mechanisms of projection and the maintenance of consciousness within a dream. The first and most important element that prevents us from flying, or prevents us from flying long enough, is emotional agitation. Simply, this is such a wonderful event that few can remain indifferent in the moment of flight. The pressure and the feeling of speed simply interrupt a dream during the first few flights as soon as we have detached ourselves from the ground and got acceleration. Even when we overcome emotional excitement over time, we will equally witness the collapse of dream during flight – visions weaken in just a few seconds with many experienced practitioners, while flying is impossible for more than half a minute. The main culprit is the lack of the most important mechanism that sustains the lucid experience, which influences the construction of the dream scenario, and that is tactile sensation. From the very exit of the body, the practitioner will find himself in a well-known void, where before he gets any vision, he will have an exclusive sense of touch. Later, the tactile sense will maximize the visual reflection of the dream in your mind; feeling everything around the practitioner will increase the intensity of the vision. But now that he is trying to fly, he will begin to lose the lighthouse that holds him to the dream port, simply because he will not have a fixed position within a dream. For the first time, his arms and legs will have no contact with the ground or walls, and he will begin to disappear from the dream in the same way the vision of a dream came, with the opposite effect. Therefore, the condition for long flying is to rub your hands and touch your elbows, shoulders, and face with your palms actively and carefully for as long as the flight lasts. Or to move the index finger of the right hand over the palm of the left, in the direction of flying, like a miniature joystick – as if directing your own flight in the course of movement of the index finger on the palm. This small detail offers everything so that the dream flight is not doomed to return to the waking state and will ensure that the vision remains solid and stable throughout the flight and after we have landed when it is necessary to strengthen clarity once again by the methods we have stated earlier.

SHADOW

There is a single phenomenon within a dream, common to many practitioners, which has such a specific aura and an extraordinary type of event that begins to twist the overall projection of the dream, like a black hole that attracts and affects the movement of the entire worlds around. It is precisely why this phenomenon is black, like the darkest and most passionate night. It is the shadow experience in our projections that usually occurs just after we leave the body, or even earlier – in the sleep paralysis phase. The appearance of a shadow is always accompanied by the appearance of primordial, horrified, and living fear inside us. It is such specific fear that it seems to have existed longer than we have been alive as if it is the fear of all beings who have walked upon this earth. What we can learn by observing the experiences of practitioners is that the closer we are to the body, the greater the appearance of this fear. It occupies our thinking apparatus and almost entirely directs the projection in its own way. We will repeat what we have stated earlier because this statement is crucial for understanding the phenomenon of shadow in lucid dreaming:

"Indeed, many Aspirants of lucid dreaming find a unique phenomenon that is the same for everyone, and that continues to shock and frighten Aspirants who cannot overcome the specific appearance of the shadow in their experiences for years. This shadow experience, which occurs in its manner of frequency, always brings the ultimate horror, terror, and insurmountable fear into a dream experience where the Aspirant has no control over the projection. Many Aspirants cite this as their worst nightmare, and that shadow usually feeds on their strangest and most ingrained childhood fears, which have such destructive power once they have risen in a lucid dream. But if lucid dreaming brings benefits in anything, it is precisely in the assimilation of this shadow. The very success in lucid dreaming is nothing compared to the experience of assimilating the shadow in a dream – which could be one of the most important undertakings of the Aspirant he may have had before Abramelin once he had found tremendous courage before the projection and managed to present it to himself as the goal of the projection, if he approaches the shadow, embraces it and to feels it illuminate. So little technical knowledge is needed for this, but so much devilish love and courage – the same one that will later take him along the whole of Abramelin operation."

It is in this phenomenon that we can find such an open action of the Vampire who haunts the Neophyte. The exploration of lucid consciousness now gives this action an altogether clearer nature. It is extremely important for the Neophyte to experience this fear and even work for some time to become aware of such projections within his lucid dream. All he has to do is that during the phantom rocking phase, when he feels that there has been a separation from the physical body, or in the void phase, he simply wants to meet the shadow. This is really all it takes to launch this terrifying experience. The shadow needs intention more than anything, as well as the initial stage of a lucid dream. It is almost impossible to find it when we teleport or after we strengthen our vision.

In practical terms, we can expect the following: after we have found ourselves motionless after waking up, as we begin with a phantom movement or turning our head back, right after a few seconds, we begin to hear buzzing – something like a fan, but on a much subtler level. As we continue with the phantom movement, this sound becomes more and more like a rattlesnake with a specific fear beginning to appear and openly growing in us. That sound is getting louder every second, we now hear a huge, massive body crawling on the floor and that fear growing in us even more.

Finally, we roll to the side, coming out of the body, falling from our bed onto the floor, start touching and move away from the body. After obtaining the vision, we find ourselves in the hallway of our apartment. All around us is the twilight, very dim light of the lamps, which prevents us from seeing the whole ambiance clearly. We have a sense of the special weight that this lucid experience radiates, and no matter how hard we try to strengthen our vision and deepen our dream, this feeling of heaviness and darkness is equally present. We continue to hear the sound of something being dragged along the floor coming from the next room and now slowly approaching our position; at the same time, the hissing intensifies. Paralyzing fear overwhelms our being while preventing us from doing anything creatively and escaping this dream scene – every second we give legitimacy to this fear by waiting for it in a daze. The sound is approaching, and we finally notice the shadow at the end of the corridor. We can hardly see anything except that it is colossal. The sound of dragging on the floor becomes even louder – now it is only a few meters away, and we suddenly see a huge creature in front of us, which is as tall as the ceiling – a huge snake almost a meter wide, with black scales that seem to breathe in a demonic way, making a suffocation-like sound. Instead of a snake's head, there is a head of an old man with slicked back black hair on top of it, with curvy eyes and an open mouth, with that monstrous sound of the hissing of a rattle and a subtle scream coming out of it. As if it is a completely independent entity, the fear in us grows and controls our reactions, making the experience completely passive on our part. That horrifying creature begins to hover over us, and the eyes of that serpent-grandsire are now staring at us, and instead of hissing, it now begins to scream and howl. Then, the whole vision disappears, and we return to the physical plane, not losing consciousness but equally holding that fear in us in the same way as it was a few moments ago. The experience of the fear that dominated our being is still in us, long after the dream, and we will have the impression that the whole next day is colored by that terror.

This would be an improvised event and a brief description of a shadow experience. It really takes a very long time to overcome such fear and approach this being. But the experience of communication and open acceptance of such a creature is one of the most authentic experiences an Aspirant can ever have. Hugging him, inasmuch as it is simply impossible as a choice in those moments, makes us experience something we will wear throughout this whole quest of ours. Such a victorious decision will give us strength and direction more than all the meditations and rituals we have performed so far. This simple movement will open more light than darkness and fear the shadow possessed at first. Because in the end, it will truly be a creation of light, while fear is only our projection towards that light. The fear of darkness is disturbing indeed, but the fear of light and fear of truth is paralyzing and terrifying, so much that it stops entire Universes in its movement.

Saying what a shadow is and what are the benefits of working with it is as poisonous as a discussion about the nature of angels and about right or wrong rituals. Simply and very concretely, the only measure in all this is our experience, so all that can be said about it is to get in touch with the shadow within a lucid dream at all costs. How this experience will be embodied in our lives will depend solely on ourselves.

It is necessary to say something more about fear, which is a very common occurrence in sleep paralysis. It can appear independently of the shadow; still, it is made up of the same part of our being as the shadow. Inexperienced practitioners may fear that they will not return to the body, that they will die trapped between worlds, that they will go insane, or have a heart attack. These are unrealistic and utterly phantasmagoric urges that always occur when we turn our attention to the side effects of getting out of the body instead of the action plan we made before the projection.

These side effects can have an infinite number of different forms and combinations: from sound distractions and hallucinations to thought creations that simply deviate from the exit procedure to visual flashes of light, color, and form in our field of vision. Such distractions are really diverse, and they all bring the practitioner to a region that is neither there nor here. Neither in a dream nor in reality, and it is in this area that our boyish fears and phobias get the opportunity to march our lives again for the first time in so many years, dominating again over our thinking apparatus, which is completely blocked in front of them. This re-survival of hellish horrors is an extremely interesting experience, and it can be said that all childhood fears are very close to our Pure Will – only if we approach them frontally, hugging and not running away from them, frightened and averted. For light is perceived only if viewed directly; every aspiration to accept it from the corner or from the side, or with the eyes closed, refracts that divine light. But not in colors, as is the case with a rainbow, but in night and darkness of our ignorance and unwillingness to embrace what we fear. And we are afraid of what is in front of us all the time – there, now, always present above us and inside us – such is the quality of the Angel, every presence in a lucid dream is, in fact, only a mechanism for alleviating that fear of looking into that light with eyes wide open. Both shadow and fear in a lucid dream are always and only routes to the Angel who tells us where to go – if we dare and if we find courage and Will. Because if we are not ready to embrace such a foreign and horrible shadow, how will we dare perform the Great Work? If we fail in our own dream, how much can we expect from ourselves in the wakefulness? Indeed, a dream is an ideal playground for the soul. Whether you weave light or shadow on this divine loom is ultimately the same thing – as long as the game is played with the same enthusiasm, the ultimate attainment will always be the same, no matter how impossible it may seem to us.

ADDITIONAL NOTES

Something needs to be said about certain details that may be important to a practitioner and that he may come across in a lucid experience. Speech within a dream should certainly be mentioned. A practitioner must not be taken aback by the impossibility of pronouncing words as he does on the physical plane. He will often find it challenging to speak in a dream. What further complicates this action is that we limit ourselves to the physical movement of the mouth, tongue, and lungs – which we do not actually have in a dream. However, if we now concentrate on the sound that needs to be heard more actively than on moving our lips, then our mouth and throat, that is, the projections of those organs, will echo what we want them to. Something similar is with flying; as long as we actively keep trying, we will have trouble, but when we focus on the final distance, the flight will start automatically. Speech without letting your voice out is also an extremely valuable trick, performed by pronouncing letters and words just within the mind and moving your tongue without opening your mouth. This is a very convenient way of performing rituals on the physical plane as well, in a way that we will almost hear within our minds what we do not say physically at all. Speech distortion in a dream is a similar phenomenon as the distortion of our image – namely, every time we look in the mirror within a lucid dream, we will always see a distorted figure. Such a distorted voice and figure can often intimidate and trigger the arrival of shadow and fear that accompanies it. These are all precious experiences to be gained, and they can be essential points of our action plan. We really believe that all experiences are not divided into good or bad, in the waking state and a dream – but to those lived through or not.

Special attention should be dedicated to the phenomenon of elevators within a dream and their use. As we have seen in teleportation experiences, our field of vision often destroys our projection by provoking overwhelming anticipation in us – so the action of passing through a certain door actually pre-projected the room or hallway we expect before we have opened that door to see what is behind. It is challenging to step out of a dream in this way; that is why we use a step backward because the sphere of gaze behind our backs does not fall under the influence of the censors of reality – simply because we do not see it and have no control over its "logic" and "reality." With elevators, the situation is completely hopeless: we enter the enclosure, after which we close the door and start moving – up or down. And as we are using that elevator, the expectation in us is shattered by the fact that we cannot see the scenario outside the elevator. All the while, our mind keeps building a reality that suits it. Suppose we include an elevator descending a couple of floors down. In that case, such descent deepens the trance with our sense of decay further, and as we are finally entering the ground floor and the elevator door is finally opening, instead of entering the expected space, we are now stepping into the entrance of hell and our own fears – those projected by our mind, as we are entering the true domain of the shadow. It will be extremely difficult to leave such a dream, partly because the mind has had too much time to construct what it needs, partly because the feeling of going down and deepening the dream has led us to descend into deeper primordial levels of our being reigned by fears and restrictions – those formed in early childhood. At the same time, the effect and the feeling of going downhill has the effect of compressing and slowing the time, which further complicates the possibility of getting out of such an awkward environment.

There is one more thing to avoid – and that is to use a phone in your dream. In fact, do you remember the last time you talked on the phone in your dream? A very inconvenient question, even those who are sure they used to talk on the phone in their dreams actually only have the feeling that they were talking, and now if they focus on that event they dreamed of, they will see that those are mostly false memories and that their experiences of talking on the phone in their dream are much rarer than they initially thought. And the ones that did happen are very vague, with eerie and incomprehensible voices. In a very similar way, it is almost impossible to read meaningful letters in a dream – they always disintegrate, twist, or melt, and even if they have a shape that can be discerned, it means nothing meaningful too often. This is mostly a simple neurological reason because the observation of visual or auditory stimuli and connecting these stimuli into meaning implies different parts of the brain spheres, which have difficulty communicating while dreaming. The situation with a phone is as serious as with an elevator; as much as telephones are usually indoors, the ringing of a telephone is usually a call from the primordial realms of our personality and often represents a call from the deepest hell. That ringing of the phone diverts our attention from the action plan or intention that rides through the dream alive and undisturbed. One ring and our perception is now completely directed to another corner of the dream, with us expressing anticipation by wondering who is calling us in this far place? And already that question flowing through our minds at the moment the phone starts ringing automatically brings the projection, and by picking up the handset after we say *"hello,"* – silence usually follows. We focus even harder to hear better who is on the other side of the line – while our mind cleverly and cunningly builds another reality, escaping from the action plan and our intentions. All this precious time, it keeps gathering an army from which there is no defense, and after a few seconds of waiting, a terrifying voice of a character who drove fear into our bones when we were children will echo on the other side of the line. Even when we hang up, it will be too late, and we can only passively watch the projection of a dream that will now rush toward us like a bloodthirsty beast chasing its prey. The first adjoining door of the room in which we find ourselves will begin to creak open, and we will see that terrible apparition which we ourselves have invoked by a completely primitive mechanism, falling for childish deception.

The use of all means is allowed, especially the two you have in your pockets. Didn't you notice them? The next time you find yourself in a lucid dream, do the following: look for one blue pill in the right pocket of your pants and a red one in the left. This will be quite enough for their projection – right now, you have placed the pills by your mind where they are needed – in the pockets of your astral pants. Accordingly, we can determine what each pill will bring as an ability or effect on a dream: when you swallow the blue one within a dream, you will get a crystal clear vision or prolong the stay in the dream. Swallowing the red one, you can get the perfect ability to fly, teleport, the power to change shape, or it will banish any presence of a shadow and fear. The most important thing is to underline the meaning of intuitive solutions and circumvent laws that limit not a dream but a dormant soul.

CHAPTER TWELVE

LIBER VII

COMMENT ON
LIBER LIBERI
VEL LAPIDIS LAZULI

Frater Alion ∴

PROLOGUE OF THE UNBORN[5]

1. Into my loneliness comes[6] ---
2. The sound of a flute in dim groves that haunt the uttermost hills.[7]

---

[5] 16 points – 16 is from Chesed – which is 4 – The place of Adeptus Exemptus. Liber VII gives a "description" of his Voluntary Emancipation from his Adeptship. 16 is seen "from the outside," from the emptiness of the Abyss.

A fantastic connection between the Probationer and the Neophyte was found primarily in the relationship between Liber 65 and Liber 7. One is worship, and the other is marriage. In the same way, the Neophyte leans on the Probationer, who projects such a resultant as his Adeptship and his "Mastery." Everything that happens in the Golden Dawn in our Order is only a slight reminder of what is found in Liber 65 and Liber 7. These two sacred texts are, in fact, all that is ever needed for the Adept to succeed.

[6] *Loneliness* – "The Hermit" – from the Supreme Triad: Declares himself as passive – the One who receives – and "understands."

[7] Darkness – Binah. *The sound of a flute* – leaves an impression on the sense of hearing which is attributed to the element of Spirit – Shin.

3. Even from the brave river they reach to the edge of the wilderness.[8]
4. And I behold Pan.[9]
5. The snows are eternal above, above[10] ---
6. And their perfume smokes upward into the nostrils of the stars.[11]
7. But what have I to do with these?[12]
8. To me only the distant flute, the abiding vision of Pan.[13]
9. On all sides Pan to the eye, to the ear;[14]
10. The perfume of Pan pervading, the taste of him utterly filling my mouth, so that the tongue breaks forth into a weird and monstrous speech.[15]
11. The embrace of him intense on every centre of pain and pleasure.[16]
12. The sixth interior sense aflame with the inmost self of Him,[17]
13. Myself flung down the precipice of being[18]
14. Even to the abyss, annihilation.[19]

---

[8] *The brave river* – description of the Universe to the edge of Chesed – *the edge of the wilderness.*

[9] "PAN" – EVERYTHING – Comprehension, understanding Everything from the Void of the Spirit. (4 = 4 elements)

[10] *Eternal snows, high above* – associates to Kether.

[11] *Perfume* – specific for 8=3 attainment; *nostrils* – the notion of "Stars" awakens and illuminates the World.

[12] The One who understands Everything "does not know" what to do with it since Everything already has its True Will and Nature.

[13] Nothing is important as a part of the Multitude, but the Wholeness of Everything is "Pan."

[14] Everything that can be understood and that is manifested is from "PAN," as an aspect and part of Everything.

[15] Trinity – *the perfume of Pan pervading;* – *the taste filling the mouth;* – *tongue and speech.* It is related to the perception of aspects of the supreme Triad of the Tree of Life: Smell, Taste, Voice.

[16] The awareness of the Whole of Everything brings the "part" to the Ecstasy of *pleasure* and *pain.*

[17] The five senses are useless – they only feel what is "lower"; *the sixth sense* is Enlightened.

[18] The Self is faced with the separation from the *being* in order to annul the Limitations.

[19] *Abyss* – where the Ego is destroyed and from which the Star is born.

15. An end to loneliness, as to all.[20]
16. Pan! Pan! Io Pan! Io Pan![21]

CHAPTER I[22]

1. My God, how I love Thee![23]
2. With the vehement appetite of a beast I hunt Thee through the Universe.[24]
3. Thou art standing as it were upon a pinnacle at the edge of some fortifed city. I am a white bird, and perch upon Thee.[25]
4. Thou art My Lover: I see Thee as a nymph with her white limbs stretched by the spring.[26]
5. She lies upon the moss; there is none other but she:[27]
6. Art Thou not Pan?[28]
7. I am He. Speak not, O my God! Let the work be accomplished in silence.[29]
8. Let my cry of pain be crystallized into a little white fawn to run away into the forest![30]

---

[20] *An end* to "Everything" – PAN "under the cloak of darkness" – even *loneliness* has been absorbed with its Opposite – as all "has."

[21] Oneness with All, Surrender of All to Nothing, Unity of the Microcosm and the Macrocosm.

[22] Chapter dedicated to 5 – MARS. It has 55 verses, 5 x 11 – The Number of the Magick of the Beast; 5 = Geburah. 55 = Nun + Heh = "Death" + "Star." 55 is the Mystical number of Malkuth, the sum of all numbers from 1 to 10.

[23] A statement of Love – The Nature of the Will: "Agape."

[24] *A beast* – Therion – chasing – IRE – Spirit.

[25] *Pinnacle* – Phallos; *Edge* – Yod; *City, fortress* – the town of SION (?); *White Bird* – plummeting from Kether.

[26] Love: AGAPE; *a nymph – white*: The One who Receives love – from the Lover.

[27] Associates to BABALON – because *there is none other, but she.*

[28] Recognition of Understanding; Recognition – as the Active Principle of the Spirit.

[29] *I am He* – Unity; insists further on the work; Working – 5 – not in Speaking.

[30] *Cry* – Birth of a Baby – *white fawn*; Hiding in the *forest* – Darkness, Binah, Passivity.

9. Thou art a centaur, O my God, from the violet-blossoms that crown Thee to the hoofs of the horse.[31]

10. Thou art harder than tempered steel; there is no diamond beside Thee.[32]

11. Did I not yield this body and soul?[33]

12. I woo thee with a dagger drawn across my throat.[34]

13. Let the spout of blood quench Thy blood-thirst, O my God![35]

14. Thou art a little white rabbit in the burrow Night.[36]

15. I am greater than the fox and the hole.[37]

16. Give me Thy kisses, O Lord God![38]

17. The lightning came and licked up the little flock of sheep.[39]

18. There is a tongue and a flame; I see that trident walking over the sea.[40]

---

[31] *Centaur* is attributed to the path of "Samekh"; "*violet-blossoms*" – Crown, to the "*hoofs*" in Malkuth – the Middle Pillar.

[32] *Steel* is attributed to Geburah; *diamond* is of Kether. All this is Perceived from the Standpoint of Understanding = Binah.

[33] Adeptus Exemptus freed himself of *body* and *soul* to awaken in the Spirit. The question is posed as a Negation.

[34] Associating that it is the Lord Horus who Initiates: *a dagger drawn across my throat*: decapitation – separation of the Highest Triad by the Flaming Sword. *I woo thee* – Intimacy with the Lord.

[35] *Blood* is sacrificed in the cup of Our Lady: it quenches the *thirst* of the Lord. Binah: a community of Saints who sacrificed their *blood*.

[36] *White* is of Kether. *The burrow Night* is the Darkness of Binah. These are L.V.X. and N.O.X. The *rabbit* is associated with the Constellation at the Foot of Orion – close to Sirius.

[37] This and the previous verse are connected because *the fox* hunts *the rabbit* hiding in the burrow. He is greater than Her because He is V.V.V.V.V.; he is PAN, Everything, he has mastered the Universe.

[38] An appeal.

[39] *Lightning* is a "product" of Union; *sheep* are Multitude (just looking white, but actually are Not).

[40] *Tongue and a flame* – HADIT. *Trident* – the sign of Apophis and Typhon – Crossing the Abyss with the release of Energy. The SON who is "taller" than the Tau-Cross. *Over the sea* – is over Binah.

19. A phoenix hath it for its head; below are two prongs. They spear the wicked.[41]

20. I will spear Thee, O Thou little grey god, unless Thou beware![42]

21. From the grey to the gold; from the gold to that which is beyond the gold of Ophir.[43]

22. My God! but I love Thee![44]

23. Why hast Thou whispered so ambiguous things? Wast Thou afraid, O goat-hoofed One, O horned One, O pillar of lightning?[45]

24. From the lightning fall pearls; from the pearls black specks of nothing.[46]

25. I based all on one, one on naught.[47]

26. Afloat in the aether, O my God, my God![48]

27. O Thou great hooded sun of glory, cut off these eyelids![49]

28. Nature shall die out; she hideth me, closing mine eyelids with fear, she hideth me from My destruction, O Thou open eye.[50]

---

[41] *Phoenix* – from Tiphareth. *Two prongs below* are Ayin, a goat, PAN "the Sinful One." The whole verse associates to the Trinity of Triads: Which Magister Templi perceives.

[42] Trinity: through addressing. *Spear* – Ultimate *Little Grey God* – Satyr. Goat – *beware*.

[43] Ascension from Low to High; overcoming: from *gray* to *gold*, from *gold* to *beyond*.

[44] Declaration. Statement of AGAPE.

[45] *Ambiguous things* – Speech is a Lie – Knowledge – description of "under" the Abyss through the Triad: *O goat-hoofed One; O horned One; O Pillar of lightning* – a PAN goat.

[46] (Again) Triad: *lightning, pearls,* and *specks* of *Nothing*: Like 3 Alchemical principles through a projection in the plane of Binah – but the Magister Templi "understands" this.

[47] Trinity: *all – one – naught* (210!)

[48] The space of *aether* – Emptiness – He is *floating* with no Stronghold, with no "Link."

[49] The essence of the Star. The desire for constant awareness.

[50] *Nature* – Binah. *Hideth* – Binah. *Closing* – Binah. *Fear* – "suffering" from Binah. *Destruction* in the Abyss, Magister Templi is *hidden* in the Silence of his Understanding – his Eye is Open (see "The Oath of the Abyss").

29. O ever-weeping One![51]

30. Not Isis my mother, nor Osiris my self; but the incestuous Horus given over to Typhon, so may I be![52]

31. There thought; and thought is evil.[53]

32. Pan! Pan! Io Pan! it is enough.[54]

33. Fall not into death, O my soul! Think that death is the bed into which you are falling![55]

34. O how I love Thee, O my God! Especially is there a vehement parallel light from infinity, vilely diffracted in the haze of this mind.[56]

35. I love Thee. I love Thee. I love Thee.[57]

36. Thou art a beautiful thing whiter than a woman in the column of this vibration.[58]

37. I shoot up vertically like an arrow, and become that Above.[59]

38. But it is death, and the flame of the pyre.[60]

39. Ascend in the flame of the pyre, O my soul! Thy God is like the cold emptiness of the utmost heaven, into which thou radiatest thy little light.[61]

---

[51] Tears are attributed to Binah. *Ever-weeping One* – Chokmah, Binah, and Kether.

[52] Denial of *Isis* and *Osiris* (in Unity): *Horus* is the Lord of the Highest Aether. He Rules Everything. He is the Child of "I," and "O." *Typhon* is the horror of the Abyss here.

[53] *Thought; evil* – Knowledge: Daath.

[54] Across the Abyss.

[55] A formula of the New Æon: a different concept of *death. Death* is a process – but it reigns beneath the Abyss. NOTHING dies. What "dies" dissolves in the Night.

[56] This is the "grade" of Understanding, not Wisdom (9=2), so it seems to be *Vilely diffracted* – in the Mind.

[57] The nature of the grade that redeems from the Suffering of Darkness. AGAPE, in Trinity.

[58] The *column* is the Middle Pillar (from Kether to Malkuth), but the *woman* is Binah.

[59] An *arrow* that reaches and unites with "the One" *Above.*

[60] The *Death* of the Ego. The "body" burns to Dust.

[61] *Flame* – 5 – flows into *the cold emptiness* – Night – Binah, N.O.X. *Thy Little Light* – "Star."

40. When Thou shall know me, O empty God, my flame shall utterly expire in Thy great N. O. X.[62]

41. What shalt Thou be, my God, when I have ceased to love Thee?[63]

42. A worm, a nothing, a niddering knave![64]

43. But Oh! I love Thee.[65]

44. I have thrown a million flowers from the basket of the Beyond at Thy feet, I have anointed Thee and Thy Staff with oil and blood and kisses.[66]

45. I have kindled Thy marble into life --- ay! into death.[67]

46. I have been smitten with the reek of Thy mouth, that drinketh never wine but life.[68]

47. How the dew of the Universe whitens the lips![69]

48. Ah! trickling flow of the stars of the mother Supernal, begone![70]

49. I Am She that should come, the Virgin of all men.[71]

50. I am a boy before Thee, O Thou satyr God.[72]

51. Thou wilt inflict the punishment of pleasure --- Now! Now! Now![73]

52. Io Pan! Io Pan! I love Thee. I love Thee.[74]

53. O my God, spare me![75]

---

[62] Microcosm dissolving = L.V.X. in *N.O.X.*

[63] The End of Everything, There is Nothing – even in *love*.

[64] *A worm* is equal to the serpent "Ouroboros." A serpent is seen by Those watching from below, and a *Worm* is seen by Those watching from above.

[65] There is a link: Love – Agape (that is why we do not talk about it at 9=2 or 10=1, but "only" at 8=3).

[66] *A million flowers* – an ecstasy of Love: Blessing of the Higher to the Lower. *Staff* – Phallos. Consecration through the Trinity: *oil – blood – kisses*.

[67] It equates life and *death*: as two sides of one "coin."

[68] *Mouth* – Phe – Mars and "the Tower." *Drinking life*: *wine* is "just a Symbol."

[69] Consuming the sacrament.

[70] Mother of Heaven – Isis: See sign of I.R. (N.O.X.)

[71] The Daughter ascends to the throne of the Mother. The soul becomes pure – to marry the Father.

[72] *Boy* – Horus. *Satyr* – PAN.

[73] The Lord determines the proper hour: but since they are one, the Magister shouts *Now!* 3 times – "he" is Binah.

[74] Unity With Everything. AGAPE PAN = Phallos.

[75] Shivering before dissolving.

54. Now! It is done! Death.[76]
55. I cried aloud the word --- and it was a mighty spell to bind the Invisible, an enchantment to unbind the bound; yea, to unbind the bound.[77]

CHAPTER II[78]

1. O my God! use Thou me again, alway. For ever! For ever![79]
2. That which came fire from Thee cometh water from me; let therefore Thy Spirit lay hold on me, so that my right hand loose the lightning.[80]
3. Travelling through space, I saw the onrush of two galaxies, butting each other and goring like bulls upon earth. I was afraid.[81]
4. Thus they ceased fight, and turned upon me, and I was sorely crushed and torn.[82]
5. I had rather have been trampled by the World-Elephant.[83]
6. O my God! Thou art my little pet tortoise![84]

---

[76] The Final Hour: the crossing of Abyss – "the Death" (Nun – Pisces – Kteis – Binah). *Death* is 50, as many as the gates to Binah.

[77] The statement of the one Above the Abyss is "absurd." This is almost a touch of 9=2 because he exclaimed the *word*: he did not keep silent in Understanding. Each last verse in this book contains a summary of a whole chapter and its overcoming. *To bind the Invisible; unbind the bound* – overcoming limitations – liberation from Adepthood, immersing into Binah.

[78] Second chapter dedicated to 3 – Saturn. It has 53 verses; Nun + Gimel – "Death" and "High Priestess." See in 777 for the value 53.

[79] The call for Oneness with the Lord. *Again, always, Forever.*

[80] Taking on the characteristic of the opposing Self. A and B (*Spirit* and *lightning*); *Thy Spirit* here is Passive, while *lightning* is Active. Kteis and Phallos.

[81] *Two galaxies* – Duality.

[82] Ending the *fight* (5) and joining forces towards the Destruction of the "third."

[83] *Elephant* – Foundation – Yesod (*Elephant* is huge, heavy, and slow – Saturn-like).

[84] *Tortoise* holds the Elephant on the Armor.

7. Yet Thou sustainest the World-Elephant.[85]
8. I creep under Thy carapace, like a lover into the bed of his beautiful; I creep in, and sit in Thine heart, as cubby and cosy as may be.[86]
9. Thou shelterest me, that I hear not the trumpeting of that World-Elephant.[87]
10. Thou art not worth an obol in the agora; yet Thou art not to be bought at the ransom of the whole Universe.[88]
11. Thou art like a beautiful Nubian slave leaning her naked purple against the green pillars of marble that are above the bath.[89]
12. Wine jets from her black nipples.[90]
13. I drank wine awhile agone in the house of Pertinax. The cup-boy favoured me, and gave me of the right sweet Chian.[91]
14. There was a Doric boy, skilled in feats of strength, an athlete. The full moon fled away angrily down the wrack. Ah! but we laughed.[92]
15. I was pernicious drunk, O my God! Yet Pertinax brought me to the bridal.[93]
16. I had a crown of thorns for all my dower.[94]
17. Thou art like a goat's horn from Astor, O Thou God of mine, gnarl'd and crook'd and devilish strong.[95]

---

[85] The tortoise is the Spirit. The Elephant represents 4 elements; it associates that the 4 elements cannot exist without the "support" of the Spirit, which sustains them together and constructs combinations.

[86] Approaching the Spirit and reconciling with the True Nature.

[87] Being undisturbed by worldly things.

[88] Value and Non-Value, no difference whatsoever.

[89] *Nubian* – Black – Binah. *Naked purple* – Yesod. *Green* – Netzach – but *green* is also as Anahata, Tiphareth.

[90] Binah source: *nipples* – "the Lovers" (from Chokmah: "the Star"). *Wine* – life.

[91] Exercise of the Will; (*house* – Bet). (*The cup-boy* – Magister Templi).

[92] *Doric boy* – from Dora – Yoni – KTEIS. Binah, but it reflects strength across the *moon*, the drunkenness of life: of the joy of Exercising the True Will.

[93] Wedding: "the Lovers" lead to 3 – Binah – He who is full of life knows what life is and what All of life is. *Pernicious drunk* is the limit.

[94] *A crown of thorns* is an allusion to the crown of Jesus and his crucifixion. Departure on the path of Binah – "Eli Eli, lama sabachthani." False crown in Daath.

[95] *Horn* is Phallos – PAN.

18. Colder than all the ice of all the glaciers of the Naked Mountain was the wine it poured for me.[96]

19. A wild country and a waning moon.

    Clouds scudding over the sky.

    A circuit of pines, and of tall yews beyond.

    Thou in the midst![97]

20. O all ye toads and cats, rejoice! Ye slimy things, come hither![98]

21. Dance, dance to the Lord our God![99]

22. He is he! He is he! He is he![100]

23. Why should I go on?[101]

24. Why? Why? comes the sudden cackle of a million imps of hell.[102]

25. And the laughter runs.[103]

26. But sickens not the Universe; but shakes not the stars.[104]

27. God! how I love Thee![105]

28. I am walking in an asylum; all the men and women about me are insane.[106]

29. Oh madness! madness! madness! desirable art thou![107]

30. But I love Thee, O God![108]

31. These men and women rave and howl; they froth out folly.[109]

---

[96] Understanding the opposites of life: "the Lovers." *Naked Mountain* – probably Abiegnus.

[97] Pronounced darkness: *moon* in waning, *clouds* covering the stars, but nature organizes *Circuits* – God is in the Center. Tiphareth.

[98] Feeding lower life from Higher spheres.

[99] Movement.

[100] Not giving a description; epithet, adjective. Everything – PAN. "He is He."

[101] *Why* is the word of Reason – limitation. Sin – the idea of misunderstanding.

[102] Crowd are exalted with themselves.

[103] *Laughter* – originates from the Multitude – Choronzon. But what is on otherworldly *laughs* to it All too.

[104] Unconditionality of the Supreme Triad; *Universe* – Binah. *Stars* – Chokmah.

[105] Kether at "that" point – in relation to the previous verses; Agape.

[106] *Men* – Chokmah. *Women* – Binah. Kteis + Pahallos, but as "multitude" – *Asylum.*

[107] Summons the *madness* of Aleph.

[108] "But" it is restrained by *love.*

[109] Confusion in Multitude.

32. I begin to be afraid. I have no check; I am alone. Alone. Alone.[110]

33. Think, O God, how I am happy in Thy love.[111]

34. O marble Pan! O false leering face! I love Thy dark kisses, bloody and stinking! O marble Pan! Thy kisses are like sunlight on the blue AEgean; their blood is the blood of the sunset over Athens; their stink is like a garden of Roses of Macedonia.[112]

35. I dreamt of sunset and roses and vines; Thou wast there, O my God, Thou didst habit Thyself as an Athenian courtesan, and I loved Thee.[113]

36. Thou art no dream, O Thou too beautiful alike for sleep and waking![114]

37. I disperse the insane folk of the earth; I walk alone with my little puppets in the garden.[115]

38. I am Gargantuan great; yon galaxy is but the smoke-ring of mine incense.[116]

39. Burn Thou strange herbs, O God![117]

40. Brew me a magic liquor, boys, with your glances![118]

41. The very soul is drunken.[119]

42. Thou art drunken, O my God, upon my kisses.[120]

---

[110] *Loneliness* – Phallos tends to marry Kteis; another association to the Trinity (*fear – control – alone*).

[111] Agape.

[112] *Pan* marries opposites within: Understanding in Binah. *Black, AEgean, marble, Roses* – Binah. The rest is the nature of Phallos.

[113] *Sunset* – the transition of the Sun into Darkness – still: Agape!

[114] *Dream"* is "Yesod." *Beautiful* – Tiphareth. But "he" transcends even reality – Binah.

[115] Exercising the Will: Magister Templi *walk in the garden* – exercise his Will, his Great Work.

[116] The True Will is the great flame, everything else is but the *smoke-ring* – irrelevant and little. *Gargantuan* is PAN – Everything.

[117] A specific scent "tied" to the experience of Binah.

[118] *Boys* – Masters of the Temple – always young – at the fountain of eternal youth.

[119] The Will of the *soul*, i.e., true nature led to the Supreme Unification.

[120] What is the Will of the "lower" – is also the Will of the "higher" – They are one.

43. The Universe reels; Thou hast looked upon it.[121]

44. Twice, and all is done.[122]

45. Come, O my God, and let us embrace![123]

46. Lazily, hungrily, ardently, patiently; so will I work.[124]

47. There shall be an End.[125]

48. O God! O God![126]

49. I am a fool to love Thee; Thou art cruel, Thou withholdest Thy-self.[127]

50. Come to me now! I love Thee! I love Thee![128]

51. O my darling, my darling --- Kiss me! Kiss me! Ah! but again.[129]

52. Sleep, take me! Death, take me! This life is too full; it pains, it slays, it suffices.[130]

53. Let me go back into the world; yea, back into the world.[131]

CHAPTER III[132]

1. I was the priest of Ammon-Ra in the temple of Ammon-Ra at The-bai.[133]

---

[121] Ecstatic Intoxication – but with clear "vision" – Understanding it.

[122] *Twice*: looking with both eyes: 6 and 9.

[123] A call for Unification.

[124] 4 qualities by which the Will is manifested.

[125] Prophecy – whoever takes the Path shall come to *an End*.

[126] O – The zero – Naught – LA "God" = AL = All = PAN – The Unity of opposites.

[127] Trinity: Madness, cruelty, restraint.

[128] A call for Unification.

[129] Agape.

[130] Scattering from Heights, permeation with the lower One.

[131] All is Manifested. *The world* = XXI = Universe.

[132] Third chapter is dedicated to 4 – JUPITER (Pillar, Support). There are 60 verses – 60 = Samekh and Sagittarius. See 777.

[133] This verse would be associated with the worship of the Sun in Tiphareth, but there is a view of how Adeptus Exemptus (7=4) actually worships the Sun as Magister Templi (8=3); i.e., it tells of worshiping the Spiritual Sun. *Amon-Ra* – Jupiter – the Sun dressed with Jupiter, in the dignity of authority.

2. But Bacchus came singing with his troops of vine-clad girls, of girls in dark mantles; and Bacchus in the midst like a fawn![134]

3. God! how I ran out in my rage and scattered the chorus![135]
4. But in my temple stood Bacchus as the priest of Ammon-Ra.[136]
5. Therefore I went wildly with the girls into Abyssinia; and there we abode and rejoiced.[137]
6. Exceedingly; yea, in good sooth![138]
7. I will eat the ripe and the unripe fruit for the glory of Bacchus.[139]
8. Terraces of ilex, and tiers of onyx and opal and sardonyx leading up to the cool green porch of malachite.[140]
9. Within is a crystal shell, shaped like an oyster --- O glory of Priapus! beatitude of the Great Goddess![141]
10. Therein is a pearl.[142]
11. O Pearl! thou hast come from the majesty of dread Ammon-Ra.[143]
12. Then I the priest beheld a steady glitter in the heart of the pearl.[144]
13. So bright we could not look! But behold! a blood-red rose upon a rood of glowing gold![145]
14. So I adored the God. Bacchus! thou art the lover of my God![146]

---

[134] *Bacchus* – Dionysus – Solar Deity. *Girls in dark mantles* – Netzach in the robe of Binah. *Fawn* – child – innocent and pure.

[135] *God!* – related to the Supreme Triad. *Rage* – Middle Triad, Geburah especially. *Chorus* – Lower Triad – Multitude.

[136] Intoxication instead of sobriety, fornication instead of chastity.

[137] Refusal to worship something specific, submission of Love under Will, exercising the True Will.

[138] The entire Consciousness, and being, and the Self, and the Soul, are harnessed to exercise the Will.

[139] Trinity: *the glory of Bacchus* (A∴A∴); *ripe and unripe* – R∴C∴ and G∴D∴.

[140] The ilex is of Geburah; *onix* – XXI; *opal* – I (8); *sardonyx* – ? (4 – ?); *malachite* – green – Netzach. All this from warm to cool.

[141] *Priapus* – Phallos; *Great Goddess* – Kteis; *shell* – Kteis.

[142] *Pearl* – grain, seed, "Yod," but Kether as well. Kether is in the shell – in the night of Pan.

[143] The Child of the Father – still hidden but overly sublime.

[144] *The pearl* is Khabs, *glitter in the hearth* is Hadit.

[145] L.V.X. Also Kether. But the symbol of Tiphareth appears.

[146] Identification with *Bacchus*.

15. I who was priest of Ammon-Ra, who saw the Nile flow by for many moons, for many, many moons, am the young fawn of the grey land.[147]

16. I will set up my dance in your conventicles, and my secret loves shall be sweet among you.[148]

17. Thou shalt have a lover among the lords of the grey land.[149]

18. This shall he bring unto thee, without which all is in vain; a man's life spilt for thy love upon My Altars.[150]

19. Amen.[151]

20. Let it be soon, O God, my God! I ache for Thee, I wander very lonely among the mad folk, in the grey land of desolation.[152]

21. Thou shalt set up the abominable lonely Thing of wickedness. Oh joy! to lay that corner-stone![153]

22. It shall stand erect upon the high mountain; only my God shall commune with it.[154]

23. I will build it of a single ruby; it shall be seen from afar off.[155]

24. Come! let us irritate the vessels of the earth: they shall distil strange wine.[156]

---

[147] He was the *priest of Ammon-Ra* – now the Magister Templi – he was released from his priesthood. He has just been born in Understanding. *Gray land* in Emperor's Scale. The gray color is from Chokmah, but also Binah. *Nile* – the river of life: going through the Triads: he was 6; he looked at many 9, and is a young *fawn of the gray land,* this as if it were a coupling of Malkuth and Binah.

[148] The combination of mobility and immobility, the combination of external and internal. New life to old sources. Newly revealed secrets.

[149] *Lover* – R∴C∴; *lords* – A∴A∴; *grey land* – G∴D∴.

[150] He who exercises his True Will has the inertia of the whole Universe by his side.

[151] Amen = 91, confirmation.

[152] *Aching* is a mystery – the revelation of Binah. A *loner* in the Multitude.

[153] As soon as the Will of the One moves, though tiny, God himself influences things to move in accordance with that Will. This is the lifting of the restriction that the Multitude fears. *Corner-stone* – on the edge of the Abyss.

[154] An association to Phallos.

[155] *Ruby* – see "Liber Stellae Rubeae."

[156] Distillation pot – Spirit of *wine* – life.

25. It grows under my hand: it shall cover the whole heaven.[157]
26. Thou art behind me: I scream with a mad joy.[158]
27. Then said Ithuriel the strong; let Us also worship this invisible marvel![159]
28. So did they, and the archangels swept over the heaven.[160]
29. Strange and mystic, like a yellow priest invoking mighty flights of great grey birds from the North, so do I stand and invoke Thee![161]
30. Let them obscure not the sun with their wings and their clamour![162]
31. Take away form and its following![163]
32. I am still.[164]
33. Thou art like an osprey among the rice, I am the great red pelican in the sunset waters.[165]
34. I am like a black eunuch; and Thou art the scimitar. I smite off the head of the light one, the breaker of bread and salt.[166]
35. Yea! I smite --- and the blood makes as it were a sunset on the lapis lazuli of the King's Bedchamber.[167]

---

[157] *Hand* – Yod – a path to Chesed. *Heaven* – Binah, where Magister Templi cultivates his garden.

[158] "Opiso Mou Teletarhai!"

[159] I+Th+U+R+A+L (?) = 10+9+6+200+10+1+30 = 266 (?) I am not sure about this. However, it looks like the Chesed aspect – because of the *strong*, especially since it worships the *invisible* – Binah.

[160] *Archangels* – belong to the sphere of Briatic forces. *Heaven* – Supreme Triad.

[161] *North* – yellow – Malkuth.

[162] Looking "from below" at Tiphareth. Gray birds from the previous verse, *with their wings* – thoughts disturbing a meditating Mind.

[163] Striving to get to the next level in Yoga (see "Eight Lectures on Yoga").

[164] Attainment.

[165] The first is the Treasurer of Wisdom, the second speaks of the Words of Wisdom.

[166] The *one* under the Abyss was killed (*bread* and *salt* – the feast of life – Tiphareth). *Bread* – Isis – Binah. *Salt* – Binah. *Black eunuch* – Binah. *Scimitar* – flaming sword that *smites* the Abyss, i.e. top from the lower part of the Tree of Life.

[167] Sacrificing the *blood* of the Saints. *King's Bedchamber* – Binah.

36. I smite! The whole world is broken up into a mighty wind, and a voice cries aloud in a tongue that men cannot speak.[168]

37. I know that awful sound of primal joy; let us follow on the wings of the gale even unto the holy house of Hathor; let us offer the five jewels of the cow upon her altar![169]

38. Again the inhuman voice![170]

39. I rear my Titan bulk into the teeth of the gale, and I smite and prevail, and swing me out over the sea.[171]

40. There is a strange pale God, a god of pain and deadly wickedness.[172]

41. My own soul bites into itself, like a scorpion ringed with fire.[173]

42. That pallid God with face averted, that God of subtlety and laughter, that young Doric God, him will I serve.[174]

43. For the end thereof is torment unspeakable.[175]

44. Better the loneliness of the great grey sea![176]

45. But ill befall the folk of the grey land, my God![177]

46. Let me smother them with my roses![178]

47. Oh Thou delicious God, smile sinister![179]

48. I pluck Thee, O my God, like a purple plum upon a sunny tree. How Thou dost melt in my mouth, Thou consecrated sugar of the Stars![180]

---

[168] Third *smite* – 3 – Binah; Comprehension – understanding the end of Thought and Speech – which are only the *winds* of Ruach.

[169] The *house* of the Goddess *Hathor* – Binah. 5=1.

[170] *Inhuman* – Divine.

[171] Victory over the winds of the Mind – Yoga. *Sea* – Binah.

[172] Binah.

[173] Shin and Nun.

[174] *Averted* – everything across the Abyss encompasses its Opposite. *Doric God* – Babalon.

[175] Binah.

[176] Malkuth.

[177] Evil – the deception of Duality, the Limitation.

[178] *Roses* – from Binah over to Tiphareth.

[179] A contradiction united in itself. Mercy is not Mercy, but it also is.

[180] *Purple plum upon a sunny tree* – Babalon with Tiphareth. *Consecrated sugar of the Stars* – Chokmah.

49. The world is all grey before mine eyes; it is like an old worn wine-skin.[181]

50. All the wine of it is on these lips.[182]

51. Thou hast begotten me upon a marble Statue, O my God![183]

52. The body is icy cold with the coldness of a million moons; it is harder than the adamant of eternity. How shall I come forth into the light?[184]

53. Thou art He, O God! O my darling! my child! my plaything! Thou art like a cluster of maidens, like a multitude of swans upon the lake.[185]

54. I feel the essence of softness.[186]

55. I am hard and strong and male; but come Thou! I shall be soft and weak and feminine.[187]

56. Thou shalt crush me in the wine-press of Thy love. My blood shall stain Thy fiery feet with litanies of Love in Anguish.[188]

57. There shall be a new flower in the fields, a new vintage in the vine-yards.[189]

58. The bees shall gather a new honey; the poets shall sing a new song.[190]

59. I shall gain the Pain of the Goat for my prize; and the God that sitteth upon the shoulders of Time shall drowse.[191]

60. Then shall all this which is written be accomplished: yea, it shall be accomplished.[192]

---

[181] Everything is manifested; it moves but stands.
[182] *Wine* – life – blood *"on these* (Her) *lips* (Phe)." Babalon.
[183] Understanding.
[184] Triad: (*body; moons; light.*)
[185] Everything that can be enjoyed and drunken with Ecstasy.
[186] Experience.
[187] Phallos – inner nature; but Kteis – Understanding – passivity.
[188] Binah.
[189] Rebirth in Understanding: *new* life, new "incarnation."
[190] Phallos and Kteis: unification of polarity in the new order.
[191] *Time* – Binah. *Goat* – Pan. *Pain* – Binah.
[192] Confirmation of the fulfillment of the prophecy of the Magister Templi – Understanding.

CHAPTER IV[193]

1. I am like a maiden bathing in a clear pool of fresh water.[194]
2. O my God! I see Thee dark and desirable, rising through the water as a golden smoke.[195]
3. Thou art altogether golden, the hair and the eyebrows and the brilliant face; even into the finger-tips and toe-tips Thou art one rosy dream of gold.[196]
4. Deep into Thine eyes that are golden my soul leaps, like an archangel menacing the sun.[197]
5. My sword passes through and through Thee; crystalline moons ooze out of Thy beautiful body that is hidden behind the ovals of Thine eyes.[198]
6. Deeper, ever deeper. I fall, even as the whole Universe falls down the abyss of Years.[199]
7. For Eternity calls; the Overworld calls; the world of the Word is awaiting us.[200]
8. Be done with speech, O God! Fasten the fangs of the hound Eternity in this my throat![201]
9. I am like a wounded bird flapping in circles.[202]
10. Who knows where I shall fall?[203]
11. O blessed One! O God! O my devourer![204]

---

[193] Fourth chapter is dedicated to 6 – SUN. There are 59 verses: Nun + Teth = 50 + 9 = 14 = Yod + Daleth; 1 + 4 = 5 = He. See 777 for 59.
[194] *Maiden* – Yod, but also "the Hermit." *Water* – Binah.
[195] Description of *God* as the Erecting Phallos.
[196] Kether with a reflection of Tiphareth.
[197] Tiphareth.
[198] *Sword* – Ruach – Tiphareth; *Moons – ooze* below.
[199] The *Universe* is as it is– "it exists" in the *Abyss of Years* – Æons – Time – Binah.
[200] Trinity: *Eternity* – the *Overworld* (the otherworld) – *the world of the Words*.
[201] "An attack" on Daath.
[202] *Circle* – O; a dying Thought.
[203] Uncertainty of the moment, ie. places when and where the Supreme Triad separates from the Lower. A dot – .
[204] Higher redemption by lower absorption – by destruction (Phe – 5 – mouth).

12. Let me fall, fall down, fall away, afar, alone![205]

13. Let me fall![206]

14. Nor is there any rest, Sweet Heart, save in the cradle of royal Bacchus, the thigh of the most Holy One.[207]

15. There rest, under the canopy of night.[208]

16. Uranus chid Eros; Marsyas chid Olympas; I chid my beautiful lover with his sunray mane; shall I not sing?[209]

17. Shall not mine incantations bring around me the wonderful company of the wood-gods, their bodies glistening with the ointment of moonlight and honey and myrrh?[210]

18. Worshipful are ye, O my lovers; let us forward to the dimmest hollow![211]

19. There we will feast upon mandrake and upon moly![212]

20. There the lovely One shall spread us His holy banquet. In the brown cakes of corn we shall taste the food of the world, and be strong.[213]

21. In the ruddy and awful cup of death we shall drink the blood of the world, and be drunken![214]

22. Ohe! the song to Iao, the song to Iao![215]

23. Come, let us sing to thee, Iacchus invisible, Iacchus triumphant, Iacchus indicible![216]

24. Iacchus, O Iacchus, O Iacchus, be near us![217]

---

[205] Falling through the "prism" of Binah.

[206] The "landing" of the experience.

[207] "Work" – 3 of Disc. *Bacchus* – Tiphareth.

[208] Binah.

[209] The relationship between the Magister and the Adept. He (MT) still absorbs both criticism and joy.

[210] Feasts of the Sun.

[211] *Lovers* – R∴C∴. *Dimmest hollow* – Binah.

[212] *Mandrake and moly* – Binah.

[213] Manifestation of the Prana of Deities.

[214] *Cup* of Babalon.

[215] *Ohe* – OAI (A∴A∴). *The song to Iao* (R∴C∴). The second time, repeated – G∴D∴.

[216] Worshiping of *Iaccush* as the Trinity of Phallos.

[217] Phallos Phallos Phallos.

25. Then was the countenance of all time darkened, and the true light shone forth.[218]

26. There was also a certain cry in an unknown tongue, whose stridency troubled the still waters of my soul, so that my mind and my body were healed of their disease, self-knowledge.[219]

27. Yea, an angel troubled the waters.[220]

28. This was the cry of Him: IIIOOShBThIO-IIIIAMAMThIBI-II.[221]

29. Nor did I sing this for a thousand times a night for a thousand nights before Thou camest, O my flaming God, and pierced me with Thy spear. Thy scarlet robe unfolded the whole heavens, so that the Gods said: All is burning: it is the end.[222]

30. Also Thou didst set Thy lips to the wound and suck out a million eggs. And Thy mother sat upon them, and lo! stars and stars and ultimate Things whereof stars are the atoms.[223]

31. Then I perceived Thee, O my God, sitting like a white cat upon the trellis-work of the arbour; and the hum of the spinning worlds was but Thy pleasure.[224]

32. O white cat, the sparks fly from Thy fur! Thou dost crackle with splitting the worlds.[225]

33. I have seen more of Thee in the white cat than I saw in the Vision of Aeons.[226]

34. In the boat of Ra did I travel, but I never found upon the visible Universe any being like unto Thee![227]

---

[218] The gate to Sun is Binah (BABALON = BAB – AL – ON).

[219] Binah whose Understanding is *healed* all the way "down."

[220] *An angel* – R∴C∴. *Waters* – A∴A∴.

[221] I = Phallos O = Kteis. The numerical value of this word is 734 or 1516 (?).

[222] Aleph – *a thousand times. Thy spear* – Phallos. *Sing* – voice – an ear hears. Ear – Spirit.

[223] *Lips* – Phe. *Eggs* – Yod(?). Mother – He, Stars. *Atoms* and *eggs* –Vau – Tiphareth.

[224] *A cat* – Bastet – Sun. *White* – Kether. *The hum* – sound – ear – Spirit.

[225] *White fur* – aura. *Sparks* – Spirit – Fire. *Splitting the worlds* – Samadhi.

[226] Æon connects Hod and Malkuth; belongs to the Astral Plane; The vision of the *cat* is from the "Mental" Plane. *White* is across the Abyss. Celebrating Iacchus as the Trinity of Phallos.

[227] *The boat of Ra* – 5=6. *The visible Universe* – bellow the Abyss; below Paroketh.

35. Thou wast like a winged white horse, and I raced Thee through eternity against the Lord of the Gods.[228]

36. So still we race![229]

37. Thou wast like a flake of snow falling in the pine-clad woods.

38. In a moment Thou wast lost in a wilderness of the like and the un-like.[230]

39. But I beheld the beautiful God at the ba[231]ck of the blizzard --- and Thou wast He![232]

40. Also I read in a great Book.[233]

41. On ancient skin was written in letters of gold: Verbum fit Ver-bum.[234]

42. Also Vitriol and the hierophant's name V.V.V.V.V.[235]

43. All this wheeled in fire, in star-fire, rare and far and utterly lonely — even as Thou and I, O desolate soul my God![236]

44. Yea, and the writing[237]

45. Eight times he cried aloud, and by eight and by eight shall I count Thy favours, Oh Thou Elevenfold God 418![238]

46. Yea, and by many more; by the ten in the twenty-two directions; even as the perpendicular of the Pyramid --- so shall Thy favours be.[239]

---

[228] *Winged white horse* – Pegasus – IRE – Spirit.

[229] Continuum.

[230] *Flake of snow* – point. White *snow* – Kether. *Pine-clad woods* – Binah.

[231] Samadhi (Atmadarshana – ?)

[232] Samadhi (Shivadarshana – ?)

[233] TARO.

[234] (41 = MA) Gold – Tiphareth. *Letters of gold* – the name of the Angel, 5=6.

[235] *VITRIOL* – distribute it inside the Hexagram. V.V.V.V.V. – Magister Templi – 5 footprints of a camel – A∴A∴.

[236] There are no Words, only the Experience of *star-fire* – Samadhi – 8=3.

[237] Some of these symbols look like "ordinary" letters; there are 16 of them... I do not understand this.

[238] 8 is Cheth- "the Chariot" – Cancer – Crab – Binah. 8 letters in "BAPHOMETh" 8=3. 8 = K.I.T. = 418; 11 = ABRAHADABRA.

[239] 10 Sephirot and 22 paths; 220 is the number of verses in "Liber AL." *Pyramid* – Phallos.

47. If I number them, they are One.[240]

48. Excellent is Thy love, Oh Lord! Thou art revealed by the darkness, and he who gropeth in the horror of the groves shall haply catch Thee, even as a snake that seizeth on a little singing-bird.[241]

49. I have caught Thee, O my soft thrush; I am like a hawk of mother-of-emerald; I catch Thee by instinct, though my eyes fail from Thy glory.[242]

50. Yet they are but foolish folk yonder. I see them on the yellow sand, all clad in Tyrian purple.[243]

51. They draw their shining God unto the land in nets; they build a fire to the Lord of Fire, and cry unhallowed words, even the dreadful curse Amri maratza, maratza, atman deona lastadza maratza maritza --- maran![244]

52. Then do they cook the shining god, and gulp him whole.[245]

53. These are evil folk, O beautiful boy! let us pass on to the Otherworld.[246]

54. Let us make ourselves into a pleasant bait, into a seductive shape![247]

55. I will be like a splendid naked woman with ivory breasts and golden nipples; my whole body shall be like the milk of the stars. I will be lustrous and Greek, a courtesan of Delos, of the unstable Isle.[248]

56. Thou shalt be like a little red worm on a hook.[249]

57. But thou and I will catch our fish alike.[250]

---

[240] *One* – Kether.

[241] L.V.X. in N.O.X. Kundalini Serpent; Serpent and Pigeon; *snake* and *singing-bird*.

[242] *Hawk* – Horus – Tiphareth – Kether. (The link between Tiphareth and Binah?)

[243] Tiphareth.

[244] The sun behind the sun; awakening in Binah. *Lord of Fire* – Horus.

[245] It is wrong to think that the Multitude can "consume" God. But He is manifested through them.

[246] Interior retreat – Behind the Veil.

[247] *Bait* – Tzaddi– Hook – !

[248] D.L.S. = 94. (93 + 1) (see 777). *Unstable Isle* – Samadhi.

[249] Tzaddi. *Worm* – bait – desired by Passion.

[250] *Fish* – Pisces – Moon – Kteis – 8=3.

58. Then wilt thou be a shining fish with golden back and silver belly: I will be like a violent beautiful man, stronger than two score bulls, a man of the West bearing a great sack of precious jewels upon a staff that is greater than the axis of the all.[251]

59. And the fish shall be sacrificed to Thee and the strong man crucified for Me, and Thou and I will kiss, and atone for the wrong of the Beginning; yea, for the wrong of the beginning.[252]

CHAPTER V[253]

1. O my beautiful God! I swim in Thy heart like a trout in the mountain torrent.[254]

2. I leap from pool to pool in my joy; I am goodly with brown and gold and silver.[255]

3. Why, I am lovelier than the russet autumn woods at the first snowfall.[256]

4. And the crystal cave of my thought is lovelier than I.[257]

5. Only one fish-hook can draw me out; it is a woman kneeling by the bank of the stream. It is she that pours the bright dew over herself, and into the sand so that the river gushes forth.[258]

6. There is a bird on yonder myrtle; only the song of that bird can draw me out of the pool of Thy heart, O my God![259]

---

[251] *Staff* – Phallos. *Fish* – Kteis. Complete change K.P. > P.K.

[252] Samadhi. No Division; above 5=6 is 8=3. *The wrong of the beginning* – 012.

[253] Fifth chapter is dedicated to 8 – Mercury. There are 48 Verses; Maim + Cheth. $40 + 8 = 12 =$ Yod + Beth. $1 + 2 = 3$ – Gimel. Maim leads along the surface of Paroketh. Cheth is $8 - 11 - 418$. See 777 for 48.

[254] *Heart* of Tiphareth – rises across the Abyss; *Trout in the mountain torrent* – Samadhi.

[255] Magister Templi, his unconditionality. *Brown* – Binah; *gold* – Tiphareth; Kether – *silver* – Gimel.

[256] Above Geburah. *Autumn* – West – Water – Chesed. *First snowfall* – Dhyana.

[257] *Crystal Cave* – Understanding (SEZAM = 667!)

[258] *Fish-hook* – Tzaddi. *A woman* is like on ATU "Star" ("Tzaddi is not a star"). *River* – ERIDANUS – 93 current.

[259] *A bird* is Ibis – the passage from 8=3 to 9=2. Magus.

7. Who is this Neapolitan boy that laughs in his happiness? His lover is the mighty crater of the Mountain of Fire. I saw his charred limbs borne down the slopes in a stealthy tongue of liquid stone.[260]

8. And Oh! the chirp of the cicada![261]

9. I remember the days when I was cacique in Mexico.[262]

10. O my God, wast Thou then as now my beautiful lover?[263]

11. Was my boyhood then as now Thy toy, Thy joy?[264]

12. Verily, I remember those iron days.[265]

13. I remember how we drenched the bitter lakes with our torrent of gold; how we sank the treasurable image in the crater of Citlaltepetl.[266]

14. How the good flame lifted us even unto the lowlands, setting us down in the impenetrable forest.[267]

15. Yea, Thou wast a strange scarlet bird with a bill of gold. I was Thy mate in the forests of the lowland; and ever we heard from afar the shrill chant of mutilated priests and the insane clamour of the Sacrifice of Maidens.[268]

16. There was a weird winged God that told us of his wisdom.[269]

17. We attained to be starry grains of gold dust in the sands of a slow river.[270]

---

[260] Pointing to the Middle Pillar (?)

[261] Voices – 8 – *chirp.*

[262] Adeptus Minor has acquired that memory, while Magister Templi gets Understanding from that.

[263] Continuity.

[264] *Boyhood* – Bebies of the Abyss; M.T. is the "degree" of "eternal youth." *Toy* – game – 8. Continuity.

[265] *Iron* – 5. *Days* – L.V.X.

[266] *Bitter lakes* – Binah. *Gold* – Kether. The connection is Beth. *Image* – smaller – Tiphareth; greater – Kether. *Crater* – Chakra – outbreak of Fire.

[267] *Good flame* – Kundalini. *Lowlands* – plane, realm. *Forest* – Binah.

[268] *Mutilated priests* and *Sacrifice of Maidens* – associates to Phallos and Kteis, but separated.

[269] Quetzalcoatl – *winged* Snake. Caduceus of Mercury 8. Sigil of the Tree of Life and Kteis and Phallos united.

[270] Kether; Binah; Chokmah.

18. Yea, and that river was the river of space and time also.[271]

19. We parted thence; ever to the smaller, ever to the greater, until now, O sweet God, we are ourselves, the same.[272]

20. O God of mine, Thou art like a little white goat with lightning in his horns![273]

21. I love Thee, I love Thee.[274]

22. Every breath, every word, every thought, every deed is an act of love with Thee.[275]

23. The beat of my heart is the pendulum of love.[276]

24. The songs of me are the soft sighs:[277]

25. The thoughts of me are very rapture:[278]

26. And my deeds are the myriads of Thy children, the stars and the atoms.[279]

27. Let there be nothing![280]

28. Let all things drop into this ocean of love![281]

29. Be this devotion a potent spell to exorcise the demons of the Five![282]

30. Ah God, all is gone! Thou dost consummate Thy rapture. Falutli! Falutli![283]

31. There is a solemnity of the silence. There is no more voice at all.[284]

---

[271] *River* – Eridanus – Universe (below the Abyss).

[272] Separation; duality; but the consciousness of Oneness does not disappear.

[273] *White* – Kether. *Goat* – Baphomet. *Lightning* – from the Eye of the Tower (links 8 and 6).

[274] Agape.

[275] 8 is dedicated to Agape.

[276] 8 through 6; the Logos originates from Agape.

[277] 8 (outside).

[278] 8 (inside).

[279] 8 (The Law of Thelema).

[280] AL – LA (Iehi Ain).

[281] Binah – Agape.

[282] *Five* – 1 – Pentagram.

[283] Destruction of Everything in Samadhi. There is no "me." *Falutli* is the Scream of Orgasm.

[284] (Magician and Exorcist) There is no 8 beyond Orgasm – "there is" Hoor-Paar-Kraat.

32. So shall it be unto the end. We who were dust shall never fall away into the dust.[285]

33. So shall it be.[286]

34. Then, O my God, the breath of the Garden of Spices. All these have a savour averse.[287]

35. The cone is cut with an infinite ray; the curve of hyperbolic life springs into being.[288]

36. Farther and farther we float; yet we are still. It is the chain of systems that is falling away from us.[289]

37. First falls the silly world; the world of the old grey land.[290]

38. Falls it unthinkably far, with its sorrowful bearded face presiding over it; it fades to silence and woe.[291]

39. We to silence and bliss, and the face is the laughing face of Eros.[292]

40. Smiling we greet him with the secret signs.[293]

41. He leads us into the Inverted Palace.[294]

42. There is the Heart of Blood, a pyramid reaching its apex down beyond the Wrong of the Beginning.[295]

43. Bury me unto Thy Glory, O beloved, O princely lover of this harlot maiden, within the Secretest Chamber of the Palace![296]

44. It is done quickly; yea, the seal is set upon the vault.[297]

---

[285] 8=3.

[286] That is a "Universal" Principle.

[287] *A savour averse* is from Adeptus Major: Magister Templi is freed of that. Experiences are without affecting the essence of Understanding (impartiality; irresistibility – only comprehension, consciousness, and Understanding).

[288] *Cone* – Phallos. *Infinite ray* – Phallos. Spiral Movement of the Universe (goat horns.)

[289] (See Liber LXV.) Unconditionality; the Spirit GOES.

[290] Rejecting an illusion.

[291] Even Tiphareth has been surpassed (outside).

[292] Eros – the inner Air that illuminates Tiphareth from Binah. Melting, "falling" in Binah. Eros is from Agape.

[293] Inner worship.

[294] A mystery that contains its opposite – across the Abyss – 8=3.

[295] *Blood* – DM – 44 – Horus. *Pyramid* – Phallos.

[296] Binah – Babalon.

[297] A∴A∴ seal.

45. There is one that shall avail to open it.[298]
46. Nor by memory, nor by imagination, nor by prayer, nor by fasting, nor by scourging, nor by drugs, nor by ritual, nor by meditation; only by passive love shall he avail.[299]
47. He shall await the sword of the Beloved and bare his throat for the stroke.[300]
48. Then shall his blood leap out and write me runes in the sky; yea, write me runes in the sky.[301]

CHAPTER VI[302]

1. Thou wast a priestess, O my God, among the Druids; and we knew the powers of the oak.[303]
2. We made us a temple of stones in the shape of the Universe, even as thou didst wear openly and I concealed.[304]
3. There we performed many wonderful things by midnight.[305]
4. By the waning moon did we work.[306]
5. Over the plain came the atrocious cry of wolves.[307]
6. We answered; we hunted with the pack.[308]
7. We came even unto the new Chapel and Thou didst bear away the Holy Graal beneath Thy Druid vestments.[309]

---

[298] NEMO.
[299] Agape (Understanding).
[300] Flaming *sword* splitting the Abyss apart (see the Invocation of Horus).
[301] *Blood* – DM – 44 – Horus; *runes* – 8. *Sky* – Binah – Nuit reflection.
[302] Sixth chapter is dedicated to Moon. It has 51 verse – Nun + Aleph; 50 + 1 = 6 – Vau, Hierophant. Death and Fool. See in 777 for 51.
[303] *Priestess* – Gimel – Moon. *Druids* – Masters and Adepts and Magicians who worshiped the Moon as the Lady of the Skies. *Powers of the oak* – Phallos.
[304] God acts openly through the Adept/Magister, and he "enters" inside – into the Secret.
[305] *Midnight* Sun – Moon – Kephra.
[306] *Waning moon* – a decrease in power. Binah – Understanding.
[307] *Wolf* – the beast dedicated to the Goddess.
[308] In harmony with the Multitude.
[309] Binah. 8=3.

8. Secretly and by stealth did we drink of the informing sacrament.[310]

9. Then a terrible disease seized upon the folk of the grey land; and we rejoiced.[311]

10. O my God, disguise Thy glory![312]

11. Come as a thief, and let us steal away the Sacraments![313]

12. In our groves, in our cloistral cells, in our honeycomb of happiness, let us drink, let us drink![314]

13. It is the wine that tinges everything with the true tincture of infallible gold.[315]

14. There are deep secrets in these songs. It is not enough to hear the bird; to enjoy song he must be the bird.[316]

15. I am the bird, and Thou art my song, O my glorious galloping God![317]

16. Thou reinest in the stars; thou drivest the constellations seven abreast through the circus of Nothingness.[318]

17. Thou Gladiator God![319]

18. I play upon mine harp; Thou fightest the beasts and the flames.[320]

19. Thou takest Thy joy in the music, and I in the fighting.[321]

20. Thou and I are beloved of the Emperor.[322]

21. See! he has summoned us to the Imperial dais. The night falls; it is a great orgy of worship and bliss.[323]

---

[310] 8=3.

[311] Understanding destroys – *poisons* the Lower Being – destroys the Ego.

[312] Hiding the L.V.X. in N.O.X. – merging into.

[313] *Thief* – Moon. *Sacraments* – 7 (also Swastika).

[314] Trinity: *groves – cells – honeycomb*.

[315] *Wine – gold* – 6. The wine is from Bacchus.

[316] Outside – inside. Within – without.

[317] Samadhi.

[318] Link: Binah – Netzach. *Stars* of Nuit – Nothingness.

[319] *Gladiator* – Fighter – Warrior – Horus.

[320] The lower soul is the Moon, the higher is Tiphareth.

[321] One satisfies the Other. Unity.

[322] *Emperor* (Tzaddi from the previous chapter – a much stronger influence here.) *Emperor* – Fire – Horus.

[323] Before Kether. The throne is the Moon – The High Priestess – Isis – Gimel. N.O.X. in which L.V.X. has a *great orgy*.

22. The night falls like a spangled cloak from the shoulders of a prince upon a slave.[324]

23. He rises a free man![325]

24. Cast thou, O prophet, the cloak upon these slaves![326]

25. A great night, and scarce fires therein; but freedom for the slave that its glory shall encompass.[327]

26. So also I went down into the great sad city.[328]

27. There dead Messalina bartered her crown for poison from the dead Locusta; there stood Caligula, and smote the seas of forgetfulness.[329]

28. Who wast Thou, O Caesar, that Thou knewest God in an horse?[330]

29. For lo! we beheld the White Horse of the Saxon engraven upon the earth; and we beheld the Horses of the Sea that flame about the old grey land, and the foam from their nostrils enlightens us![331]

30. Ah! but I love thee, God![332]

31. Thou art like a moon upon the ice-world.[333]

32. Thou art like the dawn of the utmost snows upon the burnt-up flats of the tiger's land.[334]

33. By silence and by speech do I worship Thee.[335]

34. But all is in vain.[336]

35. Only Thy silence and Thy speech that worship me avail.[337]

---

[324] N.O.X. like a veil above L.V.X.

[325] Slave – 2; *free man* –1.

[326] The veil of the Abyss.

[327] N.O.X. and stars (infinite space and countless stars in It – Nuit). *Slave* – body. A lower soul – redeemed by Spiritual attainment.

[328] Balance between "shells" (see Liber TAU).

[329] *Seas of forgetfulness* – Binah, or the Abyss.

[330] God is in All. All is One.

[331] Trinity: *a horse* upon the earth, in Water, in *enlightening foam*.

[332] Agape.

[333] *Moon* – Gimel (*ice-world* – Kadath – Binah) G∴D∴.

[334] Buddhist orange (6) – R∴C∴.

[335] A∴A∴ – He worships.

[336] Indicates an "error" if the action of either silence or speech is given for "I."

[337] In fact, it is the Lord who manifests, not the "man."

36. Wail, O ye folk of the grey land, for we have drunk your wine, and left ye but the bitter dregs.[338]

37. Yet from these we will distil ye a liquor beyond the nectar of the Gods.[339]

38. There is value in our tincture for a world of Spice and gold.[340]

39. For our red powder of projection is beyond all possibilities.[341]

40. There are few men; there are enough.[342]

41. We shall be full of cup-bearers, and the wine is not stinted.[343]

42. O dear my God! what a feast Thou hast provided.[344]

43. Behold the lights and the flowers and the maidens![345]

44. Taste of the wines and the cates and the splendid meats![346]

45. Breathe in the perfumes and the clouds of little gods like wood-nymphs that inhabit the nostrils![347]

46. Feel with your whole body the glorious smoothness of the marble coolth and the generous warmth of the sun and the slaves![348]

47. Let the Invisible inform all the devouring Light of its disruptive vigour![349]

48. Yea! all the world is split apart, as an old grey tree by the light-ning![350]

49. Come, O ye gods, and let us feast.[351]

---

[338] Trinity. The relationship of Multitude and Unity.

[339] The Lord dwells in All. "Spiritualists" channel the energy through themselves that fertilizes the world.

[340] Spiritual *gold*: "child" from IX O.T.O. (also V.I.T.R.I.O.L.).

[341] See IX O.T.O.

[342] Liber Porta Lucis and Liber Tzaddi – of the Multitude only a *few* are "chosen," but many of them are "invited."

[343] Magister Templi.

[344] K. and P. enter into the game to unite (IX O.T.O.)

[345] Trinity: *lights* – Binah; *flowers* – Tiphareth; *maidens* – Malkuth.

[346] Trinity: *wine* – Binah; *cates* – Tiphareth; *splendid meats* – Malkuth.

[347] The polarity of Prana.

[348] K. and P. Contrast that is united: understanding, comprehension.

[349] *Invisible* – N.O.X. *devouring* L.V.X. (devouring: destructive power – 5).

[350] *World* – *split apart* in Multitude – Duality of the Moon above the Abyss.

[351] *Gods* – Cosmic energies. *Feast* – unification.

50. Thou, O my darling, O my ceaseless Sparrow-God, my delight, my desire, my deceiver, come Thou and chirp at my right hand![352]

51. This was the tale of the memory of Al A'in the priest; yea, of Al A'in the priest.[353]

CHAPTER VII[354]

1. By the burning of the incense was the Word revealed, and by the distant drug.[355]

2. O meal and honey and oil! O beautiful flag of the moon, that she hangs out in the centre of bliss![356]

3. These loosen the swathings of the corpse; these unbind the feet of Osiris, so that the flaming God may rage through the firmament with his fantastic spear.[357]

4. But of pure black marble is the sorry statue, and the changeless pain of the eyes is bitter to the blind.[358]

5. We understand the rapture of that shaken marble, torn by the throes of the crowned child, the golden rod of the golden God.[359]

6. We know why all is hidden in the stone, within the coffin, within the mighty sepulchre, and we too answer Olalam! Imal! Tutulu! as it is written in the ancient book.[360]

---

[352] Trinity: *sparrow – desire – deceiver*. *At my right hand* – Binah.

[353] AL A'in - AL - LA – All and Nothing; Kteis and Phallos. Unity: "behind it" is "true nature" – AL A'in the Priest.

[354] Seventh chapter is dedicated to 7 – Venus. 52 Verses (Nun – Beth); Death and Magus; 5 + 2 = 7 – Zain, Lovers. 7 = Netzach. See 777 for 52.

[355] Magister Templi – specific scent in experience 8=3. The intoxication of external and internal. Magister Temple hears and Understands the *Word*.

[356] The Cake of Light. Trinity: *meal* – Malkuth; *honey* – Tiphareth; *oil* – Binah. The nature of Agape.

[357] Phallos that reveals its nature.

[358] Osiris is the Black God – Binah (*black marble statue*). *Pain* and *bitterness* – Binah.

[359] Osiris fulfilled his nature, which brings him to delight; he was conquered and inherited by Horus.

[360] Trinity: *stone – coffin – sepulchre*. The *answer* of OIT – Twelvefold-table.

7. Three words of that book are as life to a new aeon; no god has read the whole.[361]

8. But thou and I, O God, have written it page by page.[362]

9. Ours is the elevenfold reading of the Elevenfold word.[363]

10. These seven letters together make seven diverse words; each word is divine, and seven sentences are hidden therein.[364]

11. Thou art the Word, O my darling, my lord, my master![365]

12. O come to me, mix the fire and the water, all shall dissolve.[366]

13. I await Thee in sleeping, in waking. I invoke Thee no more; for Thou art in me, O Thou who hast made me a beautiful instrument tuned to Thy rapture.[367]

14. Yet art Thou ever apart, even as I.[368]

15. I remember a certain holy day in the dusk of the year, in the dusk of the Equinox of Osiris, when first I beheld Thee visibly; when first the dreadful issue was fought out; when the Ibis-headed One charmed away the strife.[369]

16. I remember Thy first kiss, even as a maiden should. Nor in the dark byways was there another: Thy kisses abide.[370]

17. There is none other beside Thee in the whole Universe of Love.[371]

18. My God, I love Thee, O Thou goat with gilded horns![372]

---

[361] The Book of Enoch: The Three Names of God: Gods are only parts of a whole.

[362] There is no God but Man. DEUS HOMO EST.

[363] 11 – ABRAHADABRA (Do what thou wilt shall be the whole of the law = 11).

[364] 777 (seven-fold table; Enohian). BABALON – ABADDON = Ad Babalonis Amorem Do Dedico Omnia Nihilos.

[365] Trinity: *darling – lord – master*; he is the Logos – *Word*.

[366] Invoking: A + B = C.

[367] *Awaiting*: Passive Love (Awareness of Oneness: Understanding) 8=3.

[368] The Lord does not take a particular form except that he is manifested through the Magister.

[369] The conflict of Seth and *Osiris* – opposites in the One; *Ibis* – Magus.

[370] Agape (Samadhi).

[371] All is One (Achad – Agape – 13).

[372] *Goat* – PAN (to whom Artemis surrendered). *Horns* – 8. *Gilded* – Kether.

19. Thou beautiful bull of Apis! Thou beautiful serpent of Apep! Thou beautiful child of the Pregnant Goddess![373]

20. Thou hast stirred in Thy sleep, O ancient sorrow of years! Thou hast raised Thine head to strike, and all is dissolved into the Abyss of Glory.[374]

21. An end to the letters of the words! An end to the sevenfold speech.[375]

22. Resolve me the wonder of it all into the figure of a gaunt swift camel striding over the sand.[376]

23. Lonely is he, and abominable; yet hath he gained the crown.[377]

24. Oh rejoice! rejoice![378]

25. My God! O my God! I am but a speck in the star-dust of ages; I am the Master of the Secret of Things.[379]

26. I am the Revealer and the Preparer. Mine is the Sword --- and the Mitre and the Winged Wand![380]

27. I am the Initiator and the Destroyer. Mine is the Globe --- and the Bennu bird and the Lotus of Isis my daughter![381]

28. I am the One beyond these all; and I bear the symbols of the mighty darkness.[382]

29. There shall be a sigil as of a vast black brooding ocean of death and the central blaze of darkness, radiating its night upon all.[383]

30. It shall swallow up that lesser darkness.[384]

---

[373] Trinity: OAI.

[374] *Sorrow* – Binah.

[375] *The end of the speech* is the beginning of Understanding.

[376] V.V.V.V.V.; Magister Templi – 8=3.

[377] By the power of His Truth, while living, He conquered the Universe.

[378] Agape.

[379] L.V.X. in N.O.X. – Magister Templi – Understanding.

[380] "He cultivates his garden"; Trinity again: *Sword – Mitre – Winged* Wand. Levels of achievement.

[381] Horus!

[382] N.O.X.

[383] N.O.X.

[384] Binah is just a "reflection" of N.O.X.

31. But in that profound who shall answer: What is?[385]

32. Not I.[386]

33. Not Thou, O God![387]

34. Come, let us no more reason together; let us enjoy! Let us be ourselves, silent, unique, apart.[388]

35. O lonely woods of the world! In what recesses will ye hide our love?[389]

36. The forest of the spears of the Most High is called Night, and Hades, and the Day of Wrath; but I am His captain, and I bear His cup.[390]

37. Fear me not with my spearmen! They shall slay the demons with their petty prongs. Ye shall be free.[391]

38. Ah, slaves! ye will not --- ye know not how to will.[392]

39. Yet the music of my spears shall be a song of freedom.[393]

40. A great bird shall sweep from the abyss of Joy, and bear ye away to be my cup-bearers.[394]

41. Come, O my God, in one last rapture let us attain to the Union with the Many![395]

42. In the silence of Things, in the Night of Forces, beyond the accursed domain of the Three, let us enjoy our love![396]

---

[385] There are no "positive" qualities: It is not Fullness but "Depth"; "It is" – it is not.

[386] *Not I* – NEMO (The Destruction of Ego). Destruction of the lower soul.

[387] *Not Thou* – NEMO. No separation and polarity, "You – I."

[388] Manifestation of True Nature, unconditioned. Thelema.

[389] *Woods of the world*: Kteis of Babalon: Agape.

[390] N.O.X.; N – *Night*; O – *Hades*; X – *Day of Wrath. Bear His cup* – Magister "Captain" – NEMO.

[391] *Spearmen* – Adepts of Thelema. The onset of the New Aeon

[392] *Slaves* – Elementals – they are only servants; they have no "their" consciousness.

[393] The nature of Æon. A war that brings *freedom*. (5 toward 3).

[394] Hawk – Horus. *Cup-bearers* – 8=3.

[395] Samadhi. (see Liber AL).

[396] Trinity: *the silence of Things – Night of Forces – beyond the accursed domain of the Three.* N.O.X./L.V.X. – 210.

43. My darling! My darling! away, away beyond the Assembly and the Law and the Enlightenment unto an Anarchy of solitude and Darkness![397]

44. For even thus must we veil the brilliance of our Self.[398]

45. My darling! My darling![399]

46. O my God, but the love in Me bursts over the bonds of Space and Time; my love is spilt among them that love not love.[400]

47. My wine is poured out for them that never tasted wine.[401]

48. The fumes thereof shall intoxicate them and the vigour of my love shall breed mighty children from their maidens.[402]

49. Yea! without draught, without embrace: --- and the Voice answered Yea! these things shall be.[403]

50. Then I sought a Word for Myself; nay, for myself.[404]

51. And the Word came: O Thou! it is well. Heed naught! I love Thee! I love Thee![405]

52. Therefore had I faith unto the end of all; yea, unto the end of all.[406]

---

[397] 210. Trinity: *Assembly – Law – Enlightenment* (towards N.O.X.). L.V.X. dissolving in N.O.X.

[398] Even L.V.X. is hidden.

[399] Agape.

[400] Across the Abyss is beyond *Space and Time*: Agape.

[401] *Wine* – life – blood (DM – Horus) for everyone who is (not) NEMO.

[402] The Union of Kteis and Phallos (*children from their maidens* – children in IAO).

[403] Otherworldly.

[404] *Nay* – LA – Nothing (That is a *Word*).

[405] Agape.

[406] Perdurabo – fulfillment. *The end of all.*

APPENDIX

Syllabus for the Neophyte

A CLASS

7	VII	Liber Liberi vel Lapidis Lazuli, Adumbratio Kabbalæ Ægyptiorum	Voluntary Emancipation of a certain Exempt Adept from his Adeptship. These are the Birth Words of a Master of the Temple. The nature of this book is sufficiently explained by its title. Its seven chapters are referred to the seven planets in the following order: Mars, Saturn, Jupiter, Sol, Mercury, Luna, Venus.
220	CCXX	Liber אל vel Legis	This book is the foundation of the New Æon, and thus of the whole of our Work.

B CLASS

6	VI	Liber O vel Manus et Sagittæ	Instructions given for elementary study of the Qabalah, Assumption of God-forms, Vibration of Divine Names, the Rituals of Pentagram and Hexagram, and their uses in protection and invocation, a method of attaining astral visions so-called, and an instruction in the practice called Rising on the Planes.
9	IX	Liber E vel Exercitiorum	This book instructs the aspirant in the necessity of keeping a record. Suggests methods of testing physical clairvoyance. Gives instruction in asana, pranayama, and dharana, and advises the application of tests to the physical body, in order that the student may thoroughly understand her own limitations.
78	LXXVIII	A description of the Cards	A complete treatise on the Tarot giving the correct designs of the cards with their attributions and symbolic meanings on all the planes.
96	XCVI	Liber Gaias	A Handbook of Geomancy. Gives a simple and fairly satisfactory system of Geomancy.
474	CDLXXIV	Liber Os Abysmi vel דעת	An instruction in a purely intellectual method of entering the Abyss.
489	CDLXXXIX	One Star in Sight	The structure and system of the Great White Brotherhood.
913	CMXIII	Liber Thisharb, Viæ Memoriæ	Gives methods of attaining the magical memory or memory of past lives, and an insight into the function of the aspirant in this present life.

C CLASS

811	DCCCXI	Energised Enthusiasm	*A note on Theurgy.*

D CLASS

13	XIII	Graduum Montis Abiegni	*An account of the task of the Aspirant from Probationer to Adept.*
25	XXV	The Star Ruby	*It is an improved form of the „lesser" ritual of the Pentagram. See Liber CCCXXXIII.*
28	XXVIII	Liber Septem Regum Sanctorum	*It is a ritual of Initiation bestowed on certain selected Probationers.*
61	LXI	Liber Causæ	*Explains the actual history of the origin of the present movement. Its statements are accurate in the ordinary sense of the world. The object of the book is to discount Mythopia.*
175	CLXXV	Astarte vel Liber Berylli	*An instruction in attainment by the method of devotion.*
185	CLXXXV	Liber Collegii Sancti	*Being the tasks of the Grades and their Oaths proper to Liber XIII. This is the official Paper of the various grades. It includes the Task and Oath of a Probationer.*
341	CCCXLI	Liber H.H.H.	*Gives three methods of attainment through a willed series of thoughts.*
412	CDXII	Liber A vel Armorum	*An instruction for the preparation of the Elemental Instruments.*
671	DCLXXI	Liber תרעא	*The ritual of the initiation of the Grade of Neophyte.*
671	DCLXXI	Liber Pyramidos	*The ritual of self-initiation of a Neophyte. The adaption of Liber תרעא.*

A AND B CLASSES

963	CMLXIII	Treasure-House of Images	*A superb collection of Litanies appropriate to the Signs of the Zodiac. Only the short note pertains to Class A.*	0=0 2=9

UNCLASSIFIED

No number	The Equinox Ritual	*Unpublished*	1=10

A∴A∴

THE OATH OF A NEOPHYTE

I,_____, (old motto) being of sound mind and
body, on this _____ day of_____ (An _____ Sun in _____degrees)
do hereby resolve: in the Presence of _____, a Zelator
of the A∴A∴. To prosecute the Great Work: which is, to obtain control of
the nature and powers of my own being.

Further, I promise to observe zeal in service to the Probationers under me,
and to deny myself utterly on their behalf.

May the A∴A∴ crown the work, lend me of Its wisdom in the work, enable
me to understand the work!

Reverence, duty, sympathy, devotion, assiduity, trust do I bring to the A∴A∴,
and in eight months from this date may I be admitted to the knowledge and
conversation of the A∴A∴!

Witness my hand_____

New Motto_____

THE TASK OF A NEOPHYTE

0. Let any Probationer who has accomplished his task to the satisfaction of the A∴A∴ be instructed in the proper course of procedure: which is: - Let him read through this note of his office, and sign it, paying the sum of One Guinea for Liber VII which will be given him on his initiation, and One Guinea for this Portfolio of Class D publications, B - G. Let him obtain the robe of a Neophyte, and entrust the same to the care of his Neophyte.

   He shall choose a new motto with deep forethought and intense solemnity, as expressing the clearer consciousness of his Aspiration which the year's Probation has given him.

   Let him make an appointment with his Neophyte at the pleasure of the latter for the ceremony of Initiation.

1. The Neophyte shall not proceed to the grade of Zelator in less than eight months; but shall hold himself free for four days for advancement at the end of that period.

2. He shall pass the four tests called the Powers of the Sphinx.

3. He shall apply himself to understand the nature of his Initiation.

4. He shall commit to memory a chapter of Liber VII; and furthermore, he shall study and practice a chapter of Liber O in all its branches: also he shall begin to study Liber H and some commonly accepted method of divination. He will further be examined in his power of Journeying in the Spirit Vision.

5. Beside all this, he shall perform any tasks that his Zelator in the name of the A∴A∴ and by its authority may see fit to lay upon him. Let him be mindful that the word Neophyte is no idle term, but that in many a subtle way the new nature will stir within him, when he knoweth it not.

6. When the sun shall next enter the sigh 240 (degrees) to that under which he hath been received, his advancement may be granted unto him.

   He shall keep himself free from all other engagements for four whole days from that date.

7. He may at any moment withdraw from his association with the A∴A∴, simply notifying the Zelator who introduced him.

8. He shall everywhere proclaim openly his connection with the A∴A∴ and speak of It and Its principles (even so little as he understandeth) for that mystery is the enemy of Truth.

    Furthermore, he shall construct the magic Pentacle, according to the instruction in Liber A.

    One month before the completion of his eight months, he shall deliver a copy of his Record to his Zelator, pass the necessary tests, and repeat to him his chosen chapter of Liber VII.

9. He shall in every way fortify his body according to the advice of his Zelator, for that the ordeal of advancement is no light one.

10. Thus and not otherwise may he obtain the great reward: YEA, MAY HE OBTAIN THE GREAT REWARD!

NEOPHYTE EXAMINATION

Do what thou wilt shall be the whole of the law.

1. Explore astrally all the Tattvas - pass through the door with the symbol of Tattva and explain it in detail according to your visions.

2. Same as Tattvas, explore one of the Planets and one of the signs of Zodiac - pass astrally through the door with a proper symbol and explain it according to your visions.

3. Divulge through your visions the nature of alchemical principles of Sulfur, Mercury, and Salt, and how do they differ from three Gunas and elements of Fire, Water, and Air.
    Notice - this can be changed if You decide to systematically explore astrally all the planets or all the signs of the Zodiac.

4. Make an analysis of the Zodiacal sign in four qabalistic worlds, or make an analysis of a Tarot card or Yi King hexagram, or to some other symbol of your own favor.

5. Submit a design of a Pentacle - symbolic map of the Universe as you understand it. Submit a design of Lamen - if you created it, as an image of attainment of the Great Work.

6. Write an article on your own understanding and experience of A∴A∴ Write an article about your grade or something related to your grade.

7. Create an original ritual or meditation or analyze an existing practice.

There is no time limit for the fulfillment of this task.

Love is the law, love under will.

FRATER 273

soon to be published:

Anatomy of the Abyss
The Zelator's Compendium

Sleeping Self
a lucid dreaming, astral projection, and scrying manual

Made in United States
Orlando, FL
22 November 2024

54295426R00215